The importance of J. M. Coetzee in the development of twentieth-century fiction is now widely recognized. His work addresses some of the key critical issues of our time: the relationship between postmodernism and postcolonialism, the role of history in the novel and, repeatedly, the question of how the author can combine an ethical and political consciousness with a commitment to the novel as a work of fiction.

In this study, which may be used as an introduction and by those already familiar with Coetzee's work, Dominic Head assesses Coetzee's position as a white South African writer engaged with the legacy of colonialism. Through close readings of all the novels, Head shows how Coetzee inhabits a transitional site between Europe and Africa, and it is from this position that his more general concerns emerge. Coetzee's engagement with the problems facing the postcolonial writer, Head argues, is always enriched by his awareness of a wider literary tradition.

J. M. COETZEE

CAMBRIDGE STUDIES IN AFRICAN AND CARIBBEAN LITERATURE

Series editor: Professor Abiola Irele, Ohio State University

Each volume in this unique series of critical studies will offer a comprehensive and in-depth account of the whole *œuvre* of one individual writer from Africa or the Caribbean, in such a way that the book may be considered a complete coverage of the writer's expression up to the time the study is undertaken. Attention will be devoted primarily to the works themselves – their significant themes, governing ideas and formal procedures; biographical and other background information will thus be employed secondarily, to illuminate these aspects of the writer's work where necessary.

The emergence in the twentieth century of black literature in the United States, the Caribbean and Africa as a distinct corpus of imaginative work represents one of the most notable developments in world literature in modern times. This series has been established to meet the needs of this growing area of study. It is hoped that it will not only contribute to a wider understanding of the humanistic significance of modern literature from Africa and the Caribbean through the scholarly presentation of the work of the major writers, but also offer a wider framework for the ongoing debates about the problems of interpretation within the disciplines concerned.

Already published

Chinua Achebe, by C. L. Innes
Nadine Gordimer, by Dominic Head
Edouard Glissant, by J. Michael Dash
V. S. Naipaul, by Fawzia Mustafa

J. M. COETZEE

DOMINIC HEAD

University of Central England

CAMBRIDGE
UNIVERSITY PRESS

PUBLISHED BY THE PRESS SYNDICATE OF THE UNIVERSITY OF CAMBRIDGE
The Pitt Building, Trumpington Street, Cambridge CB2 IRP, United Kingdom

CAMBRIDGE UNIVERSITY PRESS
The Edinburgh Building, Cambridge CB2 2RU, United Kingdom
40 West 20th Street, New York, NY 10011–4211, USA
10 Stamford Road, Oakleigh, Melbourne 3166, Australia

First published 1997

Printed in the United Kingdom at the University Press, Cambridge

Typeset in Baskerville 11/12½ pt [CE]

A catalogue record for this book is available from the British Library

Library of Congress cataloguing in publication data
Head, Dominic.
J. M. Coetzee / Dominic Head.
p.   cm. – (Cambridge studies in African and Caribbean Literature)
Includes bibliographical references and index.
ISBN 0 521 48232 1 hardback
1. Coetzee, J. M., 1940–   – Criticism and interpretation.
2. South Africa – In literature. I. Title. II. Series.
PR9369.3.C58Z68 1997
823–dc21   97–6959 CIP

Contents

Preface

Following the publication of his first novel in 1974, the white South African novelist J. M. Coetzee has produced, aside from his academic work and his translations, a total of seven slender novels, one every three or four yours. In terms of simple wordage this might seem a relatively modest creative output; yet the modesty is deceptive. Indeed, the importance of J. M. Coetzee to the direction of the late twentieth-century novel can scarcely be overstated. It is signalled by the weighty questions which recur in discussions of his work: how does his writing make us reconsider our definitions of postmodernism and postcolonialism? How shall 'history' be imagined in novels? What does it mean for an author to pledge allegiance to the discourse of *fiction* (rather than the discourse of politics)? Is there a function for a literary canon? What role can literary theory play in these evaluations? And what kind of ethical stance might emerge from such intensely serious and significant investigations?

The attempts to answer these questions alert us to an as-yet-undefined site of creativity. This is the crucial issue in understanding Coetzee's interim position in a very particular corner of postcolonial writing: the literature of the 'post-colonizer', which here locates a transitional site between Europe and Africa. In his collection of essays, *White Writing: On the Culture of Letters in South Africa*, Coetzee establishes a formulation which is to the point: 'white writing is white only in so far as it is generated by the concerns of people no longer European, not yet African' (*WW*, 11). His focus is on selected pre-apartheid writers of the 1920s and 1930s, but the theme of 'European

ix

ideas writing themselves out in Africa' (*DP*, 338–9) has a very important resonance to South Africa in the apartheid era and beyond. The sense of delay has very much to do with the racist underpinnings of apartheid, and the inevitable restrictions placed on ethnic and cultural identities: the literature that has emerged has been constrained, a 'national' literature only in an artificial sense, quite unable to embody a true hybridity. The peculiar problems of late-colonial and post-colonial South Africa are central concerns for Coetzee.

There is a sense in which Coetzee's writing expresses and enacts this sense of constraint, and this can be seen as a measured and appropriate writer's response to the trajectory of history 'out there'. But this also signals a turning inwards, a preoccupation with specifically literary questions. Consequently, a focus for any analysis of Coetzee is how this self-reflexiveness is to be judged, given the pressing concerns of late- and now post-apartheid South Africa, which (in some quarters) are deemed to require a more obvious gesture of engagement and commitment on the part of the writer. Coetzee's emphasis on the text and on questions of textuality, however, represents a utilization of postmodernist concerns fitted to his context. This is a considered programme of intellectual fidelity and revision, which is not only courageous, but probably visionary as well.

The focus of Coetzee's work, not surprisingly, has ensured that the novels have received a good deal of attention from academic critics, most recently from those well-versed in post-structuralist theory: both Gayatri Spivak and Derek Attridge, for example, have produced elegant and sophisticated essays on the theoretical allusiveness of some of the later novels. In the monographs, this kind of sophisticated theoretical interpretation was pioneered by Teresa Dovey's application of Lacan. An indispensable book is that by David Attwell, which is especially strong on Coetzee's various intellectual sources. Susan Van-Zanten Gallagher's study supplies invaluable information on the South African context. (Dick Penner's book, listed in the bibliography along with the other three, is also useful.) Yet the developing sophistication of much of the criticism (which the novels have certainly demanded) also presents a problem: Coetzee's novels have a power and a resonance beyond the concerns of academia, an impact confirmed by the many prestigious literary awards bestowed on them. This may be to suggest that the novels, like all very significant literary works, operate on several levels simultaneously. The difficulty, then, is how to bridge the gap between the surface lucidity and the underlying complexity of Coetzee: to indicate his intellectual importance without leaving the non-specialist behind. If this problem is not easily resolvable, this book attempts, at least, to counter the difficulty by concentrating on the novels themselves, and the unfolding reading experience they offer by virtue of their significant themes and their formal procedures. After the opening chapter, which focuses on the more complex question of Coetzee's *place* in contemporary writing, a separate chapter is devoted to each of the novels. Due cognizance is also given to the impressive and growing corpus of Coetzee criticism which supplies points of reference (and contestation) throughout the survey.

Coetzee is also an accomplished essayist: his non-fictional work is marked by an elegant lucidity which is evident even in his treatment of difficult and contentious issues. Indeed, the essays cover a range of hotly debated contemporary questions, including, for example, the nature of the modernist legacy, the nature of colonial identity and various aspects of censorship. It is beyond the scope of this book to offer an analysis of the non-fiction in its own right, but reference is made to the essays (now readily available in three separate collections) wherever they seem to illuminate an aspect of the fiction.

If there is an ambivalence in Coetzee's appeal to different reading communities, the ambivalence I am registering may also, of course, be an aspect of Coetzee's project, and another reason for his perceived importance. This 'bridging' element to Coetzee's own work was suggested in his Dawson Scott Memorial Lecture 'What is Realism?', given at the PEN International Writers' Day at London's Café Royal on 30 March 1996. Presenting a fiction instead of a lecture (which incorporated a fictionalized lecture, itself entitled 'What is Realism?'), Coetzee wove together different levels of address, including critical reflection on 'the realist illusion', an effect which this 'fiction-as-lecture' itself constantly disrupted without ever destroying. This quite astonishing duality, combining an unerring control of fictional time and space with a self-consciousness which threatens it all along, is Coetzee's defining characteristic as a novelist. It is this which enables him to allude to complex ideas within works which yet retain an elegant narrative shape. The result is a troubling and brooding resonance within finely wrought fictions which, like the characters within them, can never be finally made to yield their full significance in a reduced, extractable form.

Thanks and acknowledgements to: Abiola Irele for his helpful comments on the manuscript; to Michael Bell, Chris Nash and John Rignall at the narrative reading group, University of Warwick, for suggestions on a paper on *Michael K*; and to the School of English, UCE, for funding remission from teaching in the second semester 1995–6.

Abbreviations

AI   *Age of Iron* (1990; Harmondsworth: Penguin, 1991)

D   *Dusklands* (1974; Harmondsworth: Penguin, 1983)

DP   *Doubling the Point: Essays and Interviews*, edited by David Attwell (Cambridge, Mass.: Harvard University Press, 1992)

F   *Foe* (1986; Harmondsworth: Penguin, 1987)

GO   *Giving Offense: Essays on Censorship* (University of Chicago Press, 1996)

IHC   *In the Heart of the Country* (1977; Harmondsworth: Penguin, 1982)

MK   *Life and Times of Michael K* (1983; Harmondsworth: Penguin, 1985)

MP   *The Master of Petersburg* (London: Secker and Warburg, 1994)

WB   *Waiting for the Barbarians* (1980; Harmondsworth: Penguin, 1982)

WW   *White Writing: On the Culture of Letters in South Africa* (New Haven: Yale University Press, 1988)

Chronology

	University of Texas, Austin. Writes Ph.D. on Samuel Beckett (completed 1969).
1966	B. J. Vorster becomes Prime Minister.
1968–71	Coetzee teaches at the State University of New York at Buffalo. Commences work on first novel, *Dusklands*.
1972	Takes up teaching position, University of Cape Town.
1974	Publication of *Dusklands*.
1976	Thousands of black schoolchildren in Soweto protest against compulsory use of Afrikaans in teaching. Two students are shot dead by police resulting in nationwide protests. By 1977, 575 people are dead (official estimates).
1977	Steve Biko arrested and killed by police. Publication of *In the Heart of the Country* (CNA Literary Award).
1978	Vorster resigns. P.W. Botha becomes Prime Minister.
1980	Publication of *Waiting for the Barbarians* (CNA Literary Award; James Tait Black Prize; Geoffrey Faber Award). Symbolic attacks by Umkhonto we Sizwe (military wing of the ANC) on two oil-from-coal plants. School boycott (started by Cape Town pupils).
1983	Publication of *Life and Times of Michael K* (Booker–McConnell prize; CNA Literary Award; Prix Etranger Femina (1985)). New wave of school boycotts, which continue through 1984 and 1985.
1984	New constitution gives Asians and 'Coloureds' (not Africans) limited participation in government. Botha now state president. Coetzee becomes professor of general literature, University of Cape Town.
1985	National Education Crisis Committee (NECC) suspends school boycotts.
1986	Pass laws repealed; indefinite nationwide state of emergency proclaimed. Publication of *Foe* (Jeru-

CHAPTER I

The writer's place: Coetzee and postcolonial literature

The novels of J. M. Coetzee occupy a special place in South African literature, and in the development of the twentieth-century novel more generally. His works present a sophisticated intellectual challenge to the particular form of colonial violence embodied in apartheid, though, in some quarters, this has been seen as an oblique rather than a direct challenge. He is the first South African writer to produce overtly self-conscious fictions drawing explicitly on international postmodernism. The presence of European influences has always helped shape the South African literary tradition, so the claim, here, should not be over-stated: what Coetzee does is to import contemporary Western preoccupations which produce a stress on textuality to a degree not previously seen in his country's literature. This offers a dual challenge: first to the South African novel, usually seen as more dependent on realist conventions; and second to the broader field of postcolonial writing, which needs to accommodate the unique intermediary position that Coetzee inhabits.[1]

Coetzee was born in Cape Town on 9 February 1940, and grew up in the Karoo, the vast desert and semi-desert area of the Cape province. His family (his father was a lawyer; his mother a schoolteacher) spoke English at home, though, with other relatives, he conversed in Afrikaans.[2] He completed his undergraduate work, studying English and mathematics at the University of Cape Town, in 1961, and moved to England to work in computers in 1962. He stayed for four years, working as a programmer, during which period he wrote a master's thesis on Ford Madox Ford (MA awarded by the University of Cape Town in 1963) (*DP*, 19).

In 1965, Coetzee returned to academia: he moved to the US, to the University of Texas at Austin, where he produced his doctoral dissertation on the style of Samuel Beckett's English fiction, completed in 1969. He taught at the State University of New York at Buffalo from 1968 to 1971, during which period he worked on his first novel *Dusklands*.[3] He returned to South Africa to take up a teaching position at the University of Cape Town in 1972. Following successive promotions, he became professor of general literature at his Alma Mater in 1984.

Coetzee has held various visiting professorships in the US, and has won several prestigious literary awards, including the Booker–McConnell prize (1983), the Prix Etranger Femina (1985) and the Jerusalem Prize (1987). He must surely be a prime candidate for the Nobel Prize for literature at some future stage. If the available biographical details of Coetzee's life are sparse, this reflects the measured reflectiveness and elusiveness of the writer, who does not view himself as a public figure, someone in the public domain (*DP*, 65). (This preservation of private space is confirmed by the failure of so many interviewers to pose questions to which Coetzee fully responds.[4]) The elusiveness is also, however, entirely apposite: it is indicative of the nature of Coetzee's literary project, with its emphasis on textuality, on novels as discursive events in the world, beyond the author's controlling hand.

Coetzee's first novel, *Dusklands* (1974), is widely recognized as sounding a new postmodernist note in the South African novel, a new fictional engagement with the problems of colonialism, at the level of discourse. There is an element of hindsight, however, in the international recognition of Coetzee's importance, a belatedness signalled by the publication history of the earlier novels: it was only after the publication of the third novel, *Waiting for the Barbarians* (1980), that the previous two were properly recognized. (In Britain, for example, *Dusklands* was first published in 1982, also the year in which *In the Heart of the Country* first appeared in paperback.)

Dusklands offers an explicit challenge to the dominance of realism in African (especially South African) fiction, by distancing itself from the contemporary South African context, at first geographically and then historically. The implicit analysis of the writer's colonial context is conducted through two parallel situations, and associated discursive modes: the Defense Department analysis of the US involvement in Vietnam, and the travel writing of seventeenth- and eighteenth-century 'explorers' of the Cape. The book, comprising two separate narratives, is restricted by the two modes and their respective narrators: to be sure their perspectives are ironically undercut, their respective styles parodied, but there is still an element of re-enactment in the exposure of colonial violence. The novel requires a resisting reader, able to resist the element of enactment, and to recognize a positive self-critique in the restrictive style, a process of catharsis in which the postmodernist writer confronts (and exorcizes) the danger of self-enclosed textual play. The typical Coetzean preoccupations are all present in this first novel: the analysis of the colonizing psyche; the emphasis on textual structures; the challenge to novelistic conventions; and the self-critique.

These preoccupations are revisited throughout the novel sequence, in fresh conjunctions suited to the stylistic departure which each novel represents. There is, however, a sense of intellectual continuity through the evolution and development of ideas already present in the *œuvre*'s opening work. Consequently there is no clear sense of phases to, or clear breaks in, the sequence; rather there is a sense of consolidation and development – a looking back as well as a looking ahead – in each new work, which also represents a unique project in its own right. For this reason I have chosen, subsequently, to devote a single chapter to each novel, rather than to try and group them in an approximate narrative of creative phases.

If *Dusklands* enacts a kind of discursive entrapment, the next novel, *In the Heart of the Country* (1977), repeats the process, but offers the glimpse of a resolution. Magda, the narrating persona, and the daughter of colonialism (in an intellectual as well as an historical sense), is shown to be restricted by the generic structure of South African pastoral which, in the end, defeats her attempts to establish a new kind of fraternity – love for the people, not simply for the land.

A change of mode is found in *Waiting for the Barbarians* (1980), in that the overt signs of an austere postmodernism are relinquished. *In the Heart of the Country* had been written as a series of numbered sections (sometimes containing contradictory accounts of events), whereas *Barbarians* adopts the guise of an extended moral parable, the story of a man of conscience standing up to the terrors of imperialism, to be found within as well as without. However, the ethical awakening of the man of conscience, the magistrate who is the novel's protagonist, evolves through a dream sequence – a new kind of personal history – which is representative of the novel's circumvention of linear narrative modes.

If the surface lucidity of *Barbarians* is reproduced in *Life and Times of Michael K* (1983), there is, once more, an underlying intellectual agenda. The story of Michael K, seeking his own ethic of survival amidst the social disintegration of civil war, is a challenge (with an ecological edge) to obvious notions of political engagement. At the same time, the elusiveness of K is a grand-scale enactment of the poststructuralist idea of infinitely deferred meaning. This elusiveness, as both theme and structure, does not collapse into undecidability, but is used to define a new space of resistance.

Theories about textuality are expressed in their most direct form in *Foe* (1986), Coetzee's most obviously metafictional text; this is especially so from a literary–historical perspective as *Foe* is a postcolonial reworking of *Robinson Crusoe*, containing, also, allusions to other works by Defoe. The double operation that Coetzee performs is to associate literary and historical colonialism, and yet to redeem Defoe, fictionalized as 'Foe', as an example of that authorial insecurity, or informed self-doubting which characterizes later postcolonial writing. Coetzee's dilemma in approaching the colonized Other receives its most arresting figure in the Friday of *Foe*, the character whose history has been silenced by colonial violence: his tongue has been cut out.

When *Age of Iron* (1990) was published, it seemed to represent a clear departure for Coetzee, his most 'realistic' novel evoking the Cape Town unrest of 1986. There is certainly a brooding anger and immediacy in this novel, written between 1986 and 1989, during which period South Africa was governed under a state of emergency. At the same time, the question of help-lessness – and of guilt and complicity – is expressed through a literary project, the development of the confessional mode. With hindsight, *Age of Iron* takes its place in an ongoing, and non-linear exploration of fictional modes: the most recent novel, *The Master of Petersburg* (1994), continues the preoccu-pation with the confessional mode, and aligns the project with Coetzee's intertextual investigations. The 'master' of the novel's title is a fictionalized Dostoevsky, apparently experien-cing the events which will give rise to his novel *The Devils*, or *The Possessed* (recently translated as *Demons*).

Other critics, it should be noted, *have* detected phases, breaks or decisive points in Coetzee's career. Attwell, who detects 'three seismic shifts' in the first five novels, also sees *Waiting for the Barbarians* as 'pivotal'.[5] Derek Wright considers *Life and Times of Michael K* to mark a turning-point, 'the end of a phase in Coetzee's writing', after which it can be said 'realism has . . . gone to ground, the imperial text to earth'. Wright's argument is that the attempt to speak for a non-white protagonist is a kind of interim stage on the way to a more sophisticated postmodernism in which no attempt is made to speak *for*. The progression is confirmed, for Wright, by the self-reflexiveness of *Foe* which makes the later novel 'capable of subverting its own ethnocentricity', where, in contrast, the 'token psychological realism' of *Michael K* – the third-person mediation of the character's thoughts – evinces a restricted formalism in which a kind of paternalism is embedded. With the luxury of hindsight, after the publication of *Age of Iron* and *The Master of Petersburg*, it is difficult to concur with Wright's perception of phases in the *œuvre*. The problem of silence/voice in the representation of the Other is given a shift of focus in both of these novels, which, in any case, do not conform to the idea of a formalistic curve of increasing reflexiveness. It is true that *The Master of Petersburg* puts the issue of literary self-consciousness in a new conjunc-tion; but it also relies on certain mimetic codes, as does the earlier *Age of Iron*, to an even greater extent.[6]

In addition to Defoe and Dostoevsky, Coetzee draws on a range of European philosophers and writers in his work: Kafka and (to a lesser extent) Beckett are among the more modern prominent influences. Although such allusions are sometimes ironic, there is no simple rejection or sense of moving beyond: indeed, the Western tradition is often used to explain the postcolonial moment. Where, for example, Nadine Gordimer has immediate recourse to Frantz Fanon, a modern anti-colonial thinker, to delineate the process of decolonization, Coetzee sometimes looks back to Hegel.[7] (Coetzee has drawn especially on Hegel's conception of the master/slave or lord/bondsman relationship as mutually damaging, but also as an inverse dependency which in some measure authenticates the bondsman rather than the lord.[8]) It is common, of course, for postcolonial authors to write back to the European tradition, but, in Coetzee's case, the gesture is complex. Even when (as in *Foe*) canonicity and imperialism are seen to overlap, there is still a sense of dependency, of extending the tradition that is being subjected to critical scrutiny. The new kind of literary hybrid produced in these ambivalent operations can be seen as a kind of solution to the seemingly intractable problem of literary identity.

The question of identity, as a literary as well as an ethnic matter, has proved problematic for many white South African writers, especially those who, like Coetzee, are based in South Africa. In some senses it seems appropriate to suggest that Coetzee is not an Afrikaner, but a white South African inhabiting a very particular margin, since his background partly distances him from both Afrikaner as well as English affiliations.[9] Coetzee's own comments on his ethnic identity show him to be intensely aware of the slipperiness of his position, and of the ambivalences of this site which divides colonial from postcolonial experience. He has spoken of the term 'Afrikaner' as having three different applications, the first two of which would disqualify Coetzee from Afrikaner group membership. The first is linguistic and cultural: English rather than Afrikaans is Coetzee's first language, and he is not 'embedded' in Afrikaner culture, such as the Reformed Church. In its second sense, 'Afrikaner' becomes an ideological tool, moving from an anti-British political agenda in the 1880s, to an anti-black Nationalism in the later years of apartheid. By this definition, those who do not share the political vision – whether or not they are Afrikaans-speakers – can be expelled (or can remove themselves) from affiliation with the group.

The third application of the term is the external activity of naming, a brand imposed on the basis of historical association. Here, Coetzee suggests, he does not have the power 'to withdraw from the gang', from the guilt by association with the crime committed against Africa by the whites of South Africa. Indeed, he indicates that his writing – he cites the second section of *Dusklands* as an example – sometimes draws its validity from this sense of complicity (*DP*, 342–3).

This complex issue of identity is of vital importance in establishing the niche of postcolonialism which Coetzee inhabits. If he is unwilling, or unable to resist the external appellation of 'Afrikaner', this has to do with historical revision, the uncovering of contamination in the colonial legacy. At the same time, he strongly resists the contemporary taint, affiliating himself with an indeterminate, but growing, ethnic-linguistic group who

are merely South Africans (itself a mere name of convenience) whose native tongue, the tongue they have been born to, is English. And as the pool has no discernible *ethnos*, so one day I hope it will have no predominant color, as more 'people of color' drift into it. A pool, I would hope then, in which differences wash away. (*DP*, 342)

In resisting the descriptive label, Coetzee here identifies himself with a utopian drive towards cultural and biological hybridity in South Africa, the projected 'rainbow country'. It is very important to recognize that this affinity with the process of decolonization, for someone like Coetzee, also *depends upon* the more passive acceptance of historical guilt: 'Afrikaner' is an identity to be both rejected/acknowledged in the present process of historical revision.

Over this border position, which to some degree is an inevitable situation for the white anti-apartheid writer, looms the shadow of compromise. A familiar critical debate in

Coetzee studies concerns the question of historical engagement, and the appropriate fictional response to the apartheid
regime. If Coetzee is accurately represented as South Africa's
most significant postmodernist writer, a doubt may legitimately
emerge concerning his credentials in dealing with the particular historical moment. Is it possible, in other words, to
engage simultaneously with the sophisticated literary questions
posed by the poststructuralist/postmodernist turn and, directly,
with the key social and political issues of the day? There is no
doubt that Coetzee's engagement with history *seems* oblique
when his work is compared with the forms of gritty realism
associated with black prose fiction, or, for example, with the
novels of Nadine Gordimer (the usual touchstone).

The problem of realism in connection with Coetzee turns
out to be a problem of definition. Here the dominance of
various forms of realism in South African prose fiction, as
almost the 'unquestioned means of bearing witness to, and
telling the truth about, South Africa', inevitably makes the
technical innovations of a writer like Coetzee contentious.[10]
Indeed, his avoidance – and criticism – of a certain concept of
realism is a reaction against a perceived norm.

The standard invoked in this debate about South African
fiction (and African fiction more generally) derives from the
writings of Georg Lukács, especially his work on 'critical
realism' in the novel. A focus of Lukács' prescription for the
novel is the realization of individual characters coupled with an
understanding of the historical dynamic, a representation of
public and private realms in which one is not subordinate to
the other: instead there should be a dialectical interaction
between public and private realms. It is through the typification
of character that this is achieved: in the Lukácsian novel of
critical realism a character is the representation of both
individuality and typicality. In such a character 'the determining factors of a particular historical phase are found . . . in
concentrated form'.[11] This formula for the capture and concentration of historical forces has proved compelling, in an
ethical sense, as a prescription for the fictional recording of, or
bearing witness to, life in South Africa.

In her review of *Life and Times of Michael K*, Nadine Gordimer invokes Lukács' concept of typicality as a yardstick to assess the portrayal of Michael K as representative of the victimized black population of South Africa. It is a measure which finds Coetzee's character wanting, since it leads Gordimer to find K's passivity historically unfaithful: Coetzee, she suggests, 'does not recognize what the victims, seeing themselves as victims no longer, have done, are doing, and believe they must do for themselves'. The fault is a distortion of 'the organicism that George Lukács defines as the integral relation between private and social destiny'.[12] In *The Black Interpreters* (1973), Gordimer had made a keynote defence of realism in a broader context, to explain the importance of the developing fiction of black African writers. Her model of Lukácsian critical realism, as inherently socially progressive, was amenable to this purpose.[13]

Coetzee stands fundamentally opposed to this kind of normative prescription, and he conceives the novel as a genre as having moved beyond such formulae: commenting on 'the "typical" characters that a theorist like Lukács advocates', he has suggested that the novel is now after 'bigger game than that'.[14] In Gallagher's account, Coetzee flatly rejects this kind of realism, and instead 'opts for a non-realistic, self-referential fiction that constantly highlights its own unreliability'.[15] It is, however, possible to overstate the *effect* of Coetzee's self-consciousness, which does not present unreliability to disrupt the surface reading experience in the way that some post-modernist works do. In fact, there is a strong contrary pull operating simultaneously, an attempt to resuscitate aspects of realism (even while they are undermined). In *Life and Times of Michael K*, for example, Coetzee draws on the principle of third-person omniscience, a convention of realist fiction, in order to approach Michael K and release this character's thoughts. Simultaneously, the novel curtails this omniscience, and reveals dubious associations in the narrative authority it implies. But the reading experience is not severely disrupted. Indeed, one of the remarkable things about Coetzee's fiction – exemplified in *Michael K* – is its capacity to retain an aspect of 'realist illusion', in tandem with a self-consciousness that might be expected to destroy all such effects.

This *formal* duality suggests that, in fact, Gordimer and Coetzee are not so far apart as is often assumed, since it reveals a political understanding operating on the very *structure* of Coetzee's work; but there is still the question of how an appropriate form can be fashioned to demonstrate *commitment*. Gordimer's criticism of *Life and Times of Michael K* derives from an idea about commitment in literary form. Lamenting the novel's apparent 'revulsion against all political and revolutionary solutions', she suggests: 'I don't think the author would deny it is his own revulsion.'[16] A similar concern governs Stephen Watson's important essay 'Colonialism and the Novels of J. M. Coetzee', in which Watson ultimately distances himself from the charge, which he articulates in detail, that Coetzee's recourse to mythical structures represents an evasion of history. In effect, Watson finds reason to praise Coetzee's work for its limitations. The shortcomings, ambivalences and contradictions of the novels are productive in so far as they afford insight 'into the colonising mind, as well as the dissenting colonising mind'. But, by a different measure, Watson suggests, the novels would not fare so well. They will be found wanting by the critic seeking something more than an oblique representation of the material circumstances of colonialism – or, indeed, by the critic seeking a 'new history' – because 'the solid core of his work lies elsewhere, outside the works themselves, in something that is effaced, implicit, barely alluded to'. Lacking the core of history, the novels contain 'little more than an artfully constructed void'.[17]

This 'different measure' presents the argument in a confrontational manner, assuming consensus concerning what 'history' denotes. However, Coetzee's resistance of history may be a challenge to this consensus rather than a reluctance to engage with the problem of historical representation. In a talk from 1987, 'The Novel Today', Coetzee addresses the problem (also in an apparently confrontational manner): 'In times of intense ideological pressure like the present, when the space in which the novel and history normally coexist like two cows on the same pasture, each minding its own business, is squeezed to almost nothing, the novel, it seems to me, has only two options: supplementarity or rivalry.' The crucial point here is that Coetzee locates his argument historically. He is describing a strategy – in this talk given in Cape Town during the 1986–1990 State of Emergency – which is a direct response to late-apartheid South Africa. Specifically, he is challenging a sense that it is *de rigueur* for the committed anti-apartheid writer to tilt his or her writing towards a preconceived style of intervention: that is, the documentation of, the bearing witness to, the supplementation of, an agreed history. *Rivalry* with historical discourse, Coetzee suggests, will produce 'a novel that operates in terms of its own procedures and issues in its own conclusions, not one that operates in terms of the procedures of history and eventuates in conclusions that are checkable by history'. A concentration on the development of novelistic form – also a response to a precise political moment – embodies a rivalry with a pointed dialectical agenda, for such a novel would 'evolve its own paradigms and myths', in rivalry with (or 'even enmity' towards) history, which may consequently be demythologized.[18]

Coetzee is arguing for a position that has affinities with a broader postcolonial revision of history. In his talk, he goes on to discuss the novel and history as different kinds of competing discourse, suggesting that his own role as a novelist is to counter the claims of history to primacy.[19] But is this not, in a sense, also *atypical* of postcolonial revisionism? Where the usual model is one in which a displaced or hidden history resurfaces in the process of decolonization, Coetzee appears to be making a more fundamental challenge to the *idea* of history. For some commentators this challenge – which does not *necessarily* discriminate between, say, Afrikaner mythology and anti-apartheid revisionism – might appear to lose its political edge. This is a crucial nexus, where the conflation of postmodernism and postcolonialism places stress on discourse as power, on the world as text. The importance of a novelist such as Coetzee turns on how this problem is viewed. In fact, Coetzee has a more complex view of how the idea of history functions, an amplification of the argument in 'The Novel Today'.

In one of the interviews with Attwell, Coetzee offers a
sophisticated deliberation on the question of literature and
history. This comment explains the nature of Coetzee's 'obliquity', and how this is produced by his context, in terms
which are quite specific to his intellectual and political identity
as postcolonial. A key observation is that 'History may be . . . a
process for representation, but to me it feels more like a *force* for
representation, and in that sense . . . it is unrepresentable.'
This quality of being unrepresentable is given an extended
explanation, emerging from Coetzee's response to a poem by
the Polish poet Zbigniew Herbert. The poem is about five
condemned prisoners who spend their last night reminiscing
about such things as girls and card games, before being shot
when morning arrives. The focus is on the poet's rationale for
his oblique representation, in 'a poem . . . justifying poems that
stand back from calls to revolutionary action':

Herbert doesn't talk about History, but he does talk about . . . the
spirit of the barbarian (embodied in such people as Stalin), which is
pretty much the same thing as history-the-unrepresentable. Herbert's
strength is that he has something to oppose to the barbarian . . . It is
because Herbert feels himself so deeply to be a European and
believes, with whatever hedgings and reservations, in the vitality, the
social vitality, of the literature of shepherds, roses, and so forth, in the
power of poetry to bring those symbols to life, that he can oppose
poetry to the great shambling beast of history . . . But in Africa . . .?
In Poland one can still address the five men in the cell, or their
executioners in the yard, indirectly, via the almost infinite lattice that
a shared European culture provides. In Africa the only address one
can imagine is a brutally direct one, a sort of pure, unmediated
representation; what short-circuits the imagination, what forces one's
face into the thing itself, is what I am here calling history. 'The only
address one can imagine' – an admission of defeat. *Therefore*, the task
becomes imagining the unimaginable, imagining a form of address
that permits the play of *writing* to start taking place. (*DP*, 67–8)

The ending of this passage supplements the enigmatic idea that
history is unrepresentable. At the conclusion of this extract,
Coetzee acknowledges that the unmediated presentation of
history *is* imaginable – it is the obvious option, in fact – even if
it is the enemy of imagination or creativity. This warning

against the easy compromise obliges us to reconsider the sense in which Coetzee views history. If it is all too easy to succumb to the pressure to attempt a straightforward representation of history, then 'unrepresentable' carries an ethical imperative, an exhortation to resist the dynamic of history.

The account of Herbert's poem is wistful in that Coetzee is affected by Herbert's recourse to a heritage to which he does not have easy access himself. The power of European poetry, with its traditional symbols, produces a '*social* vitality' to set against history/the barbarian spirit. The opposition is startling: unmediated history – ethically unrepresentable – is associated with barbarianism (exemplified by Stalinism), and is seen as the enemy of social vitality. And, if Coetzee is wistful about the unavailability, in Africa, of the kind of shared values he associates with the European literary heritage, this is revealing about the provisional position of his literary project, this imagining of the unimaginable. Coetzee has recourse to the idea of a European literary genealogy as an *example* of a shared cultural language, that which might positively oppose the force of history. It is a resource which Coetzee must sometimes draw on (as in this discussion) as an ambivalent touchstone in his own fiction. This is an essential aspect of the discursive play he is attempting. At the same time, Coetzee does not separate European culture from the field of colonial domination, so that the recourse to a European tradition, in the battle with history-the-unrepresentable, is already an interrogation of historical forces. The interrogation is produced by the self-conscious complicity in Coetzee's wistfulness about this heritage – here, as in his fiction. This kind of gesture is symptomatic of a complex style of writing-against-itself.

A question to explore more fully is exactly what kind of postcolonial writer Coetzee is. Where is he situated through this embattled play of writing, with its various intellectual and cultural allegiances? The first point that needs to be stressed (a point implicit in the preceding pages) is that the orientation of his writing leads him to gesture beyond the late-colonial situation of South Africa under apartheid. However, there is still a sense of historical embroilment in this moment of fading colonialism that might invite a special formulation: Attwell, for example, employs the term 'colonial post-colonialism' to describe the South African situation to which Coetzee responds (especially in *Foe*).[20] Yet there are affinities between the textual decolonizations that Coetzee performs and features of the broader postcolonial dynamic. In exploring these affinities, it is necessary to confront the problem of postmodernism, and the intellectual affiliation implied in the poststructuralist/postmodernist turn.[21]

Superficially, postmodernism and postcolonialism appear to share the same goals: in both cases, the rejection of imperial discourse, with its in-built centre/margin hierarchical opposition, seems part of a broader dismantling of Eurocentric master codes. However, critical opinion is divided as to whether there is a common project, or whether the surface similarities mask essential differences in context and political orientation. It is important, here, to distinguish between different manifestations of postcolonial writing, some of which are less appropriately bracketed with postmodernism than others.

Simon During formulates a positive conflation, broadly appropriate to Coetzee's situation: During characterizes postmodern thought as 'that thought which refuses to turn the Other into the Same', thus opening up 'a theoretical space for what postmodernity denies: otherness'. Even so, there is a problem in the voicing of the Other: 'postmodern thought also recognizes, however, that the Other can never speak for itself as the Other. One should hesitate to call a discourse which revolves around these positions either for or against postmodernity, but it is certainly not simply consonant with it.'[22] This is to acknowledge the potential for complicity, whilst also insisting on the necessary distinction between postmodernism and postmodernity (without which all postmodernist expression, creative or critical, must be in thrall to late capitalism).

But are these elements of criticism and complicity in a simple balance? Kumkum Sangari argues that postmodern scepticism is 'both symptom and critique of the contemporary economic and social formation of the West', but the symptomatic element overshadows the critique, resulting in a catastrophic complicity.

In Sangari's account, postmodernism tends 'to universalize its epistemological preoccupations', a tendency found 'even in the work of critics of radical political persuasion':

On the one hand, the world contracts into the West; a Eurocentric perspective . . . is brought to bear upon 'Third World' cultural products; a 'specialized' skepticism is carried everywhere as cultural paraphernalia and epistemological apparatus, as a way of seeing; and the postmodern problematic becomes *the* frame through which the cultural products of the rest of the world are seen. On the other hand, the West expands into the world; late capitalism muffles the globe and homogenizes (or threatens to) all cultural production – this, for some reason, is one 'master narrative' that is seldom dismantled as it needs to be if the differential economic, class, and cultural formation of 'Third World' countries is to be taken into account. The writing that emerges from this position . . . gloomily disempowers the 'nation' as an enabling idea.

Of course, the complex colonial situation of South Africa would require a different model than the West/'Third World' opposition Sangari is working with, especially as the idea of a new 'nation' in post-colonial South Africa is an inevitably compromised one, more implicated in colonial structures than elsewhere in Africa. Even so, this analysis of postmodernism needs to be considered, for it is based on the worrying suggestion that postmodernism (which here includes poststructuralist criticism) represents a new kind of intellectual imperialism, a natural extension of late capitalist expansionism in the information society. Sangari makes an appeal to resist this totalizing impetus:

If the crisis of meaning in the West is seen as the product of a historical conjuncture, then perhaps the refusal either to export it or to import it may be a meaningful gesture, at least until we can replace the stifling monologues of self and other (which, however disordered or decentered, remain the orderly discourses of the bourgeois subject) with a genuinely dialogic and dialectical history that can account for the formation of different selves and the construction of different epistemologies.[23]

The rejoinder might be that an understanding of complicity is a familiar theme of postmodernism, though this may well be manifested as a peculiarly Western crisis. Postmodernism may have gone further in experimenting with dialogical discourse and dialectical representations of history than Sangari allows, but this may not be a project that speaks *for* all postcolonial experience. This raises an issue of immediate relevance to the political significance of the broader field of postcolonial studies: the problem of provenance. The familiar poststructuralist appropriation of postcolonial texts often assumes a shared agenda, which might also be chance, coincidence. The experience of colonization might well produce a particular, and independent, decentring drive with a political content unavailable to more purely theoretical areas of the postmodern. Elleke Boehmer argues that 'to quibble about provenance in this area of postmodern and postcolonial co-operation is unproductive' since 'both discourses are . . . spin-offs of . . . the disintegration of Western cultural and political authority in its imperial form'.[24] If this does not fully answer the charge of a new kind of intellectual imperialism, it does acknowledge the political responsibility of discursive formations. It also signals a conflation between postcolonialism and postmodernism which is appropriate to Coetzee's intellectual position. Any clear distinction between the two may, in fact, be exploded definitively by the position of the white academic-as-writer in South Africa.

Linda Hutcheon, whilst sensitive to the differing politics of postcolonialism and postmodernism, also suggests that an important area of overlap might be a shared complicity: the characteristic postcolonial mode of irony (also typically postmodernist) is 'a trope of doubleness', and has affinities with the simple binary codes of colonialism. Hutcheon suggests that 'the post-colonial is . . . as implicated in that which it challenges as the *post-modern*' by virtue of its partial allegiance to Eurocentric concepts. The sense of identity produced by postcolonial texts is consequently already contaminated.[25] But is the taint of contamination the same as the guilt of complicity? Diana Brydon offers an important qualification of this argument, pointing out that there is 'a leap from the recognition that the post-colonial is "contaminated" by colonialism . . . to the conclusion that such "contamination" necessarily implies complicity'. Where Hutcheon suggests that post*modernism* is politically ambivalent, Brydon argues it might be more appropriate to refer to the contradictions of post*colonialism* which produce a different aesthetic, and a different sense of the political: 'the name "post-modernism" suggests an aestheticizing of the political while the name "post-colonialism" foregrounds the political as inevitably contaminating the aesthetic, but remaining distinguishable from it'.[26] This version of postcolonialism may be modified to allow for a revised perception (rather than a rejection) of postmodernism. It also, very significantly, creates the space in which an autonomous aesthetic expression can be recognized.

Yet the particularity of individual postcolonial discourses needs to be stressed to supply the content of this politicized aesthetic. Simon During draws a distinction between the 'post-colonized', who 'identify with the culture destroyed by imperialism and its tongue'; and the 'post-colonizers', those who, 'if they do not identify with imperialism, at least cannot jettison the culture and tongues of the imperialist nations'.[27] The situation of the English-speaking writer in South Africa complicates these categories, because the English language cannot be seen as an imperialist tongue in South African literature in any simple sense.[28] One should also remember that Afrikaans has been perceived as the imperialist language in recent history. (The Soweto riots of 1976–7, for example, stemmed from protests against the enforced use of Afrikaans in teaching, the perceived language of the oppressor.) As a producer of English-language novels, Coetzee occupies a qualified site as 'post-colonizer', in which the sense of guilt and taint – a tempered complicity – can help structure a new space of aesthetic autonomy.

It should be acknowledged that a different construction of the contamination/complicity cusp is possible, one which casts doubt on the separation of 'colonial' from 'post-colonizer'. In his reading of *In the Heart of the Country*, Ian Glenn associates Coetzee's formal innovations with both modernism and 'the colonial world experience' of modernity, concluding that 'Coetzee has produced the novel of identity for the multinational age by focusing on the colonial as a kind of generic

precursor of the multinational.'[29] This is an arresting observation, from which it is tempting to extrapolate a more general
argument about Coetzee, though Glenn is concerned only with
the second novel. The logic of Glenn's designation of Coetzee's
internationalism is to see its root in his preoccupation with the
colonizing psyche. Without denying this focus, it may be
necessary to resist any implication that Coetzee is a colonial
writer, a designation which would appear to deny a new
politicized aesthetic, the existence of a new space beyond
colonial writing.

The idea of the post-colonizer allows for the engagement
with Western influences *within* postcolonial writing, in a way
that is not flatly ironic or parodic. This is the corner of
postcolonial culture described by Helen Tiffin where 'decolonization is process, not arrival'. The process involves an interaction between the European and the local, a 'dialectic
between hegemonic centrist systems and peripheral subversion
of them; between European or British discourses and their
post-colonial dis/mantling'.[30] This formulation is entirely appropriate to 'white writing' in South Africa – that writing which
is 'generated by the concerns of people no longer European,
not yet African' (*WW,* 11) – and may also help to explain
Coetzee's international resonance. If Coetzee is seen as a post-
colonizer, this resonance is Janus-faced, admitting the presence
of colonialism in a new world-view. It is precisely here that the
postcolonial offers a politicized corrective to the homogenizing
tendencies of both colonialism and postmodernity.[31]

It is in this spirit that Brydon detects a pointed critique in the
postcolonial text, a 'search for a way out of the impasse of the
endless play of post-modernist difference that mirrors liberalism's cultural pluralism'. Postcolonial writing and criticism are
united in the search for 'a new globalism' which 'simultaneously asserts local independence and global interdependencies'
by thriving 'on an interaction that "contaminates" without
homogenizing'. Such a 'new globalism' is conceived as 'neither
the old universalism nor the Disney simulacrum'.[32]

Coetzee, it seems, provides a test-case for defining this new
globalism which, in an apparent paradox, ties together the

general and the particular. Coetzee's importance, that is to say, stems from his specificity as a post-colonizer, and from the credibility given to the international moment of decolonization by the scrupulous specifics of its constituent parts. This duality – the peculiar force of which may hold good for only a narrow historical moment – may account for Coetzee's stature in the field of postmodernist literature, and better than any naive notion of 'universal' appeal: it is his exemplary role as post-colonizer that speaks to a broad international community, with a shared experience, while continuing to offer very precise discursive interventions in a given context.[33]

This discussion – in implicitly marking some kind of line between the modernism upon which Coetzee draws, and his own brand of postmodernist expression – sketches a definition which is based upon the writer's intellectual and historical locations taken together. Yet this is not to imply a clear break, which would evidently dilute Coetzee's continual insistence on his position as partly determined by intellectual as well as historical complicity. This, necessarily, is an evolving definition in which the 'post' in postmodernism may be taken to indicate both an extension of modernism, and a challenge to it, and to the broader impulses of modernity it may contain. This apparent paradox – involving both extension and challenge – is crucial to the dialectic of any ethically oriented postmodernism.[34]

In acknowledging this site of diverse pulls and influences, Michael Chapman argues that 'we can "Africanise" Coetzee's stories without denying their attachments to the projects of modernity'. The dialectic, however, involves a simultaneous *detachment* from such projects:

What distinguishes Coetzee from the latter-day colonial's penchant simply to copy the Western culture, for example, is his scepticism about the master narrative of the West itself: according to his reiterated view, the ideas of the enlightenment have translated themselves in the 'third world' as imperialisms, more latterly global-isms, that through superior technology are likely to continue to impose their will on others.

Accordingly, Chapman sees no reason 'to denigrate [Coetzee's] post-modernism since he does not revel in the simulacra of the consumerised image, but holds the global hyper-realities to third-world account'. We cannot, however, look for simple solutions, since Coetzee's 'suspicions of Western totalism' are not countered by a romantic evocation 'of indigenous cultures'. Indeed, 'it is no use invoking lost pasts, whether Afrikaner or African: the greater responsibility is to understand, modify, and re-imagine the symbolic narratives and the maxims by which we construct and construe our "reality"'.[35] This is a post-modernism which is based on a notion of hybridity which embraces literary and intellectual identity, as well as a particular historical moment: apparent simple binary oppositions – modernism/postmodernism; first world/third world – are reconstituted in a more complex transitional model. If this is the essence of Coetzee's postcolonialism, it seems to conform in some measure to the 'postcolonial contramodernity' which Homi Bhabha has defined, involving a 'postcolonial time-lag' which allows the discourse of modernity to be properly written from a postcolonial perspective:

Without the postcolonial time-lag the discourse of modernity cannot, I believe, be written; with the *projective past* it can be inscribed as a historical narrative of alterity that explores forms of social antagonism and contradiction that are not yet properly represented, political identities in the process of being formed, cultural enunciations in the act of hybridity, in the process of translating and transvaluing cultural differences.[36]

A modified understanding of how political identity and cultural hybridity is manifested in actual late-colonial South Africa must obtain, since these are, inevitably, areas of suppression. But Coetzee gestures continually towards newly conceived political identities, through fictions which are themselves pointed acts of hybridity.

   A specific feature of Coetzee's work, which is also a recurring theme of postcolonial writing and criticism, is allegory. The creation of allegory, as a procedure for creative writing, is complex in Coetzee's work, since it unites the different aspects of his literary identity. The role of semiotics in contemporary literary theory raises an idea of allegory to a position of

unprecedented importance in literary history, with the implication that all language and all literature is allegorical in
forming a network of deferments of meaning, of allusions to
(and substitutions for) an unattainable referent.[37] The fluidity
of contemporary allegory, implied in contemporary theoretical
accounts, chimes also with the transition from modernism to
postmodernism, helping us to place Coetzee within this development. This involves, also, a supplanting of the (overprivi-
leged) symbolic mode, as Fredric Jameson suggests:

If the symbolic is (overhastily) assimilated to various organic concep-
tions of the work of art and of culture itself, then the return of the
repressed of its various opposites, and of a whole range of overt or
covert theories of the allegorical, can be characterized by a generalized sensitivity, in our own time, to breaks and discontinuities, to the
heterogeneous (not merely in works of art), to Difference rather than
Identity, to gaps and holes rather than seamless webs and triumphant
narrative progressions, to social differentiation rather than to Society
as such and its 'totality'.

The allegorical method which results 'is very much what is
demanded and mobilized by the periodizing schema of the
modernism/postmodernism break'. It is also 'overhasty' to
associate the symbolic with a cultural dominant, because the
drift of Jameson's outline argument is to associate the modernism that is challenged by postmodern allegory with a
unifying mode that it had already begun to disrupt. However,
this does help us to map out general tendencies, and to see
which features, incipient in modernism, are intensified in the
postmodern turn. In the category of 'the allegorical', Jameson
includes the range of critical orientations and theories, emerging in postmodernism, which embody a pluralistic and provisional approach to the problem of interpretation. For allegory
(as a creative and a critical mode) this involves a new
grounding, or ungrounding:

The newer allegory is horizontal rather than vertical: if it must still
attach its one-on-one conceptual labels to its objects after the fashion
of *The Pilgrim's Progress*, it does so in the conviction that those objects
(along with their labels) are now profoundly relational, indeed are
themselves constructed by their relations to each other. When we add

to this the inevitable mobility of such relations, we begin to glimpse the process of allegorical interpretation as a kind of scanning that, moving back and forth across the text, readjusts its terms in constant modification of a type quite different from our stereotypes of some static medieval or biblical decoding.[38]

In a more static conception, allegory can be seen as a device for concealing (and so for disseminating) transgressive, or 'heretical' ideas (associated, for example, with secret brotherhoods, or the victims of religious persecution), since the encoding of a message makes it harder to recover. Possibly just such a static understanding of allegory has had a bearing on the failure of Coetzee's novels to invoke the disapprobation of the South African censors: his work has been judged (he surmises) too indirect to be a genuine threat (*DP*, 298). Coetzee is clear, however, that such strategic writing is fruitless since 'the game of slipping Aesopian messages past the censor is ultimately a sterile one, diverting writers from their proper task' (*GO*, viii). In Jameson's very different conception, however, allegory becomes a radical investigation of its own grounding. In the case of Coetzee, this self-analysis often manifests itself in a blurring of the two parallel planes of signification – the allegorical and the literal referent – notionally held apart in separate (corresponding) levels. This is especially clear in *In the Heart of the Country*: if Magda's 'spinster fate' *allegorizes* the international isolation of South Africa, the novel's action – with its inversion of the master/servant relationship – seems a more literal representation of a South Africa on the brink of revolution. The distinction is sometimes slippery, of course, but it is based on the assumption that metonymy is dominant in more mimetic modes of representation, whereas allegory is governed by an impulse to metaphor: Coetzee consistently elides the metonymic and the metaphoric.

The example of postcolonial allegory illustrates how a more abstract theoretical model can perform very precise and necessary textual decolonizations. Stephen Slemon's theory of postcolonial allegory accounts, appropriately, for Coetzee's ambivalent use of the mode. For Slemon, postcolonial allegory effectively represents a challenge both to the structures of colonial thinking, and to theoretical ideas concerning the function of allegory, its cultural bases and its relationship to history. The postcolonial perspective suggests that history embodies either the imposition of the colonizer, or 'a cultural absence', which means the effectiveness of postcolonial writing depends on its 'strategies for transcending or going "beyond history"', a focus which tallies with Coetzee's own complaints about history as category. Allegory is prominent among these strategies, representing a historical revisionism which draws its radicalism from an emphasis on history as discourse, something which 'destabilise[s] history's fixity'. In this kind of revisionism 'received images of history are projected into an implied level of meaning that runs in parallel to the literal level of the text'. History exists, that is to say, as an extra-textual presence which is alluded to through the process of allegorical correspondence. The reader has an active role in this dialectic of discourses:

> The point for post-colonial allegory is that historical material must be *read*, and read in *adjacency* to a fictional re-enactment of it. Two separate 'lenses of language' require focusing; the reader's gaze must be binocular; and binocular vision enables depth perception. In post-colonial allegory, the field of vision for this depth perception is our inherited concepts of history itself.
>
> In this way, post-colonial allegorical writing builds the provisional, discursive nature of history into the structure and narrative mode of the text so that it becomes approachable only in an act of reading that foregrounds its secondary or conditional nature, its link to fictionality.

This model of the dialectical interaction of discourses implicitly develops and undermines a more static model of allegory which can be associated with the colonial project: if a fundamental impulse of allegory is to set a literary text 'against a pre-existing master code' then 'a similar process of interpreting signs has been used in imperial thinking to read the world and to legitimise the power relations it establishes within it'. The colonial reliance on a pre-given master code of interpretation, projected onto the object of colonization, suggests an *allegorizing impulse in imperialism*, and this requires that allegory itself be interrogated in postcolonial writing. Slemon offers Coetzee's

Waiting for the Barbarians as an illustration that 'allegory can . . . be used to dismantle the system of allegorical thinking that underwrites the act of colonisation'.[39] This ambivalent model – the use of allegory against itself – is typical of Coetzee, as is his emphasis on discursiveness in allegory and in myth-making, an emphasis which already opens up the closural tendency of colonial history.

This overview of Coetzee's literary and cultural identity is based on the assumption that the local and the international determinants of the writer are inseparable, complementary influences. Is there, however, a narrower allegiance for Coetzee, as member of an academic community with its own agenda? Ian Glenn suggests that 'if Coetzee is organically connected to or representative of any class in South Africa, then it must surely be that of professional academics at the traditional English-speaking universities'. Implicitly, this is offered as an explanation of Coetzee's novelistic manner, since the University of Cape Town 'has had the greatest interest in proclaiming the international nature of knowledge, in claiming not to be involved in the local applications of apartheid but to adhere to universal notions of academic freedom and disinterested academic inquiry, and in arguing that apartheid is but one manifestation of other issues over which the intellect can triumph'. Coetzee's own comments on his identity, and the way it is determined by the specific colonial situation of South Africa would seem to distance him from 'universal' or 'disinterested' academic matters. Yet how his academic identity determines his literary identity is crucial, not, perhaps, at the level of an individual institution, but in an international dimension as Coetzee is one of a new breed of critics-as-writers.[40]

With regard to Coetzee's 'dual allegiance to creative and critical disciplines', Glenn considers one consequence to be 'that Coetzee the critic may be said to have attempted to make his works critic-proof', so that they 'understand his critics better than the other way around, anticipating their readings and objections'.[41] This imputes a deliberate pre-empting to the novelist's design, a focus on academic reception rather than fictional expression. However, Coetzee's self-conscious doubts about such a project are a matter of record in his essay on Nabokov's *Pale Fire*.[42] One might expect a critic-as-writer to make full use of his or her intellectual and theoretical resources, and it is not certain that this necessarily implies anticipation of the critics. Huggan and Watson speculate that 'Academe would have invented J. M. Coetzee had he not already existed, so sympathetic do his concerns seem to be to critical theory and many of its current preoccupations.' This means that Coetzee 'represents in himself a new kind of author, in whom academic critic and writer, formerly regarded as distinct, are melded as never before – even more closely than is the case with, say, an American novelist such as John Barth'.[43] The consonance between the fiction and the preoccupations of theory (as a *presence* in the fiction) is well observed. But this may not result in a sympathetic correspondence, even though this seems to be the obvious conclusion. A different emphasis may be apposite. In an interview with Jean Sévry, Coetzee is asked whether he sees continuity or disruption between his activities as a writer and as a linguist, and he responds in these terms:

Much of my academic training was in Linguistics. And in many ways I am more interested in the linguistic than the literary side of my academic profession. I think there is evidence of an interest in problems of language throughout my novels. I don't see any disruption between my professional interest in language and my activities as a writer.[44]

Attwell cites this response to indicate that Coetzee 'admits to being a linguist before being a writer', an observation that may need a gloss.[45] What Coetzee actually admits to in the interview is a greater interest 'in the linguistic than the literary side of my *academic* profession', which establishes a distinction between linguistics and literary analysis (rather than creative writing). This makes sense of Coetzee's focus on questions of language in his literary criticism, without suggesting that an interest in language theory anticipates the fiction. Of course, his theoretical reading is a pervasive influence in the fiction, but in ways that are by no means straightforward: there is no formulaic application of theory specifically designed to pre-empt the critics. It may be more appropriate to give some credence to the distinctions Coetzee has implicitly drawn (at Attwell's prompting) between creative and critical work. Resisting the invitation to offer some interpretation of the motif of resistance in *Michael K*, Coetzee articulates his discomfort by drawing a clear distinction between the critical and creative acts. He talks of the novel becoming, in the writing process, 'less a *thing* than a *place* where one goes every day for several hours a day for years on end. What happens in that place has less and less discernible relation to the daily life one lives . . . other forces, another dynamic takes over . . . In contrast, as I talk to you today, I have no sense of *going anywhere* for my answers. What I say here is continuous with the rest of the daily life of a writer-academic like myself.' Coetzee talks of the respect he is obliged to cultivate for the writing process, without feeling the equivalent respect for his interpretative comments, whatever integrity they may have (*DP*, 205). The import of this response is to stress the process of creative writing as wholly other to critical and interpretative comment, of which Coetzee is, in another interview, dismissive: 'what is criticism, what can it ever be, but either a betrayal (the usual case) or an overpowering (the rarer case) of its object? How often is there an equal marriage?' (*DP*, 61).

Nadine Gordimer, expressing distrust of the critic's tendency to emphasize the presence of theory in the fiction, argues that Coetzee 'forgets the language and thought-patterns of literary theory' in the process of creative writing.[46] This bald dismissal ought, perhaps, to be set against the distinction Coetzee makes: this notion of 'forgetting' is at odds with his usual insistence on the unavoidable presence of traces, influences.

Another way of approaching this problem may be to situate Coetzee in a broader cultural cross-fertilization. This is the impetus of Attwell's rejoinder to Gordimer's complaints: he suggests that after poststructuralism the writer/critic boundary is inevitably breaking down where different cultural discourses (including those of the critic and the writer) face an increasingly well-informed mutual interrogation.[47]

Coetzee's distrust of criticism, his refusal to see it as an object deserving of respect, does not, of course, deny the presence of theoretical ideas as inspiration for his fictional motifs. But the insistence on the uniqueness of the creative process must alert us to the special ways in which such ideas are fictionalized, and make us sceptical of finding the theorist's agenda untransformed. In fact, fictional transformations of theoretical ideas abound in Coetzee's novels, and these, together with the other innovations in literary form alluded to in this chapter, comprise the determining features of this post-colonizing literature.

CHAPTER 2

Writing violence: 'Dusklands'

It has become a truism in criticism of Coetzee that *Dusklands* (1974) introduces a new postmodernist strain in the novel from South Africa.[1] Gordimer, it is true, is progressing towards a discursive self-consciousness at this time (notably in *The Conservationist*, also 1974); but *Dusklands* offers no mimetic representation of the South Africa with which it is contemporaneous: it also introduces the characteristic Coetzee style, in which an interrogation of the chosen narrative modes is an integral aspect of the fiction.

This interrogation, at one level, is straightforward, relating to different discourses of imperialism which are parodied in the novel. At another level, however, the interrogation becomes more complex, designating a reflexive self-critique which implicates the austerity of postmodernist expression itself (or at least the *idea* of this austerity). The impetus of this built-in critique is to anticipate a charge of moral failure, an absence of judgement on the horrors depicted. An incipient ethical stance emerges, often where a self-consciousness about discourse – postmodernism in caricature – is made to betray its own will-to-power.

The book is divided into two main sections (each with its own subsections), though it is probably wrong to speak of these two sections as separate novellas as their meaning is dependent upon their interrelationship, and the development of theme and motif.[2] The first section, 'The Vietnam Project', details the collapse into insanity of its narrator, Eugene Dawn, writing an analysis of the psychological war in Vietnam for the US Defense Department. One subsection is an extract from Dawn's report, which parodies the pseudo-rationality of this kind of analysis. (The point of reference, here, is a collection of Hudson institute reports, published in 1968 with the title *Can We Win in Vietnam? The American Dilemma*. Coetzee's epigraph is taken from this volume.[3])

The second section, 'The Narrative of Jacobus Coetzee', with its subsections and attendant apparatus, is based on the travel writing of seventeenth- and eighteenth-century 'explorers' of the Cape (the original Jacobus Coetsé was a distant ancestor of the author) (*DP*, 52). This structure invites us to draw parallels between a moment of contemporary imperialism and the origins of Afrikaner domination, and to examine the question of authorial complicity, both as a general issue, and through a recognition of the specific self-analysis of Coetzee's historical associations.[4]

Those critics who have found fault with *Dusklands* have tended to concentrate on the obliquity of the book's method: Coetzee is condemned for failing to offer a more direct rejection of the colonial violence he represents. The more damaging corollary of this is the charge that the book is somehow itself complicitous with the excitement of colonial self-aggrandizement. Peter Knox-Shaw, for example, feels this to be 'an art that can only re-enact', while W. J. B. Wood considers the book to be 'curiously symptomatic of the very thing it purports to diagnose'.[5] Actually, complicity is a theme of the novel, and is inevitably enacted in the sequence of first-person narratives, where each narrating subject is exposed as a product and perpetrator of colonial projects. The complaint does raise larger questions about the adequacy of postmodernist expression, and its avoidance of a centred authorial judgement, but the significant technical question, for a close reading of the novel, is how the exposure of colonialism is generated. The principal vehicle for this is irony, and the success of this will be a matter for individual readers to determine. Knox-Shaw doubts whether irony is adequate for the treatment of the brutality the novel depicts.[6] My view is that the ironic undercutting is extensive enough – indeed it pervades the novel – to make the question of judgement ultimately unequivocal. And there are places where a position of implied authorial judgement is evident, certainly when one bears in mind the overall structure of the book, and the effects produced by pattern and juxtaposition.[7]

Of the two sections, the second – 'The Narrative of Jacobus Coetzee' and its related apparatus – is the longer, suggesting that this is where the emphasis lies, and this is what one might expect: the analysis of US involvement in Vietnam is a prelude to the consideration of Dutch expansionism in eighteenth-century South Africa. Significant parallels are drawn, and the first section acts as an overture to the second. This is important because many themes which are introduced in 'The Vietnam Project' are treated less directly in Jacobus Coetzee's narrative, so that the implied judgement of the second section sometimes depends upon the cumulative reading experience. Attitudes and key terms recur, acquiring significance as the novel progresses.

Eugene Dawn, the narrator of 'The Vietnam Project', is shown to have been driven insane (to a position of disconnected amorality) by his work as a mythographer for the US military. Connections are made between the dehumanizing effects of war, and the psychological impact of defining racial and cultural differences in the furtherance of military tactics. A broad concept of patriarchy is implicated in this, though central to this analysis is a consideration of how Western consumerism defines woman as commodity for consumption. These, in outline, are the forces which produce the psychological collapse of Eugene Dawn. The section ends with his institutionalization, resisting the probes of his psychiatric doctors, after kidnapping and then stabbing his son. At one level, the book reveals an allegorical connection between Dawn and the US itself: if both are unnatural fathers, the association concerns not only the paternal imperialism of the US, but the nation's role as the sometimes inhospitable host to a complex migrant multi-culturalism.

Eugene Dawn's inability to participate in a community – in a civilization of mutual interaction – produces a solipsism which governs his narrative. Inextricably tied to this solipsism is a pervasive brutality, a consequence of the inability to perceive the Other as human. The result is that all self-expression (like all colonial self-interest) is something that is enacted upon the Other, dehumanized, and rendered a fitting object for violence, willed or actual. Dawn describes his wife as 'the swimwear model I married' (*D*, 39), thus reducing her to the fetishistic sexual icon of Western consumerism, and her name Marilyn reinforces this with its echo of Marilyn Monroe.[8] Dawn's description of sex with Marilyn concentrates on his own lack of satisfaction:

Before the arrival of my seed her pouch yawns and falls back, leaving my betrayed representative gripped at its base, flailing its head in vain inside an immense cavern, at the very moment when above all else it craves to be rocked through its tantrum in a soft, firm, infinitely trustworthy grip. The word which at such moments flashes its tail across the heavens of my never quite extinguished consciousness is *evacuation*: my seed drips like urine into the futile sewers of Marilyn's reproductive ducts. (*D*, 8)

The desire to impose physical contact on the Other becomes a motif in the book, brutality expressed as a psychological need. It is clearly significant that this need is presented, initially, as a phallocentric concern. In the absence of male pleasure, sex is presented, here, as defilement. The term 'evacuation' has a particular proleptic function as it plays a crucial part in the ironizing of Jacobus Coetzee, as we shall see. A related idea emerges in Coetzee's later essay (1988) on D. H. Lawrence and *Lady Chatterley's Lover*, where Coetzee considers Lawrence's view that an excremental idea of sex is at the root of the porno-graphic imagination. This notion of sex as dirty – as an act of soiling done to woman by man – is something which Coetzee sees as tainting Lawrence's own imagination in key essays on obscenity and on *Lady Chatterley*. Also implicated in this 'taint' is Lawrence's justification of phallic possession. Coetzee is not necessarily critical here of Lawrence's novel itself; indeed he feels Lawrence's justifications represent a betrayal of its achievements. Neither does Coetzee come to firm conclusions in defining the pornographic. It is the *idea* of male seed as tainted, and the associated *idea* that an excremental view of sex underlies the pornographic – ideas broached not by Lawrence's novel, but by his defence of it – that chime with *Dusklands*. Here these are presented as aspects of the imperialist psyche (*DP*, 302–14).[9]

   The novel's first section invites speculation on the nature of the pornographic, how it can be defined and what its psychological effects might be. Marilyn, Dawn reports, associates his problems with a series of photographs of war atrocities (*D*, 10), and this connection is swiftly established. Having reported the discovery of a photograph of Marilyn naked – the product of an affair, Dawn assumes – he goes on to describe some of his photos, admitting the 'delicious shame' and arousal they produce in him (*D*, 15). The matter of visual control is an obvious additional component of the colonizing identity, expressed again in phallocentric terms; as, for example, when Dawn expresses a voyeuristic interest in seeing Marilyn through another man's eyes, because, as he admits, he is excited by 'new perspectives' (*D*, 11). The photographs are his obsession, and they offer a distillation of imperialist violence. The horror of the photos is effectively underscored by Dawn's confused and inappropriate responses to them. The first, apparently, is an image of child rape, a hefty sergeant copulating with a Vietnamese female. Dawn calls her a woman, though suggests she could be a child. However, in giving the photograph the caption 'Father Makes Merry with Children' Dawn indicates his preferred interpretation (*D*, 13).

   The second photo depicts two smiling sergeants brandishing, as trophies, the severed heads of three Vietnamese. (The association with John the Baptist – beheaded by Herod for 'political' reasons – may not be accidental.) Dawn reports that he finds a severed head ridiculous, and giggles at the thought of a grieving mother retrieving the head of her son, carrying it away in a sack, like a supermarket purchase (*D*, 15–16). A lunatic and dehumanized reaction is presented through the pointed association of Western commodification and sadistic enjoyment.

   The third image, a still from a propaganda film of caged prisoners on Hon Tre Island, is the most significant. In the film, Dawn explains, a commander jabs at a prisoner in a cage with a cane, calling the prisoner a bad man and a communist for the benefit of the microphone. Dawn has two enlarged photographs of this prisoner; the second, in greater magnification, he describes:

The glint in the right eye has become a diffuse white patch; shades of dark gray mark the temple, the right eyebrow, the hollow of the cheek.

I close my eyes and pass my fingertips over the cool, odorless surface of the print. Evenings are quiet here in the suburbs. I concentrate myself. Everywhere its surface is the same. The glint in the eye, which in a moment luckily never to arrive will through the camera look into my eyes, is bland and opaque under my fingers, yielding no passage into the interior of this obscure but indubitable man. I keep exploring. Under the persistent pressure of my imagination, acute and morbid in the night, it may yet yield. (*D*, 16–17)

The desire, through 'exploration', to make the image of the man 'yield' its 'interior' is palpably at one with the desire for colonial domination. Yet the desire is a haunting obsession, tainted by the fear of the man's direct glance, a fear forever artificially postponed through the arrest of the film. The wielding of power through the control of technology gives specificity to the context – US imperialism in Vietnam – and also supplies an example of Coetzee's significance in contemporary intellectual thought. Here he presents an arresting conjunction between US imperialism, technology and the experience of postmodernity. If this is a familiar set of connections to us now – (Fredric Jameson places the Vietnam experience in this kind of intellectual history, for example[10]) – it seems remarkably prescient expressed in a novel in 1974. Through the evocation of quiet evenings in the suburbs, Coetzee also presents what is now a familiar theme in American literature and (especially) film: that beneath the surface normality of suburbia, an arrested time, seethes a tide of latent violence.[11]

The opening part of Dawn's narrative ends with an articulation of US policy as an expression of the selfsame desire:

Our nightmare was that since whatever we reached for slipped like smoke through our fingers, we did not exist; that since whatever we embraced wilted, we were all that existed. We landed on the shores of Vietnam clutching our arms and pleading for someone to stand up without flinching to these probes of reality: if you will prove yourself, we shouted, you will prove us too . . .

But like everything else they withered before us . . . If they had walked toward us singing through the bullets we would have knelt and worshipped; but the bullets knocked them over and they died as we had feared . . . We forced ourselves deeper than we had ever gone before into their women; but when we came back we were still alone, and the women like stones. (*D*, 17–18)

The presentation of imperial violence as a quest for ontological reassurance anticipates a main preoccupation of Jacobus Coetzee. The vicious circularity of this need, which produces increasing levels of brutality, is evidently self-defeating. Again, the presentation is phallocentric: the desire for contact and self-confirmation manifests itself in ever more violent rape, producing inevitably dehumanized victims.

To some extent, there is, in such passages, an enactment of the brutal pseudo-rationality that the novel would reject. Consequently, one is required to be a resisting reader, and this is signalled quite obviously. When Dawn kidnaps his son, and his madness becomes overt, this is merely confirmation of what has already been demonstrated. When tracked down by his wife and two court officers, Dawn stabs his son, and describes the act with the same pseudo-rationality that governs his narrative. He considers, for example, the memory of the child's skin popping, and speculates dispassionately on the nature of this sensation (*D*, 42). In this scene, the past tense occasionally intrudes into a sequence of events described mainly in the present, indicating that Dawn is recollecting through his madness – as therapy, perhaps – and reliving the scene. Clear signals are given, here, not simply that the lucid narrating voice is unreliable, but that a process of concealment is operative: the amorality of an unhinged psyche is 'cloaked' (but actually revealed) by a discourse of attempted rational justification. This is a principle that holds good for the novel as a whole. It also raises the issue of how self-justification undermines itself, and this has direct ramifications, by analogy, for Dawn's assimilation of brutality, and for his work as mythographer. The broader parodic aspect of Dawn's self-justification draws in the discourses of post-Enlightenment rationality, and hence the ideological rationalization of Western colonialism.[12]

In an important section in the first part of Dawn's narrative, he gives an account of print as a medium which ties these concerns to the broader project of writing. Here, print is said to be sadism, a 'hard master' before whom writer and reader are equally abased. Into this discussion Dawn introduces a consideration of pornography, finding something liberating in the impulses he assigns to it:

The pornographer is the doomed upstart hero who aspires to such delirium of ecstasy that the surface of the print will crack beneath his words. We write our violent novelties on the walls of lavatories to bring the walls down . . . Pornography is an abasement before the page, such abasement as to convulse the very page. Print-reading is a slave habit. I discovered this truth, as I discovered all the truths in my Vietnam report, by introspection. (*D*, 14)

The final sentence here alerts us to the dubious provenance of this 'truth', another product of Dawn's catastrophic solipsism. Dawn's introduction of the topic of pornography is also a hostage to fortune. He is defining it as a written genre, but there is clearly a connection between this topic, and the photographs of atrocities which induce in him shame and arousal. Dawn considers printed written pornography to be heroic in the sense that it disrupts the slavish reception of print, threatening to crack its surface, much as he desires somehow to penetrate the smooth surface of the print of the prisoner (*D*, 16–17). The desired transgression is one of liberation through violence, and this indicates another area in which the novel gives signals requiring us to resist any sense of re-enactment. Pornography is often said to have an insidious normalizing effect: excitement is induced, so this argument runs, by presenting as normal that which is sensed to be indecent. This is the logic of desensitization which suggests devotees of pornography must, once one level of thrill is normalized, progress to another more 'indecent' level until that, too, is normalized. (Coetzee considers this argument in his later work on censorship (*GO*, 66–7).) This dynamic of dehumanization – and this version of the pornographic –

supplies a partial explanation for Dawn's reactions to his photos. More important, however, is that his own account of the pornographic has a different emphasis: it is an overt disruption of the printed medium which he defines, an heroic transgression through violence, acknowledged as such.

There is a contradiction, then, between Dawn's own justification of that which is transgressive and liberating, and how he appears actually to have been desensitized himself. The *effect* of his own narrative, however, conforms more to the model of overt transgression, since what we read is disruptive and dissonant, the opposite of that which normalizes the indecent, the unacceptable. This is the best guarantee that the novel as a whole (for this principle, too, is pervasive) does more than enact the colonial fantasy: we are continually disturbed by the internal contradictions of this fantasy, highlighted by the fissures and disruptions in the two narratives. In effect, Coetzee programmes into the novel a hunt for 'the obscene'; the reader learns to look for obscenity in the ideological positions of the successive narrators. In this sense, the evocation of the pornographic is instrumental in advancing a broader analysis. (Latterly, Coetzee points out that the obscene is not coreferential with the pornographic (*GO*, 20).[13])

In 'The Vietnam Project', Dawn's discussion of propaganda, in his official report, includes a section on 'the father voice', where bombing raids – authority from the sky – are associated with propaganda on the radio waves (*D*, 21). This explicit cultivation of patriarchal authority as the instrument of imperialism recurs in 'The Narrative of Jacobus Coetzee', initially when Jacobus imagines his Hottentot servants see him as their father (*D*, 64). In the second, brutal expedition of retribution, the boy Adonis, pleading in vain for his life, calls Jacobus 'my father' in an attempt to appease the mad egotist who still shoots him (*D*, 101).[14] Another (associated) motif is that of visual control. For Jacobus, this is the determining image of his objectives:

Only the eyes have power. The eyes are free, they reach out to the horizon all around. Nothing is hidden from the eyes. As the other senses grow numb or dumb my eyes flex and extend themselves. I become a spherical reflecting eye moving through the wilderness and ingesting it. Destroyer of the wilderness, I move through the land cutting a devouring path from horizon to horizon. There is nothing from which my eye turns, I am all that I see. Such loneliness! . . . What is there that is not me? (*D*, 79)

The 'freedom' that is articulated is the freedom to destroy and consume. This is colonization as total imposition, a god-like refashioning of everything in the image of the colonizer. As for Eugene Dawn, the will-to-power results in self-defeating solipsism, with all notions of the Other effaced. Later, bemoaning the lack of penetrative violence displayed by the Namaquas, Jacobus claims that blue eyes are needed for penetration; Coetzee thus introduces a hint of Aryan domination into the theme of visual control (*D*, 97).

Another facet of Jacobus' self-projection, and its built-in contradiction, is *cultural* imperialism. The would-be colonizer is unable to respond to indigenous culture on its own terms. The Namaqua dance which Jacobus witnesses, for example, distresses him. Jacobus describes the dance as an imitation of the courtship behaviour of the dove, combining a sense of the chase with different representations of sexuality which clearly convey a certain dignity. Yet Jacobus is distressed by the complexity: 'Nothing would have relieved me more than for the rhythms to simplify themselves and the dancers to drop their pantomime and cavort in an honest sexual frenzy culminating in mass coitus. I have always enjoyed watching coitus, whether of animals or slaves' (*D*, 86). The 'relief' he desires is that of debasing the cultural expression, reducing it to a visual scene he fully understands and controls. The phallocentric view – a defining characteristic of Jacobus – is explicitly presented as contradictory. Early in the narrative he indicates that 'Bushman girls' (the oxymoron reveals the limits of colonial taxonomy) are preferable to Dutch girls who 'carry an aura of property with them'. The Dutch girl's baggage of family and property results in a loss of freedom for the man, whereas the Bushman girl, depicted as having just witnessed the colonizer shooting her menfolk, 'is tied into nothing'. She is 'a rag you wipe yourself on and throw away' (*D*, 61). This enthusiasm for murder, rape and defilement as the route to freedom is not left simply to offend on its own terms: its own terms are undermined, since the necessary material acquisitiveness of the colonizer is at odds with the sexual violence – satisfied by a non-materialistic connection – that is also part of this identity.[15]

Jacobus, in short, is barbaric. His solipsism, philistinism and phallocentric aggression are all impulses inimical to civilization. The obvious master–savage inversion that we witness in his narrative is quite clearly stated when he is reduced to leading a Bushman's life (as he imagines it) (*D*, 98–9), though by this stage his savagery is already self-evident.

The ironic undercutting of Jacobus is at its most effective in the discrepancy that emerges between his perception of himself as heroic, god-like explorer, and the dismissive way he is treated by the Namaquas. Indeed, in this section of the novel Coetzee is able to inject the respite of humour into what is otherwise an intensely bleak work.

When the Namaquas are encountered, Jacobus rehearses in his mind the sequence of events he imagines will follow. These involve various scenarios of violence and the struggle for power, and, in the sequence they are imagined, ultimate victory for – and reverence of – himself as demigod (*D*, 65–6). This anticipation sets up a bathetic descent in the section which immediately follows, headed 'Sojourn in the land of the Great Namaqua'. The heading catches the pomposity and self-importance of Jacobus which the narrative now debunks. Far from the awe-inspiring explorer, Jacobus is ridiculed. He has brought with him tobacco and rolled copper to buy goodwill, but he is robbed even of the power to dispense these bribes: the Namaqua men crowd round his wagon chanting their demand for 'presents' (*D*, 68), and soon they appropriate all of Jacobus' goods, his oxen and his wagon, and most of his servants defect. Neither is Jacobus treated with any respect in the Namaqua settlement: the boys call him 'Long Nose', and a woman performs an insulting dance to taunt him (*D*, 72, 74). Soon Jacobus is suffering from severe diarrhoea, and is becoming delirious. (He wonders if he has been poisoned (*D*, 97), although this can be read as a paranoiac interpretation of motive, based on self-projection: the Namaqua express no unprompted violence towards him.) His weakness overtakes him in a futile attempt to escape the camp, during which his one faithful servant, Jan Klawer, holds him in position while, as he puts it, 'I evacuated myself heroically over the tailgate' of the wagon (*D*, 75). These repeated evacuations, evidently far from heroic, comprise the most significant mark Jacobus is to leave on the land on this exploratory expedition. In this sense, they are representative of his project. The term 'evacuation' also recalls the term when used by Eugene Dawn in describing sex with his wife. Through this deliberate association, the defilement of woman is connected to the defilement of colonization.

Back in the camp, the delirious Jacobus, effectively under house arrest, is confined to one of the huts reserved for menstruating women, in a further indignity. These huts, beyond a stream marking the boundary of the rest of the village, are a place of confinement and temporary expulsion. Jacobus, fed on scraps and suffering from a large carbuncle near his anus, makes a slow recovery. At one point, he makes an expedition across the stream towards the village proper, having to hold his buttocks apart as he walks to ease the pressure on the carbuncle. Once spotted he is summarily ordered back to his hut. He turns, and realizes that it would be injudicious to hold his buttocks in the same way on the return journey: 'My buttocks grated on each other but I could not afford a wrong gesture' (*D*, 85). Even at the height of his humiliation, Jacobus retains his false sense of himself as an emissary of civilization. The gesture he is fearful of risking is one that may be judged abusive, invoking wrath, yet this fear for himself is couched in terms that suggest the power of negotiation is still available to him. The comedy is generated by Jacobus' *lack* of humour, and, in such moments, the undermining of Jacobus is fully accomplished, since his discourse – and the lack of self-knowledge it reveals – is shown to be directly at odds with his situation.

The humour generated by Jacobus' bathetic descent is short-lived, however, since his brutality manifests itself even in this section. Revenging himself on a group of mocking children, he attacks them, biting an ear off one. The Namaqua adults declare him to be mad. As with Eugene Dawn, insanity is confirmed, and externally verified, after the physical attack on a child (*D*, 90–1).

Jacobus Coetzee, like Eugene Dawn, justifies the colonial project as a need for ontological reassurance, and again the illogicality of this reasoning is manifest in the manner of its presentation. After his second expedition of vengeance, in which the Namaqua village is razed to the ground, its inhabitants raped and slaughtered, Jacobus asks himself what has been achieved through all of these deaths. His explanation is confused and wild, despite the self-confidence of the construction:

Through their deaths I, who after they had expelled me had wandered the desert like a pallid symbol, again asserted my reality. No more than any other man do I enjoy killing; but I have taken it upon myself to be the one to pull the trigger, performing this sacrifice for myself and my countrymen, who exist, and committing upon the dark folk the murders we have all wished. All are guilty, without exception. I include the Hottentots. Who knows for what unimaginable crimes of the spirit they died, through me? God's judgment is just, irreprehensible, and incomprehensible. His mercy pays no heed to merit. I am a tool in the hands of history. (*D*, 106)

Jacobus Coetzee remains a symbol – a vivid rather than a pallid one – of the colonizer, and this passage concentrates the pseudo-rationality of the colonizing psyche. The need for self-confirmation is a primary feature, though the solipsist's attempt to confirm his own reality through contact is always self-defeating. The unnecessary assertion that his countrymen exist reveals the ontological insecurity. Further, the appeal to incomprehensible divine judgement, through the excuse that the colonizer is merely extending the Christian world, is undermined: first, because the white man's volition is implicated in the violence ('the murders we have all wished'); and, second, through the appeal to history, which invokes the history of colonial struggle rather than the religious epoch Jacobus appears to imply.

There are moments where Jacobus is (implicitly) aware of

the contradictions of his position, as, for example, when he envisages his faithful servant Klawer turning the tables on him. Here Klawer is deemed to be

representative of that out there which my eye once enfolded and ingested and which now promises to enfold, ingest, and project me through itself as a speck on a field which we may call annihilation or alternatively history. He threatens to have a history in which I shall be a term. Such is the material basis of the malady of the master's soul. (*D*, 81)

This 'turning of the tables' states, very economically, the history of post-colonialism in the sense that Klawer, representative of the colonized, is presented as having the power of assertion through the marshalling of his own history. Jacobus, however, projects the impulses of the colonizer onto the colonized – specifically that of self-advancement through consumption of the Other – and this supplies a continuing justification of violence, history as annihilation, one way or the other. (The uncompromising ethos parallels the way Dawn envisages his 'duty toward history' as the pursuit of US war aims (*D*, 29).)

Coetzee's essay 'Idleness in South Africa' (1982) indicates the importance to him of understanding the impetus of colonial discourse, the *written* representation of the Other. The essay begins with an account of the reports about the Khoi people of the Cape of Good Hope – 'Hottentots' as they were then labelled – written by European travellers from the mid-seventeenth century. In these accounts, the veracity of which is sometimes suspect, the various authors express horror and disgust at the Hottentot life style. Unfavourable observations abound on such things as diet, hygiene, the sound of the native language and, especially, a perceived idleness. Coetzee shows, however, that whatever appears so shockingly different to the European eye can only shock in this way because it offends a presupposition of commonality, an implied framework of 'samenesses'. The travellers' accounts are based on an implicit set of (up to nineteen) categories, covering all aspects of European civilization, from economy and government to social customs and physical appearance. The imposition of this grid represents an assumption of sameness in that it tacitly announces Hottentot society to conform to the rules of organization discernible in other (all other) human societies. Without expecting these early travellers to conceive a different schema, sensitive to cultural difference, Coetzee nevertheless shows how the Eurocentric grid may well misrepresent the codes of Hottentot society. In effect, Coetzee is ascribing to the eye of the European colonizer a limited structural anthropology; and, in condemning this tendency, which celebrates sameness, Coetzee tacitly aligns himself with a (poststructuralist) privileging of difference which grows out of the criticisms he makes (*WW*, 13–15).

The immediate importance of the essay to *Dusklands* is that its analysis takes discourse as a focus of the critique. The distinguishing feature of the grid Coetzee detects is that it signals the attempt to impose a false order: apparent idleness is defined as such because it denotes behaviour (which might be otherwise defined) that does not fit the grid of seventeenth-century travellers with a Protestant inheritance. The scandal of idleness is an offence to a mode of perception; the grid is used to aid the composition of the traveller as *writer*, but the Hottentot frustrates the desire to write, preferring to lie about, instead of supplying the traveller–writer with data for his categories (*WW*, 23). The essay demonstrates that the analytical eye of these early travellers – among them the first Afrikaner settlers – generates a cultural violence embodied in discourse. The disappointment is of the desire to assimilate an alien culture to the *word* of European explanation. The latent violence of this desire is explicitly presented, in *Dusklands*, as the colonizer's dismay at finding no receptor worthy of his violent probes.

The essay extends the analysis of discourse to show how the European mode of perception reveals its own gaps when the synchronic descriptive mode – that grid of cultural norms – is forgotten. When the travellers introduce into their accounts a basic diachronic element, in describing a sequence of daily events, the Hottentot is revealed to be far from idle: Hottentot life is then shown to be busy with a variety of social concerns, to do with intrigue and surveillance, as well as subsistence. In the discourse of their *own* history, that is to say, the Hottentots undermine the travellers' discourse of descriptive assimilation. Jacobus anticipates precisely this disruption in the threat of Jan Klawer, his Hottentot servant, to have a history (*D*, 81).

The essay, however, is not prescribing a salutary combination of descriptive analysis with history, even though one might expect such a fusion of synchronic and diachronic modes to represent the basis of a poststructuralist resolution to the flawed structural anthropology examined. In fact, Coetzee detects a version of this kind of fusion, already present, in the early discourse of the Cape. This hybrid discourse combines chronological sequence as 'narrative' with the descriptive mode, though the latter is really disguised by the former. The result is advantageous to the traveller, who now has access to the immediacy of narrative, and the ability to recount events for interpretation, without relinquishing the 'God's-eye organization' afforded by categorical description. This is the idea of narrative as manipulation and control, and the account of Jacobus Coetzee is projected as a *narrative* in precisely this sense.

'Idleness in South Africa' ends with a consideration of the apartheid era, and some of the central planks of its early legislation, the Immorality Act (1950) and the Mixed Marriages Act (1949). Coetzee speculates that these cornerstones of racial separation, outlawing interracial relationships, were designed to protect white working men from the temptation to drop out of the working class by settling down to idle lives with 'brown women', and presiding over large and unproductive mixed-race families. This is a speculation which suggests that the fantasy of native idleness had a part to play in the racist mythology of apartheid, and this evidently reinforces the political engagement of *Dusklands*: the novel re-enacts the impulse to cultural domination implicit in the early discourse of the Cape, a discourse which, Coetzee argues, is a formative part of apartheid thinking (*WW*, 23, 15–16, 35).

Such links, however, are not dependent on the external evidence provided by interviews or essays. The novel itself incorporates this kind of bridge, most explicitly in the apparatus concerning S. J. Coetzee, the 'editor' of Jacobus' narrative whose work on this subject, so the 'Translator's Preface' tells us, was part of a series of annual lectures on early explorers in South Africa, delivered between 1934 and 1948 at the University of Stellenbosch (*D*, 55). This period, immediately prior to the election of the first Nationalist government, was one in which the mythology of apartheid was fashioned, a mythology which leant heavily on the idea of the Afrikaner pioneering spirit, and the inheritance of the white colonizers' achievements. The 'Afterword', originally some of S. J. Coetzee's lecture material, extends the historical linkage. This is achieved, mainly, through the association of discourse: S. J. Coetzee, whose pseudo-intellectual work is located, historically, in the run up to 1948, is shown to reproduce the pseudo-rationality of Jacobus. He excuses the exploitation of indigenous African peoples, for example, by appeal to religious mysticism. Exploitation, in this light, is recast as a necessary step in a divine plan for global civilization, the exploiters playing merely the role of God's emissaries (*D*, 110). The 'Afterword' undermines itself repeatedly in this way, most importantly, perhaps, over the question of ownership of the land. Afrikaner claims to the territory of Southern Africa rested on a spurious notion of 'discovery', and a disregard of the historical presence of indigenous peoples. In this spirit, S. J. Coetzee reasons that, since the area which Jacobus traversed was vast, the historian may legitimately think of its features as unknown – even if known to indigenous eyes – until 'discovered' by European eyes (*D*, 115–16). The spuriousness of this argument is reproduced, pointedly, in the privileging of European descriptive codes:

When Bushmen first saw the grass which we call *Aristida brevifolia* and spoke among themselves and found that it was unknown and called it *Twaa*, was there not perhaps an unspoken botanical order among them in which *Twaa* now found a place? And if we accept such concepts as a Bushman taxonomy and a Bushman discovery, must we not accept the concepts of a frontiersman taxonomy and a frontiersman discovery? (*D*, 116)

The legitimacy of a frontiersman taxonomy is predicated on the acceptance of a pre-existing Bushman taxonomy, an evident paradox since the Eurocentric code is favoured to displace that which is adduced to justify its existence in the first place.

The question of control through discourse, both through the imposition of an explanatory grid, and through the manipulation of narrative, implies an affinity between the colonial project and the playing-out of a game or contest. When Jacobus rehearses in his mind the different possible outcomes of his encounter with the Namaquas, he betrays a fascination with permutation, in which ethical choice ('the inner debate') is merely functional, a point of crossover in the random exploration of alternative scenarios (*D*, 65–6). Coetzee's work on Beckett supplies some of the intellectual context to this. His essay on *Lessness*, for example, concentrates on the permutations of the words Beckett uses.[16] This is not to suggest, however, a direct influence on the book's content: Coetzee's indication that the positive intellectual content of *Dusklands* does not emerge from his reading of Beckett seems correct (*DP*, 26–7). More significant may be Coetzee's view, with hindsight, of the period in which his work on Beckett was conducted. In the last interview in *Doubling the Point* – which is really an autobiographical excursus rather than an interview – Coetzee sees this work as belonging to a time when he had a narrow conception of literature, a conception matched by the narrowness of the texts he chose for analysis, 'from a period in Beckett's life when Beckett too was obsessed with form, with language as self-enclosed game' (*DP*, 393). This rejection of the Beckett studies betrays a self-critique, an understanding of the limitations of the excessive formalism of his computer-generated stylistic studies. In *Dusklands*, the self-critique is extended beyond a personal exorcism and is given a general resonance, at one level through the motif of the game or contest.

Indeed, the idea of the game supplies a vital linking and framing theme in the book. Jacobus considers his survival after his treatment at the hands of the Namaqua to be a game between himself and 'an indifferent universe', something he undertakes 'inventing rules' as he goes. He considers other possible versions of the contest, one of which is a prediction of the revenge mission he subsequently undertakes (*D*, 98). This idea of the contest is one in which only one cognitive self is acknowledged; all else is incorporated into an indifferent universe which can be mastered by the invention of new rules. The colonizing impulse is thus represented as self-interest, excluding all other interests, and pursued through a wilful manipulation of circumstance.

Jacobus' distillation of his activities into a solipsistic contest has affinities with the 'rational' discourse of Eugene Dawn's report in which, for example, a formula for the probability of hits in air strikes is discussed: in a paradoxical plea, statistical analysis is combined with a projection of warfare through terror, emotion (*D*, 28–9). It is at this point, significantly, that Dawn's report begins to fall apart, the discourse of pseudo-rationality cracks, and an account of his personal problems is incorporated (*D*, 29).

In the book of Hudson Institute reports, *Can We Win in Vietnam?*, there is a cool evaluation of 'Ten Scenarios on Vietnam', ranging from 'Shameful and Undisguised Abandonment' to disguised US takeover. Herman Kahn, the author of this piece, actually offers eleven scenarios: 'we will not consider the final possibility', he writes, and then promptly sketches this scenario 'in which the United States acts as an imperial power and institutes even a limited but permanent *de jure* and/or complete *de facto* takeover of South Vietnam'. The calm evaluation of alternatives has obvious affinities with the speculative hubris of Jacobus: just as Jacobus' disastrous lack of self-knowledge prompts him to imagine his potential reign as demigod as he is on the brink of humiliation, so did the actual difficulties in Vietnam (not merely the final outcome) make Kahn's range of scenarios seem fanciful. In his report, Kahn even adopts the terminology of gaming and probability in discussing the 'domino theory' of cause and effect to denote the wider implications for Southeast Asia for US intervention in Vietnam. It is true that there is no evident enthusiasm in a report like Kahn's for this terminology, but the willingness to engage with it links the report with the range of self-projecting colonial discourse that Coetzee uses and parodies in the novel.[17]

A more important parallel with Jacobus on this topic, however, may be Dawn's supervisor, 'Coetzee', someone who 'made his name in game theory', and whose 'career has been built on the self and its interests' (*D*, 32).[18] The shadowy supervisor, Coetzee, who has a deleterious psychological effect on Dawn, inevitably becomes associated with the author Coetzee, just as the discussion of the Dutch Coetzee lineage in the apparatus of Jacobus Coetzee's narrative implicates the author in the historical fact of colonization. The specialism of supervisor Coetzee – game theory – adds another dimension to the novel's treatment of guilt and complicity, for now the idea of guilt is extended into the kind of writing the novel represents. More recent debates about postmodernism are often preoccupied with the influence of theoretical ideas on creative work, and whether or not writers, who put into creative practice ideas drawn from their poststructuralist theoretical milieu, are inevitably divorcing art from life. This is the (now) familiar idea of literature as an end in itself, the playing-out of textual games which refer to nothing but themselves. In *Dusklands*, it seems that Coetzee has considered this charge *avant la lettre* (and evidently before it could be levelled at his own work, since this is his first novel).

Of course, the impetus of the novel is to reject the kind of short-circuited gaming that Jacobus indulges in, or which is involved in the strategies of warfare. There is, however, a limit to the kind of intervention the novelist can make, and this is acknowledged in the association of names: J. M. Coetzee is partially tainted with the intellectual and privileged withdrawal of supervisor Coetzee. The business of the novel writer, experimenting with narrative form and perspective, is to diagnose this as a problem, and the carefully ordered composition, with its structured ironies, achieves this very well. A bleak consequence of the contrast of styles is that it functions to connect two different histories and locations, implying the persistence of the colonial impulse and its continuing tendency to depredation. The sense of 'decolonization', therefore, is concentrated in the analysis of the authorial role. The 'Coetzee theme' is extensive: if Dawn's supervisor Coetzee establishes a link with the author, so, more obviously, does the translator of Jacobus' narrative, one 'J. M. Coetzee', son of the South African scholar, S. J. Coetzee; and, of course, the actual Jacobus Coetsé was a distant ancestor of the author.

The proliferation of 'Coetzees' in the novel is an economical channel for making explicit the linking themes. These emerge as the metafictional interrogation of narrative modes, and the author's sense of complicity in the will-to-power of imperial thinking, both as a Western intellectual with the guilt-laden leisure to write, and as someone whose own ancestry is implicated in the early colonial discourse which is the focus.

It may be the element of complicity and its acknowledgement which justifies the composition of such a text as the second section of *Dusklands*. Indeed, Coetzee has himself expressed the view that the writing of such a text, without historical complicity, might be morally dubious (*DP*, 343). It is in this diagnostic sense that the negative can be seen as positive. The title imagery functions in much the same way: the encroaching historical night of the interior 'dusklands' which are represented (a bleak psychological landscape) is offset by the anticipation of a different kind of dawn. Even if the insane Eugene Dawn is not the herald of the desired new day, his exposure, at least, removes his programme from the agenda.[19]

The wrong kind of love: 'In the Heart of the Country'

Through its explicit exploration of authorial complicity, *Dusk-lands* establishes a ground rule which can subsequently be taken as a given. In his first novel, Coetzee identifies his historical links in the literature of the post-colonizer, making the re-present-ation of a directly personal guilt superfluous. In *In the Heart of the Country* (1977), the question of complicity, and an associated metafictional preoccupation, is taken in a new direction.

In some ways, *In the Heart of the Country* is Coetzee's most difficult and forbidding novel. It is a disruptive and disturbing book which offers an implicit admission of the semi-impotence of the white intellectual/writer in South Africa, and an oblique reflection on South African literary culture, and Afrikaner mythology. This has a particular resonance for South Africa after the Soweto riots (1976–7), which galvanized Black Consciousness, and produced a disregard for white assistance, at this time, in the anti-apartheid struggle. A full understanding of all the Coetzee novels, of course, depends upon a knowledge of the South African context, but, where the allegorical dimen-sion of, say, *Waiting for the Barbarians* invites broader reflections on power and morality, this novel is explicitly inward-looking. In the South African edition, in fact, the dialogue was presented in Afrikaans, with the rest of the narrative written in English.[1] If other editions – written entirely in English – represent a concession to the international English-speaking audience, the original conception suggests that the Afrikaner was Coetzee's principal target reader. The publication history of the novel (as with *Dusklands*) also betrays a lack of initial international enthusiasm – it did not appear in paperback, for example, until

1982, two years after the publication of *Waiting for the Barbarians*, Coetzee's next (more immediately accessible) novel.[2]

It has also been remarked that the novel has received less critical attention than some of Coetzee's other works. Sheila Roberts (before offering a useful reading of the novel as a problematic feminist text) considers different possible explanations for this comparative neglect: the female narrator, perhaps, has been of less interest to some critics as a 'representative of coloniality' than Jacobus in *Dusklands*, or the Magistrate in *Waiting for the Barbarians*; or, perhaps, the 'flawlessness' of the text discourages the 'rewriting' involved in critical commentary; or, perhaps, the novel's self-consciousness supplies the explanation, since the narrator offers her own sophisticated 'explanations for her predicaments', thus usurping the critic's function.[3] A closer look at the novel, however, indicates that the book demands interpretation in several areas. Despite Magda's 'explanations', the inconsistencies in her accounts require explication; and the contradictions of the style itself, for all its apparent 'flawlessness', have a significance which is opaque. There is also (as a sideline issue in this novel) a deliberation about allegory, a coinciding use and interrogation of its procedures. If all allegories are encoded with the demand for interpretation, this ambivalent use of the structures of allegory adds a second element of required interpretation, at the level of metafiction.

The novel is written as a kind of journal, or first-person monologue, revealing the psychological identity of the speaker, Magda, who emerges as the symbolic daughter of colonialism, in both an intellectual and an historical sense.[4] Her account is presented in two hundred and sixty-six numbered sections, in which contradictory accounts of events are frequently given. In this way, the distinction between event and imagination is deliberately blurred. The emphasis is on how Magda constructs her first-person narrative, and what it reveals about her. The stories she tells thus have an inward-looking impetus. She tells of her father with a new (apparently imaginary) bride, and of her brutal double axe-murder of the newlyweds. In another scenario, she tells of her father's seduction of 'Klein-Anna', the

wife of the black servant Hendrik, and of her shooting of her
father in bed with his new mistress. After the burial of the
father, a significant section of the narrative concerns Magda's
failed attempts to establish rapport with Hendrik and Anna.
This colonial outpost is ultimately overrun, however: Magda is
humiliated and raped by Hendrik, and he and Anna eventually
desert Magda, leaving her alone on the farm, reflecting on
portentous messages about her historical role from 'sky-gods' in
the air. In the final lyrical sections, the father is resuscitated as
a companion in Magda's nostalgic paean to the old rural ways.

Essentially, this is an unstable interior monologue in which
the narrator enacts the psychological breakdown attributable
to, and representative of, the divisive colonial mind. Consequently, Magda has a dual function as both victim and
perpetrator of the colonial structure. The landscape plays a key
role in this presentation of colonial failure: this is a space which
is shown to be inhospitable to colonial organization. Indeed,
Magda's problems stem from the lack of community, unsustain-
able in the remote veld. The result of this lack is that family
relations, labour relations and sexual relations become disas-
trously confused, though these confusions do highlight the
ideological problems inherent in the systems themselves. The
precise historical reference is to a farm of the late nineteenth or
early twentieth century, as suggested, for example, by details of
transportation (horse, bicycle and train). However, the element
of historical reference is treated unrealistically, and its significance is widened accordingly. The appearance of aeroplanes at
the end of the book, and the request for taxes for municipal
services received by Magda brings us into the late twentieth
century (*IHC*, 124–6). On the basis of such details, Gallagher
surmises that the novel 'spans the period of approximately
1870–1960'.[5] One might quibble with the precise dates, but
this, broadly, is the impression created; and one effect of this, as
in *Dusklands*, is to make implicit connections between historical
Afrikaner identity and the contemporary situation in South
Africa.

There is a positive political potential in Magda's account,
which is transgressive in various ways: the double parricide is

merely the most obvious factor in her challenge to the patriarchal order.[6] Gallagher, perhaps, argues more strongly than
most critics for a positive reading of this transgressiveness,
suggesting that 'the meditations of Magda – with their contradictions, fluid quality, and feminine imagery – embody a
counter-myth, an alternative story to the patriarchal history of
Afrikaner nationalism', in which the notion of woman as
maternal fount is central.[7] In my reading, Magda turns her
back on the positive potential of her narrative in the crucial
concluding section, and this is representative of the novel's
structure in other respects: there is a dominant dynamic of
circularity which short-circuits the forward-looking impulse.
This principle of negation is a little less bleak than it is in
Dusklands, since a resolution is glimpsed; but the circular
dynamic is ultimately diagnostic, serving to uncover Magda's
own confusion: her consciousness is both representative of, and
produced by, the schizophrenic psychology of colonial society.

For some critics, the use of allegory is a central problem in
the novel, a point highlighted in Penner's claims that this novel,
more than any of Coetzee's others, 'has prompted readings in
which the characters and events are seen as an allegory of
modern South Africa'.[8] A perceptive reading is that of Hena
Maes-Jelinek, who feels that Coetzee places an emphasis on
how power is wielded through language, suggesting that
Magda herself abuses this power. As a consequence, her own
long monologue can be read as an allegory of the situation in
South Africa, her 'spinster fate', in particular, referring to the
nation's international isolation.[9]

Caution is needed in this connection, and it may sometimes
seem more appropriate to speak of representative, rather than
allegorical, resonances or possibilities where the level of
abstraction is minimal or not sustained. There is a self-
conscious problematizing of this distinction, however: the
novel's action can be seen as allegorizing a South Africa
apparently on the brink of revolution, but also as unfolding a
microcosmic representation of this context, with Coetzee
offering some negative future projections, as an admonition.
Hendrik's appropriation of patriarchal power – in adopting the

'master's' garb, and inverting the mistress/slave relationship in his humiliation and control of Magda – is portentous. By unsettling the rigidity of allegory as category, Coetzee offers an exemplary instance of Fredric Jameson's postmodernist allegory, which is 'horizontal rather than vertical': if there is a structure of parallel levels of significance, there is also a sense that the objects signified are 'profoundly relational'. The writing of such an allegory is itself interpretive, 'a kind of scanning that . . . readjusts its terms' in a way which is in tune with the postcolonial interrogation of 'given' systems.[10]

If allegory is understood in this transitional sense, Penner's reading is helpful: he argues that if the farm is seen as a microcosm of South Africa, then the novel appears to be an allegory of impending swift and violent revolution, establishing an uncertain situation of continuing violence and misunderstanding. This indicates that the political dimension to the novel is radical, an important observation of a novel (and a novelist) sometimes seen as disengaged from political questions.[11]

At a more general level of signification, the novel's touchstone is the issue of fading colonialism, to which is attached a consideration of the nature of knowledge. The black servants' quarters on the farm formed, originally, the schoolhouse for the settler children in the region, attended, perhaps, by Magda's father, her grandfather and herself. The children were educated to be

heirs of all the ages familiar with the rotation of the earth, Napoleon, Pompeii, the reindeer herds of the frozen wastes, the anomalous expansion of water, the seven days of Creation, the immortal comedies of Shakespeare, geometric and arithmetic progressions, the major and minor modes, the boy with his finger in the dyke, Rumpelstiltskin, the miracle of the loaves and the fishes, the laws of perspective, and much, much more. But where has it all gone now, this cheerful submission to the wisdom of the past? (*IHC*, 46)

The schoolhouse, the basic outpost for the dissemination of colonial knowledge, has passed into the hands of black Africans, a partial reclamation representing the beginning of the transition towards a genuine postcolonialism. The kinds of knowledge which comprise this heritage are significant. This is a combination of different kinds of certitude: faith in scientific and religious explanations; faith in canonical values; and a belief in the power of narrative to yield formative moral lessons. The decolonizing aspect of this has two dimensions. The first is in relation to the Afrikaner national identity, nurtured by myths of heroism and supremacy.[12] The second, broader dimension, which encompasses the first, links the passing of this colonialism to the moment of postmodernity more generally, and its distrust of grand theories/metanarratives, on the grounds that they can mask an unacknowledged ideology. The 'cheerful submission' to this kind of knowledge is a thing of the past, and it is in this spirit that Magda bitterly questions the validity of her father's upbringing and education: 'What did he learn from Hansel and Gretel about fathers who lead their daughters into dark forests?' (*IHC*, 46). The implication is that the moral lessons of colonial knowledge, its explanatory narratives, may reinforce, while appearing to admonish, the central impulses of colonialism.

Much of this analysis unfolds through direct, metonymic association, and even the use of figurative ideas can be direct: the question of the land and its ownership is raised straightforwardly through the association of Magda with the hermit crab – usurper of other creatures' 'homes' – an idea which evidently implicates Magda in the colonial appropriation of land (*IHC*, 43, 136). There is, however, a more abstract, and related motif in the book (which is, nevertheless, overtly self-conscious): this is the image of the body being inhabited by the body of another. Coetzee uses this idea in *Dusklands*, in Eugene Dawn's narrative, when Dawn talks of 'a hideous mongol boy who stretches his limbs inside my hollow bones' (*D*, 39), a metaphor for the *effects* of an imperialistic ideology which has taken root inside him: the image encapsulates a self-defeating solipsism which inverts and subverts a natural (biological) human progression. The uses of this motif in the second novel are various. Initially Magda imagines her body being taken over as a kind of death-in-life, a loss of identity which is a succinct representation of her ongoing self-analysis (*IHC*, 53–4). The next occurrence of the motif is more arresting, invoking the idea of 'the law' for the purpose (aside from the allusion to Kafka) of introducing Magda's emerging reflections on power, and her place in the hierarchy of the farm:

How can I say that the law does not stand fullgrown inside my shell, its feet in my feet, its hands in my hands, its sex drooping through my hole; or that when I have had my chance to make this utterance, the lips and teeth of the law will not begin to gnaw their way out of this shell, until there it stands before you, the law grinning and triumphant again, its soft skin hardening in the air, while I lie sloughed, crumpled, abandoned on the floor? (*IHC*, 84)

This passage is complex in that it adds several important political issues to the question of Magda's identity. The law is the law of language and command, which possesses Magda as much as she possesses it. (It is unavailable to her servants, who are not literate (*IHC*, 84).) The personification of the law (male) inhabiting, and parasitically devouring, Magda's body, makes a crucial point about the ambivalence of woman's role in colonial systems, whereby she is obliged to support a hierarchical system not of her devising, to which her own identity must be subordinate.[13] The phallocentrism is presented as a kind of rape from within, and the devouring is a silencing of the female voice. The parasitism is also a monstrous birth, destructive of the female, and the idealized role of maternal fount. After the rape scenes, Magda, trying to understand Hendrik's violent invasions of her, wonders if he is trying to inhabit her by cramming his own frame within hers (*IHC*, 108); Magda is thus established as the target of violent impositions from both sides in the colonial power struggle. The circuit of violence is completed in the next appearance of this motif when Magda expresses the wish to inhabit another:

I would like to climb into Klein-Anna's body, I would like to climb down her throat while she sleeps and spread myself gently inside her, my hands in her hands, my feet in her feet, my skull in the benign quiet of her skull where images of soap and flour and milk revolve, the holes of my body sliding into place over the holes of hers, there to wait mindlessly for whatever enters them, the songs of birds, the smell of dung, the parts of a man, not angry now but gentle. (*IHC*, 108–9)

The purport of this is ambivalent in several ways. Magda

extends her deliberations on Hendrik's motives in the rape scenes to her own desire to displace the rapist's wife; in doing so, she implicates herself in the motif of invasion and possession. Her desire to experience whatever Klein-Anna experiences is tainted with a dubious need to possess the Other, and this echoes the ontological uncertainty of the colonial self examined in *Dusklands*. At the same time, Magda's desire to experience the world through Klein-Anna's sensations has positive connotations. Imagining herself as Hendrik's sexual partner in different circumstances, Magda tries to undo the psychological wrong of the sexual violence, and, by wishing to experience the veld from Anna's point of view, she shows herself, at this moment, open to other cultural representations of farm life.

Part of the allegorical resonance has to do with how the colonial identity has constructed itself, and Magda's doubts about this construction – evident, for example, when she desires to experience an alternative version of life on the veld – are supported by an uncertainty in the narrative treatment of event and time.

This uncertainty results in a typically (almost stereotypically) postmodernist structure: a sequence of numbered sections, in which some 'events' are logically discredited by subsequent accounts, or are given in various, competing versions. In Penner's view, this makes it 'impossible to ascertain whether any of the events Magda describes happen anywhere but in her mind'.[14] Perhaps we can recast this observation to account for Magda's own summary of her narrative: 'I make it all up in order that it shall make me up' (*IHC*, 73). The principle of composition, in other words, places an emphasis on the construction of identity, so that the reader learns to stop puzzling about the 'veracity' of what is related. Instead, we consider narrated events in terms of what they tell us about Magda, though, of course, a lack of plausibility may be a factor in our judgement.

In establishing this principle in the novel, however, Coetzee does rely on certain expectations in his readers. The tension in the opening, for example, rests, to some extent, on the assumption that Magda's father has, indeed, come home with a new bride and that this is a genuine source of her psychological anxiety.[15] Magda's double axe-murder of the newlyweds (*IHC*, 11), is accepted initially as a narrative event, an acceptance reinforced by Magda's concern about being discovered, and by her anxiety in disposing of the bodies (*IHC*, 13–15). When, however, the father appears to be alive after all, the first clear indication of the book's treatment of event is given (*IHC*, 16) (though there are hints even before this). The book starts, then, with a shock tactic in which a reader's expectations are evidently undermined in order to emphasize the focus on the narrating self and the manner of its creation.

Even so, it is not true that all subsequent events are treated with an equal distrust, deemed to be entirely internal to Magda. In one sense, of course, the whole book is Magda's self-invention to which everything is partly subordinate. But there are pointed differences in the treatment of certain episodes. Very shortly after the murders of the newlyweds, an account is given of Hendrik's arrival on the farm with his new bride on a donkey-cart (*IHC*, 17). This is a parallel scene to that of the arrival of the father and his bride on the dog-cart in the opening section, and might appear, at first, to be part of an emerging series of fictional weddings (*IHC*, 1). Yet this second arrival has a different status. Hindsight makes this self-evident, since the initial 'fictional' wife is soon expelled from the novel, whereas Hendrik and Klein-Anna play crucial roles from this point onwards, and so become fixtures in the narrative development. Even on an initial reading, however, one can detect a difference in treatment. One difference is that the arrival of the father and his bride, and their descent from the dog-cart, is described more than once. The first description, on the first page, is followed by sections which delineate the new family tensions; then, in section 22, we are taken back to the moment of arrival, with Magda watching (from a chink in a curtain) as her father lifts his wife from the cart (*IHC*, 9). The effect of this is to suggest the possibility of a restart to the narrative, the possibility of a different version. The emphasis on Magda *watching*, here, also makes her centrally implicated as a source of implausibility and uncertainty. From here, perhaps, we learn to look askance at accounts of those events which have an immediate emotional impact on her. In Marion Hänsel's film version of the novel, *Dust*, an attempt is made to place emphasis on Magda as constructor of events, by freezing the scene of the newlyweds' arrival, outside Magda's window, as she puts the shutter back into place.[16]

The account of Hendrik's arrival with Klein-Anna is different for several reasons. First, it is a retrospective account of an event that occurred six months in the past, and this provides a relative veracity when set against the arrival of the other couple, described initially in the immediate past ('today' (*IHC*, 1)), and then revisited in the present tense (*IHC*, 9). More important, perhaps, is the stress on material mundaneness in the description of Hendrik and Klein-Anna, the hand-me-down garments of Hendrik, and the details of the marriage bargaining in which Hendrik has paid money and livestock. Because these are details of an impoverished life beyond Magda's personal experience, the account has a plausibility which is immune to her most extreme interference. The distinction between the arrival of the different couples – however slight it is – also serves to privilege the arrival of the black couple, as an event of greater narrative stability.

The problem of different versions comes to a head in Hendrik's raping of Magda, which is described five times in consecutive sections, in a sequence of startling brutality (*IHC*, 104–7). For Attwell, the repeating of the rape scene serves to deny it the status of an event, establishing it instead as 'a colonial fantasy' of Magda's.[17] This reading may be supported by an earlier section in which Magda 'reports' a bedroom conversation between Klein-Anna and Hendrik in which Hendrik imagines the rape (*IHC*, 86–7): the element of imaginary projection may colour the rape itself, when it occurs. Penner points out that, in successive versions of the rape scene, the violence of perpetrator and victim diminishes, while the victim's acceptance increases, and this might also support the idea of a colonial fantasy.[18] It is important, however, not to lose sight of Magda as victim in these scenes, something which is surely reinforced by the repetition which, it seems to me, serves to intensify rather than ameliorate the impression of ordeal. To make sense of this, one needs to keep the allegorical dimension in view: the motif of bodily invasion, as in *Dusklands*, suggests a literal violence, but is simultaneously metaphorical. Only now the colonized, too, is presented to be manifesting the same desire for self-expression through bodily invasion, a reciprocal violence. In this sense, it makes no difference whether or not the rape is a fantasy of Magda's. The allegorical point is that the colonizer is necessarily the instigator of revolutionary counter-violence. There also a sense that Magda is a psychological victim, alienated from the 'native' Other through her internalization of the rape fear/fantasy, a recurring topos in the discourse of racism.

The construction of Magda is ultimately a textual problem, in the sense that she is shown to be the product of different textual influences. Her narrative is peppered with quotations from, or allusions to, many important figures in modern Western literature and philosophy, including Blake, Hegel, Kierkegaard, Freud, Kafka, Sartre and Beckett.[19] The fact that she is versed in contemporary literary theory makes her seem, in the words of Ian Glenn, 'a kind of Emily Dickinson with therapy and a thesis in critical theory'.[20] Clearly, the extraordinarily rich and diverse composition of Magda's intellectual identity underscores her position as a metafictional device to facilitate the exploration of character construction, and the nature of the 'I-figure' in fiction. A structural vehicle in the narrative for this preoccupation with textuality is the subversion of the *plaasroman* tradition, a procedure which, as Gallagher suggests, concentrates on 'the Afrikaner identity created in and sustained by the cultural texts of these traditional genres'.[21] However, Coetzee's subversiveness here is typically complex.

In his essay 'Farm Novel and Plaasroman', Coetzee distinguishes between the English-language farm novel and the *plaasroman* proper, the Afrikaner novel of idealized rural and farm life (*WW*, 63–4). This essay has an interesting connection with *In the Heart of the Country*, for it argues for an antipastoral

tradition in the English-language novel of South African farm
life, a tradition to which Coetzee's novel belongs.

In the essay, Coetzee considers the antipastoralism of Olive
Schreiner and the idealistic pastoral of Pauline Smith. Coetzee's own novel extends Schreiner's antipastoral vision – very
much more self-consciously – and seeks to highlight the social
gaps in the kind of pastoral idyll represented by Smith. Indeed,
when Coetzee considers Schreiner's African farm to be a
'microcosm of colonial South Africa', he also summarizes his
own novel. A point that he makes about Schreiner's *Story of an
African Farm*, given its symbolic impetus, is that it makes no
attempt to engage with the materiality of farm life and the
process of wealth production: life on Schreiner's farm is the life
of insects rather than of sheep (*WW,* 65, 64). This apparently
slight observation may be of greater significance to *In the Heart
of the Country* than it appears, since another recurring motif in
the book concerns insect life.

In the light of the essay, the insect motif in the novel can be
taken to evoke the sense of futility in which a purposive farm
life is supplanted by the thriving of insect life: the most obvious
example of this is the attraction of flies to the dying father, left
in his fouled bed, his shotgun wound festering (*IHC,* 77). The
flies feed off the patriarch, explicitly denoting the demise of
colonialism in the language that Schreiner initiated. Magda
imagines the same fate for herself, her skeleton sucked clean by
flies (*IHC,* 79).

In the examples given, the role of insect life can be taken to
represent a natural terrain which is resistant to the imposition
of a colonial order.[22] In Coetzee's usage, however, the motif is
complicated by a reverse association. In the burial of the dead
father, sewn up in a grey tarpaulin, a parallel is made between
insect life and the activities of the colonist himself. Magda
describes the corpse as a grey larva, with herself as its mother
stowing it for incubation (she does crawl into the tomb in order
to drag the corpse into place) (*IHC,* 92–3). The inversions, here,
are very much to the point: the daughter taking on the role of
mother is a detail which underscores the distorted familial
situation, as does the ironic parallel between incubation/

rebirth and the incarceration of the parricide victim. Imagining the intimacies of her father and Klein-Anna, Magda compares their actions to those of flies glued together (*IHC*, 57). Later, Magda says 'this is a land made for insects who eat sand and lay eggs in each other's corpses and have no voices with which to scream when they die', a haunting summary of this circular parasitism, in which desires are silenced in mutually destructive familial and social relationships (*IHC*, 108). The insect motif, determined by a principle of enclosed circularity, thus encompasses colonial activities (affecting both the colonial community and the subjugated population), as well as the reciprocal activities of the colonized community slipping its chains.

Another key point in the essay 'Farm Novel and Plaasroman' is the silence concerning the place of the black man in the South African pastoral idyll (*WW*, 81). Coetzee's second novel offers a practical engagement with this question, articulated in theory in the later essay. The central roles of Hendrik and Klein-Anna have this literary–historical significance.

A contemporary literary parallel that is worth considering in this connection is Gordimer's Booker prize-winning novel of 1974, *The Conservationist*. Coetzee mentions Gordimer's book in his discussion of the farm novel, seeing it as belonging to that antipastoral tradition of Schreiner's *Story of an African Farm*. Coetzee's discussion of this occasions a consideration of the fundamental postcolonial problem of how the white man can live in South Africa. He evaluates the pastoral resolution of the problem, the prescribed withdrawal into an independent rural existence, and the argument that this solution is refuted in the symbolic logic of Gordimer's novel: in *The Conservationist*, the presence of a black man, buried in a shallow grave on a white man's farm, provides a symbolic decolonization when it resurfaces after a storm. Coetzee is pessimistic about such literary gestures, in that he doubts whether the ghost of the pastoral can be laid, a pessimism which shows his determination not to underestimate this aspect of Afrikaner ideology (*WW*, 81). The motif of burial and exhumation is a recurring one in *In the Heart of the Country*, although, in comparison with Gordimer's mythic tale of decolonization, the treatment is more negative. Where

Gordimer uses the idea to overturn the history of black African dispossession, Coetzee places an emphasis on the white corpse, betraying an insistence on the obstacles to the postcolonial moment. In the novel, for example, Magda speculates on how to dispose of the bodies of her father and his new wife, fearing that, if she buries them, they will eventually be washed out of the earth again (*IHC*, 15). The burial motif in Coetzee, quite distinct from Gordimer's utopianism, concentrates on the immutability of the colonizer.

Much of the ambivalence of the novel can be traced to the style of Magda's narrative. When she claims that lyric rather than chronicle is her medium, attention is drawn to the mode of the narrative, an important issue for all of Coetzee's novels (*IHC*, 71). In a broader sense, lyric rather than chronicle is Coetzee's medium. As the novel sequence progresses, he develops the lyricism of his writing, though this mode is put to different uses in different contexts, making the development a complex matter. Magda's lyricism, ultimately, is restricted by the circularity that is the irresolvable restrictive feature of her narrative. It is a lyricism which stems from the desire to recuperate the pastoral dream of white independence. Magda, like Coetzee, senses the loss of the traditional in her story: 'what was once pastoral has become one of those stifling stories in which brother and sister, wife and daughter and concubine prowl and snarl around the bedside listening for the death-rattle, or stalk each other through the dim passages of the ancestral home' (*IHC*, 70). This passage effectively summarizes the literary self-consciousness of the novel, its deliberate anti-pastoralism in which the dying patriarch becomes the focus of a new power struggle through which new social relations are negotiated.

The effort to recuperate the pastoral is centred on the novel's ending. However, before the attempt to reinvoke this kind of lyrical mode, problems have already manifested themselves in Magda's lyricism: the poetic purple passages in her narrative are often disturbingly misdirected, as in this description, following the account of the parricide, of how her father ought to have died:

His final experience must have been an unsatisfactory one, a groping with dulled muscles toward an illusory zone of safety. He lies head and arms over the edge of the bed, black with his heavy blood. It would have been better for him to have yielded the gentle ghost, following it as far as he could on its passage out, closing his eyes on the image of a swallow swooping, rising, riding. (*IHC*, 14–15)

Passages like this have several functions, the most obvious of which, perhaps, is to highlight the disjunction between form and content: the lyrical mode, with its utopian impulse, might well conceal a dystopian content (which is here made quite explicit). In this way, the novel trains its readers to be wary of its lyricism; at the same time, however, the symbolic dimension to the father's role gives this passage coherence, since the imagined demise of the father – the quintessential Afrikaner patriarch – is appropriately associated with the 'dying fall' of the pastoral mode, exposed as ideologically questionable.

The sense of questioning and rejection is reinforced by the sequence in which Magda claims to be addressed by voices speaking in Spanish from flying machines passing overhead. The voices are voices of criticism and commentary on the colonial situation. They are associated with a utopian future, since their language is a Spanish of universal meanings (Magda understands it though she knows no Spanish), evoking the unifying ideal of Esperanto (*IHC*, 126). The voices are also associated with a future – they come from aeroplanes – to which Magda must try and accommodate herself, the post-colonial world of the late twentieth century. However, Magda's responses to the voices represent a failure to meet the challenge. She does realize that she stands indicted by the voices, and she senses that their message is of value to her (*IHC*, 133, 130); but she fails to grasp the full significance of these indictments. Her response to the first message – '*when we dream that we are dreaming, the moment of awakening is at hand*' – makes this clear. This kind of portentous pronouncement emphasizes overtly the purport of the allegory – of spinster Magda, representative of South Africa. But it is also a tacit self-justification of Coetzee's method in this novel: dreaming about dreaming is, in another sense, bringing to consciousness a representation of an illusion (in this context, becoming self-conscious about ideological distortion/political mythos). If such self-consciousness heralds a political awakening, this novel, dramatizing a psyche struggling with its ideological construction, announces itself as belonging to a moment of impending awakening and political change. Magda, however, feels sure that this critique does not refer to her present state, indicating that, for her, political awakening is not imminent (*IHC*, 127). In addition to her extended reflections on the voices, Magda 'writes' (by arranging stones on the ground) a more terse response in the form of a poem, in which she betrays only a faint understanding of the charges against her. For example, the first line of the poem – referring to the proffered hope of waking to a new political dawn – translates as 'you offer me a desert' (*IHC*, 133), a negative rejection of the future.[23] The other messages address dangers specific to Afrikaner identity, in particular the circular introspection of a self-perpetuating mythology (*IHC*, 128), and the damage done to all participants in the master/slave bond in both social and psychological terms (*IHC*, 130). In each case, Magda considers the charge, but too narrowly to deal with the full significance.

Magda's narrative closes by turning away from the messages of the 'sky-gods' and with a gesture of ambivalent lyricism. A couple of pages from the end, Magda offers an extended account of a nostalgic speech addressed by her to her father, whose death is symbolically reversed *as if on account* of Magda's failure to see through the political significance of her narrative. Here she offers memories of a holiday at the seaside, of family pets and former servants (revealingly mentioned in association), and of sundry isolated moments on the farm (*IHC*, 136–7). Magda evinces an understanding of the negative purport of this nostalgic withdrawal in the novel's final section, but effectively sees this as a legacy she cannot surmount:

There are poems, I am sure, about the heart that aches for Verlore Vlakte, about the melancholy of the sunset over the koppies, the sheep beginning to huddle against the first evening chill, the faraway boom of the windmill, the first chirrup of the first cricket, the last twitterings of the birds in the thorn-trees, the stones of the farmhouse wall still holding the sun's warmth, the kitchen lamp glowing steady.

There are poems I could write myself. It takes generations of life in the cities to drive that nostalgia for country ways from the heart. I will never live it down, nor do I want to. I am corrupted to the bone with the beauty of this forsaken world. If the truth be told, I never wanted to fly away with the sky-gods. My hope was always that they would descend and live with me here in paradise, making up with their ambrosial breath for all that I lost when the ghostly brown figures of the last people I knew crept away from me in the night. (*IHC*, 138–9)

The ambivalence of Magda's conclusion is a matter of self-knowledge. The novel's title can now clearly be seen to designate exactly this throwback nostalgia, the idea of former country ways embedded in the heart, a prop for an Afrikaner identity in need of reconstruction. Magda shows understanding of this as a way of life which is no longer sustainable: the nostalgia represents an aesthetic of the rural which is 'corrupt', now applied to a 'forsaken' world. Magda is tacitly aware of the racial significance of her 'loss' of 'the ghostly brown figures', and this suggests, at one allegorical level, the broader catastrophe of racial separation. Because Magda cannot fully address the significance of the sky-gods' messages, her nostalgic withdrawal represents a failure in social terms, a fantasy sustained by an anticipated divine intervention that might smooth over the problems of social division.

The culmination of Magda's yearning in the misguided lyricism of the novel's ending has also a narrow (and paradoxically) positive significance. What Coetzee does, in essence, is to make Magda's limitations emblematic of broader inevitable limitations, especially for the writer trying to make a worthwhile imaginative intervention in South Africa. In *Doubling the Point*, Coetzee and Attwell draw together material, which is relevant to the novel, under the heading 'The Poetics of Reciprocity'. This phrase provides an umbrella category for all investigations of relationship and consciousness germane to the postcolonial situation, and which are explored throughout the *œuvre*. In his interview with Coetzee, which touches on *In the Heart of the Country*, Attwell does, however, supply a particular focus: the apparent impossibility of reciprocity given

Coetzee's comment, in his later Jerusalem Prize acceptance speech (1987), about the failure of love in South Africa (*DP*, 58). The text of this speech makes clear the political context of the remark. Coetzee here attaches great significance to the legal opposition to miscegenation in early apartheid legislation. He shows how the outlawing of sexual relations between white and black (established by the Mixed Marriages Act (1949) and the Immorality Act (1950)) formalized what one might call familiar colonial disorders: the denial of the desire to 'embrace' the Other, and a fear of a reciprocal embrace.[24] The passion of the colonizer in South Africa is consequently displaced:

At the heart of the unfreedom of the hereditary masters of South Africa is a failure of love. To be blunt: their love is not enough today and has not been enough since they arrived on the continent; furthermore, their talk, their excessive talk, about how they love South Africa has consistently been directed toward *the land*, that is, toward what is least likely to respond to love: mountains and deserts, birds and animals and flowers.

There is much here that can be applied directly to Magda, especially as, in his developing discussion, Coetzee suggests 'fraternity' – implying community – as a replacement for 'love' (*DP*, 97). Magda's experiences appear to re-enact the misplaced love of the 'masters' of South Africa, especially in the pastoral nostalgia of her conclusion where a celebration of the land, its flora and fauna, pointedly supplants her gestures towards fraternity.

Yet there is an ambivalence, here. In interview with Attwell, in fact, Coetzee offers an apparently opposing interpretation of Magda's passion, suggesting that it is of the order of love he appeals for in the Jerusalem Prize speech, the love of the country and its people, not just the land. The ambivalence is suggested when Coetzee acknowledges that Magda is an anomaly because she finds herself in a literary genre (pastoral) to which her passion does not belong. In generic terms, this produces (for Coetzee) a particular kind of antipastoral – Cervantean he calls it – in which a self-conscious critique of generic convention comes from a character within the text (*DP*,

61–2). In these terms, Magda attempts to lay the foundations for the right kind of passion, the fraternity she seeks to establish through her overtures to Klein-Anna and Hendrik. But she is contained within a generic structure that defeats her, and which obliges her to have recourse to the wrong kind of love, the passion of an unregenerated pastoral. Magda's failure has also to do with the uncomprehending rebuff she receives from Klein-Anna and Hendrik: Hendrik, indeed, offers a vengeful violence by way of response, and here there is another literary allusion which gives meaning to the failure of contact. In the Jerusalem Prize speech, Coetzee also makes reference to Alan Paton's *Cry, the Beloved Country*, and the day of reckoning prophesied by one of the black characters given the whites' failure to love: 'I have one great fear in my heart, that one day when they are turned to loving we will find we are turned to hating' (*DP*, 97). Magda's passion, emblematic of the long-awaited white love, is spurned by Hendrik, now turned to hating, in accordance with this kind of prophecy. Paton's novel is a classic statement of Christian-liberalism through which such a disastrous eventuality is implicitly circumvented: hope is proffered on the basis of a (frankly apolitical) conception of individual co-operation. By dramatizing the dark prognosis of hate unleashed, Coetzee distances himself from the classic liberalism of Alan Paton, presenting the bleak scenario Paton was at pains to try and outflank.

The ambivalence surrounding Magda dictates, also, the reflexivity of the novel. We have seen how Coetzee raises questions about the South African pastoral mode by showing how his character's best intentions make her ill-suited to the conventions of this genre. Beyond this, Coetzee's reflexivity raises a larger question concerning the role of imaginative literature in South Africa under apartheid. This topic is also broached in the discussion of love in the Jerusalem Prize speech, where Coetzee considers how apartheid has produced a psychological stuntedness and deformity. The consequence of this, for the writer, is to be obliged to produce inevitably stunted and deformed representations, in order to capture this distorted inner life successfully. There is a despair in this speech, a sense of being overwhelmed by political reality, the 'truth' which 'swamps every act of the imagination'.

Admittedly, there is a sense in which this rhetoric is fitted to the public statement: Coetzee's longing for a different world, a freedom from 'pathological attachments' in which his occupation might have more meaning, is accurate as a political commentary rather than as an evaluation of his own achievements (*DP*, 98–9). Indeed, it is the careful delineation of pathological attachment that gives *In the Heart of the Country* its power and historical resonance. Even so, this does raise a serious point about the adequacy of the Coetzee style to his given historical situation: the novel, after all, dramatizes, through Magda, a misguided lyricism which evokes (even while it subverts) South African pastoral. The self-consciousness is pointed – more than an end in itself – but there is still a sense of circularity in the way the novel places itself in South African literary history, a circularity which parallels the cultural imprisonment of Magda (and her nation).

The European literary models which impact on Magda's identity are also shown in a compromising light, and this diffidence is rooted in doubts about the arrival of postmodernism in the novel in South Africa. The presence of Beckett has a broad denotative function in this connection, as he occupies a border between modernism and postmodernism. As Caroline Rody points out, Magda, in one sense, is 'a garrulous talking head straight out of Beckett', a role she tries to resist:[25]

If I had been set down by fate in the middle of the veld in the middle of nowhere, buried to my waist and commanded to live a life, I could not have done it. I am not a philosopher. Women are not philosophers, and I am a woman. A woman cannot make something out of nothing . . . I am not a principle, a rule of discourse . . . I need more than merely pebbles to permute, rooms to clean, furniture to push around: I need people to talk to, brothers and sisters or fathers and mothers, I need a history and a culture . . . I need a moral sense and a teleology before I will be happy, not to mention food and drink. (*IHC*, 119–20)

Magda rejects the philosophical abstractions of Beckett, and makes a direct appeal to the Real, and to an end-oriented understanding of history – in short, to those transparencies that are discredited in postmodernism. Rody points out that this section demonstrates that Magda 'does not want to be the Beckett persona she resembles because a woman needs life, not just words. Voicing in the female a desire for connection to people, to nature, to life itself, Coetzee's text uses feminism to challenge the limits of the postmodern.'[26] If these limits are challenged, however, it is in a spirit of resignation. Magda, in making her defiant appeal, simultaneously reaffirms her place in her textual prison: she reveals herself to be an artificial postmodernist product, familiar with *Happy Days*, and with Beckett's fascination with permutation. She is placed by the marks of a European literary tradition which invalidate her desires.

There is a sense that Magda's intellectual inheritance (as Coetzee's creation), involving that range of European literary and philosophical influences, is shown as misplaced, if not barren and unsustaining. In this metafictional sense, Magda's spinsterhood is the mark of a colonial dead-end. There is, however, a paradox, since this might suggest an uncomplicated exposure of intellectual colonization which is not present: it is also *through* the novel's allusiveness that the authority of its analysis emerges. An example is the reference to Hegel's work on the master/slave, or lord/bondsman dialectic. Teresa Dovey points out that Magda offers a translation of a key section from Hegel's *Phenomenology of Spirit* (*IHC*, 130).[27] The observation of Hegel's, to which Magda makes reference, concerns the paradoxical bond between lord and bondsman. The pertinent aspect of Hegel's argument is that the lord depends for his mastery on the self-consciousness of the bondsman, and so fails to achieve the independent status that the self-consciousness of *his* position requires. The position of *genuine* self-consciousness, paradoxically, is the bondsman's, not the lord's: each occupies the reverse position in the relationship to the one presumed.[28] In this relationship there is an inverse authenticity which validates the bondsman. Coetzee is not following Hegel in his interest in the discipline of service and obedience; but he does *project* an authenticity in the process of overturning thraldom.

Coetzee's appropriation of this inverse authenticity has a metafictional orientation: the model of decolonization has also a literary parallel, implying the need for a kind of formal hybridity, in which the post-colonizer's intellectual inheritance can be exploited and interrogated simultaneously. Such an inheritance can be justified, or authenticated in its own right, by being utilized to reveal the anterior authenticity of the oppressed Other. Formally, this involves striking a balance between contesting claims.

There are, however, various pressures operating to produce this formal hybridity. Coetzee has expressed his own concerns on a parallel issue which is pertinent here, articulating a 'wistfulness' for the immediacy of an uncomplicated idea of the real. Yet he is also dubious about realism as a mode of intervention in South Africa, another kind of obedience to codes which need interrogating (*DP*, 63–4). The Coetzee style is, in effect, a carefully worked out compromise between political obligation or duty, on the one hand, and intellectual integrity, on the other. There is an expectation, Coetzee suggests, that the writer in Africa should find a transparent way of rendering the history operating on him (*DP*, 67–8). Imagination, in this conception, becomes subordinate to moral duty. But this is, necessarily, a defeat of imaginative literature, and also a betrayal of the intellectual obligations of a poststructuralist writer, trained to interrogate the codes of writing. The required compromise is one which keeps history in view, without losing a focus on the medium. *In the Heart of the Country* is evidently an illustration of this kind of compromise, a novel in which the codes of writing are bound up with the presentation of historical identity. And, if the novel itself is caught on the horns of this particular dilemma, that may be the best justification of its historical relevance: it is an expression of simultaneous intervention and self-doubt, by a writer aware of his own sense of complicity, seeking to balance competing demands. In this sense, the presentation of the paradox – which captures the political instability – is a perfectly faithful record of the historical moment, and so an *ethical* solution in its own right.

This necessary paradox is embodied in the lyricism at the novel's end. As Peter Strauss argues, the lyrical mode itself (through which Magda's idyllic vision is expressed) has an important duality, since it can 'imprison the mind as nothing else can', but is 'also uniquely able to press a mind beyond itself, to press it beyond its own strictures'.[29] This, I think, is a perceptive account of the *potential* of the lyrical mode in Coetzee's work. This potential, which is barely realized in this novel, begins to be developed in important ways through Coetzee's *œuvre* from this point onwards.

CHAPTER 4

An ethical awakening: 'Waiting for the Barbarians'

The process of self-confrontation in the first three novels reaches a kind of plateau in *Waiting for the Barbarians* (1980). This is signalled through the idea of a personal awakening – that which is ultimately beyond Magda's reach in *In the Heart of the Country*, but which becomes a determining structural feature in this novel.

Waiting for the Barbarians crystallizes the central issue of debate concerning the ethical vision of Coetzee's fiction, and his importance as a novelist. This novel about the destructiveness (and self-destructiveness) of an imperial regime – obstructed by one man of conscience – has obvious ramifications for the white opponent of apartheid South Africa in 1980, the year of publication. The parallels, however, are vague in that the time and place of the novel's setting are imprecise. At one level, this is an allegory of imperialism and, as such, it inevitably widens its significance. Yet, if the parallel political situations are various, the novel may still be shown to have its compositional roots in a set of specific responses to contemporary South African concerns, and it is this achieved duality which lends credibility and resonance to the allegorical style: through a broadening and questioning of its one-to-one significance, the novel reinvigorates the allegorizing impulse.

The novel centres on a frontier outpost in an unknown land at an unknown time, a settlement – a walled town – under the auspices of the portentously termed 'Empire'. The omission of the definite article helps to widen the connotations of 'Empire', which becomes available as an emblem of imperialism through history. The narrator of the novel is the long-time magistrate of the settlement, and it is he who focuses the condemnation of Empire, principally through an involved, painful, and ambivalent process of self-evaluation and self-critique: the uncovering of the magistrate's own complicity helps him to a deep understanding of the nature of Empire's imperialism, and to a burgeoning ethical stance.

For Attwell, *Waiting for the Barbarians* occupies a pivotal position in Coetzee's *œuvre*, since there is a 'process of formal stabilization' at work which produces (by comparison with the previous novels) a greater degree of conventionality in the descriptions, in the narrative voice and in the treatment of time. Attwell considers that these changes represent, not a relapse into realism, but rather an exorcism of its ghost. The key to this pivotal position is a new presentation of history which, in the earlier novels, was presented as 'an absolute horizon to consciousness', but which now emerges as a question of discourse, an ideological structure: 'the objectification of history-as-myth'.[1] This properly identifies the seminal place of the presentation of 'history', but the narrative alternative the novel generates seems to me to be more involved in certain realist codes than this account acknowledges. The novel is more typical of the *œuvre*, more representative of the dominant mode of formal hybrid, than Attwell's pivotal position implies.

One critic finds an unresolved tension in the novel between a postmodernist 'voice' creating ambiguity and doubt, on the one hand, and an alternative 'voice' conveying the moral concerns of Leavis' Great Tradition, a more stable element representing an 'enduring code of ethics'.[2] While a (typically postmodernist) dialectic between different traditions may be present, this may also involve a mutual interrogation of these different traditions from which a synthesis, an alternative postcolonial ethic, might emerge.

At the beginning of the narrative, Colonel Joll and his men from Empire's Third Bureau arrive at the settlement to begin operations to deal with the perceived barbarian threat. (The frontier marks the point beyond which the Empire's domain gives way to territory inhabited by the nomadic barbarians.) Joll and his men are torturers and interrogators, driven by the

directive to discover the 'truth', a 'truth' predetermined by
Empire's Manichean ethos, and its own schema for self-
assertion. Joll and his men round up prisoners and interrogate
them. One of the torture victims, a young barbarian girl, has
been nearly blinded, and has deformed ankles, which were
broken by her captors. The magistrate develops an ambivalent
interest in her – which reveals to him his affinity with her
torturers – and she becomes the catalyst for his journey of self-
discovery. The magistrate takes the crucial decision to return
her to her own people, and takes a small party on an
expedition to this end. On his return, he is branded a
collaborator with the barbarian 'enemy', tortured and reviled.
The novel ends with the abandonment of the settlement by the
Third Bureau garrison: they have been out-thought by those
they interpellate 'barbarian', the elusive nomadic people (who
have avoided direct confrontation, but have undermined and
sabotaged the Empire's operations by stealth). The novel closes
as a reduced population at the settlement (many have fled),
now abandoned by their supposed protectors, remain waiting
for the barbarians.

The novel takes its title from a poem of the same name by
the Greek poet C. P. Cavafy, which presents an anticipation of
decolonization which does not occur. The poem offers an
image of the Roman Empire in decadent stasis, awaiting the
arrival of 'the barbarians' who will take over the mantle of
government – the legislative process – as well as the titles and
trappings of high office. The barbarians, in failing to arrive, in
ceasing to exist, can no longer offer 'a kind of solution'. In one
sense the 'waiting' is a waiting for the imperialist self-prophecy
to be fulfilled. This prophecy is partly a teleology of imperial
history, justified by the presence of a preconceived Other: it is
as if everything has built up to this moment. Yet the fulfilment
of this prophecy would also be a negation of the imperial
enterprise, its death-knell. It is this ambivalence and contradiction identified in the Cavafy poem that Coetzee's novel
echoes.[3]

In the novel, there are different connotations of waiting, for
Colonel Joll and for the magistrate. Joll needs the barbarians to

arrive for his mission, and Empire's function, to be validated. For the magistrate, however, the barbarians have already arrived in the form of Empire's militia: he has been waiting for Empire's barbarity to manifest itself, so that he can begin the process of disentangling himself from its ideology of power and justice.[4]

At a basic level, the magistrate's story suggests an allegory of the situation of the contemporary South African liberal, facing the fact of complicity in apartheid. Yet, as with the earlier novels, one does not find the kind of detailed correspondences that one might expect of a sustained, old-style political allegory, and this raises familiar questions about the kind of intervention the novel makes. For one critic, it is precisely the lack of specificity that gives the novel, as allegory, its potential to undermine the codes of the specific political hegemony: 'in a situation of such extreme political and economic oppression as South Africa's – where even visions, if they are too specific, can seem to impose a history – an unspecified, ahistorical allegory may make a more acceptable offering, which is, because more acceptable, perhaps even politically more efficacious'.[5] The lack of specificity may signify a subversive elusiveness. This need not be taken to suggest a style of writing designed to deceive the censors through obliquity (the sterility of which activity Coetzee identifies himself (*GO*, viii)). This is a different kind of revisionist nonconformity, the writer's pursuit of new codes under the guise of following older ones: what appears to be a universal allegory or parable about power and oppression – as a stable set of relations, or a given master code – may really be a special refusal and an interim gesture.

In a similar vein, Attwell defends the lack of specificity in the novel's milieu, an imprecision sometimes taken to denote 'a form of ethical universalism': the alternative is to see the lack of precision as a deliberate strategy and an immediate response to events in South Africa in the late 1970s. The (I think convincing) argument is that the fictional Empire is a fictionalization of the apartheid regime, a parody of its paranoid machinations, its implausible (and so insubstantial) manipulations of history.[6]

There are, in any case, some uncomfortable contemporary associations, despite the vagueness of the setting. A direct echo of the contemporary context – and the particular climate of moral choice it engendered – is suggested in the inhabitants' abandoning of the settlement in the face of fears of barbarian attack. An obvious parallel is the choice of white South Africans to emigrate in the 1970s and 1980s, to pursue professional careers in other developed countries, divesting themselves of responsibility for the threat of violence in their country. In the novel, the sense of guilt and fear is clear in the subterfuge required by those abandoning the settlement, and in the reprisals meted out (*WB*, 128, 130).

Susan Gallagher points persuasively to another specific issue in the contemporary context which is decisive in the composition of *Waiting for the Barbarians*: torture. Gallagher correctly observes that an international concern for human rights was focused on the South African regime following the Soweto riots in 1976–7, and the death of Steve Biko in 1977. This is the immediate resonance of the torture scenes in the novel.[7]

Coetzee also makes this a literary and theoretical topic, through allusions which reveal affinities between the novel's investigations of torture, and Foucault's comments on this in *Discipline and Punish*.[8] A still more dominant presence, however, is Kafka, evident in the brutal scene in which a line of barbarian prisoners are flogged. The word 'ENEMY' is written on their backs in charcoal, and they are then thrashed until the word is effaced (*WB*, 104–6).[9] Through his allusions, as well as specifically in this scene, Coetzee investigates an association between torture, identity and writing. The specific reference is to Kafka's story 'In the Penal Colony', the influence of which extends beyond the one scene in *Waiting for the Barbarians*. The story concerns a device for execution which kills by scoring on the condemned body a phrase deemed appropriate to the determined sentence. An explorer visiting the penal colony is invited to witness an execution: the colony's Commandant apparently seeks external condemnation of the lingering practices of the previous Commandant's regime. The condemned man is a soldier, sentenced to death for insubordination, and the words 'HONOUR THY SUPERIORS!' are to be inscribed on his body: the idea is that the prisoner, rather than being informed of the sentence, will 'learn' the lesson inscribed as sentence is carried out.[10] The turning-point in this twelve-hour process, this torture-as-execution, is deemed to be at six hours, after which, presumably, death is certain. The officer in charge of the apparatus – who is now its sole open proponent – speaks of this moment as one of 'enlightenment', when the transfiguring effect of justice can be witnessed on the dying man's face.[11] Perceiving that the explorer will not speak up for the system of justice, the officer frees the prisoner and takes his place, resetting the machine to inscribe the legend 'BE JUST!'. The machine, neglected in this new regime, goes wrong and kills the officer quickly and violently, without making the inscription. The dead officer's face betrays no sign of the promised redemption.[12]

In several ways, Coetzee's novel draws on the psyche of the officer in the story. His unquestioning faith in judicial procedures, his refusal to doubt guilt, the association he perceives between pain and truth/enlightenment, his fascination for the tortured body – these are all factors in the novel's analysis of Empire. There is, however, a shift of emphasis in the scene which suggests the allusion. In Kafka's story, the process of inscription is an expression of power, as well as an exposure of the self-destructiveness this involves. In Coetzee's novel, the process of inscription has more directly to do with identity and the interpellation of the subject (as 'enemy'), and the element of self-defeat, though equally pronounced, is oriented differently. As in Cavafy's poem, the operations of Empire require the existence of the barbarian as enemy, and here the beating away of the charcoal inscriptions is an ironic purgation of the Manichean difference upon which Empire depends.

In an essay written in 1986, Coetzee describes *Waiting for the Barbarians* as a novel specifically about torture and its impact on the 'man of conscience'. He goes on to consider the reasons for, and the pitfalls involved in, the South African novelist's fascination with torture. The first reason is abstract: the connection between torturer and tortured is an extreme,

compelling metaphor for authoritarian oppression more generally. The second reason, however, links this general with the
particular: the novelist is drawn to the analysis of acute human
experience, and there is no individual interaction more private
and extreme than that which occurs in the torture chamber.
Coetzee's implication is that the novelist feels a moral duty to
interrogate this hidden 'vileness', which is also suggestive of an
archetypal situation of fictional creativity, in which are found
dark human mysteries (*DP*, 363).

It is in discussing the pitfalls of this fascination that the
political edge to Coetzee's deliberations is sharpened. The
basic dilemma in the treatment of torture is that the writer fails
either by ignoring it, or, potentially, by reproducing it through
representation. Resolving this dilemma is the writer's task, in
seeking to establish the authority to imagine torture and death
on his or her own terms (*DP*, 364). This is a call for an effective
reappropriation, and simultaneous analysis of state violence.
Waiting for the Barbarians can, quite properly, be seen as an
extended treatment of these concerns. It is at once an investigation of the archetypal dark chamber, and a reimagining of
state violence as a response to a specific political situation.

Coetzee conducts this reimagining in the novel as a process
of discovery in which different ways of thinking it through are
broached. In the essay, Coetzee castigates Sipho Sepamla for
his treatment of torturers in *A Ride on the Whirlwind*. One
problem is that Sepamla attempts to make his torturers both
too satanic, and yet 'too easily human', explaining how one
man has developed a split personality to survive the stresses of
his work as torturer (*DP*, 365). Similar issues are raised in
Waiting for the Barbarians, begging the question as to whether
Coetzee establishes a subtly new approach, or whether he
might be condemned by his own bench-mark. When, for
instance, the magistrate ponders on Joll as once a torturer-
initiate, does this make him seem 'too easily human'? Here is
the relevant passage:

Looking at him I wonder how he felt the very first time: did he,
invited as an apprentice to twist the pincers or turn the screw or
whatever it is they do, shudder even a little to know that at that

instant he was trespassing into the forbidden? I find myself wondering too whether he has a private ritual of purification, carried out behind closed doors, to enable him to return and break bread with other men. (*WB*, 12)

The impulse of this wondering bewilderment is to establish the *difficulty* of the torturer's return to everyday human activities, to express incredulity that such a thing is feasible. Even so, there is also an element of empathy, an engagement with the idea of transgression and initiation; but this empathy also fails to introduce a humanizing element. The affinity hinted at here between the magistrate and Joll is part of the magistrate's self-critique, an understanding of his own propensity for inhuman behaviour. Sexuality and torture are linked here (as elsewhere), through the idea of personal thrill and sensation through entry into the forbidden.

A similar episode occurs much later when the magistrate questions Mandel, his own torturer, about how he can reconcile his duties with his daily existence:

'I am only trying to understand. I am trying to understand the zone in which you live. I am trying to imagine how you breathe and eat and live from day to day. But I cannot! That is what troubles me! If I were he, I say to myself, my hands would feel so dirty that it would choke me – '

He wrenches himself free and hits me so hard in the chest that I gasp and stumble backwards. 'You bastard!' he shouts. 'You fucking old lunatic! Get out! Go and die somewhere!' (*WB*, 126)

The persisting incredulity denies any normalization of the torturer's role, but the issue of what is 'human' is also scrutinized. Where, for Coetzee, Sepamla presents his torturer as too easily human, able to compartmentalize brutality within his everyday existence, Coetzee implies Mandel is unable in some measure to cope with the internal division: the honest question provokes an outburst of genuine violence, physical and verbal, an emotional response quite different to the clinical cruelty of the torture chamber.

The violence offered to the magistrate includes a public beating, the force-feeding of gallons of salt water and a mock-hanging (and near strangulation). His treatment, however, is gratuitous in that he is not being tortured for information. The purpose of the random violence is, as the magistrate puts it, 'to show me the meaning of humanity' (*WB*, 115). Aside from the immediate irony, there is a different aspect to the reimagining of torture in this notion of humanity. If a torturer can be presented as too easily human, so, too, in an associated way can the onlooker – until, that is, the onlooker becomes the victim. The magistrate realizes the purpose of the lesson he is being taught through torture: that high-minded notions of justice can be retained only by the healthy body. The tortured body will lose its grasp of such principles (*WB*, 115). If ironic, the 'lesson' is also salutary, indicating that principles, if backed up by the requisite degree of humanity, may have to pass the test of personal suffering.

This is an ambivalent episode, however, and one might equally wonder if Coetzee courts one of the dangers he mentions in his essay on torture, the danger of reproducing the effects of repressive state violence. One feature of this unintentional buttressing would be the perpetuation of fear, and one might wonder if the magistrate's experiences replicate the principled observer's fear of being drawn into a situation that he or she could not endure, a situation which would break their principled stance (clearly the torturer's goal). Yet the magistrate does not lose his principles; nor are the descriptions of his experiences presented in a way which conveys extreme pain or suffering. Still more important is the fact that the magistrate, as narrator, has control of the account: he cannot be objectified as victim, dehumanized by a sustained external view. The torturer's perspective on him, in other words, cannot be reproduced. These are all important strategies which ensure that close control over the imagining of torture is retained. Allied to this is the affinity between the magistrate and the psyche of the torturer (that of Joll in particular). The exploration of this affinity might suggest that the distinction between oppressor and oppressed is fudged, with the effect that there is a dangerous engagement with (or reproduction of) the state's activities. The strategy, however, has the reverse effect. The presence of affinity overcomes the danger of demonizing the oppressor, and mythologizing his power. And it is through this process of demythologizing the psyche of Empire that the magistrate is able to discover – and begin to see more clearly – his ethical differences from it.

A useful point of reference for the novel's investigation of language and power is Coetzee's essay, 'Isaac Newton and the Ideal of a Transparent Scientific Language' (1982), in which he points out the formative role of language on the expression of thought. In this particular case, the structures of a language are shown to help determine the couching of scientific 'laws'. Coetzee considers the possibility that causality can be confused in this process, that one may unconsciously project the structure of one's own language on to the phenomena one is trying to describe, thus producing 'truths' which are really predetermined by a particular linguistic conception. Coetzee goes on to point out a contradiction between the impulse of the scientist to find an unambiguous and transparent language through which to translate scientific truth, and the tendency of language towards ambiguity. Even science, Coetzee shows, has recourse to the ambivalent trope of metaphor, for example. Indeed, scientific theories – the argument in Newton's law of gravitation that two bodies *attract* each other, for instance – are necessarily expressed in metaphorical language, since they are conveying new claims for which no literal explanation exists. In interview, Coetzee rehearses the philological argument that languages go through a particular evolutionary process in which a middle stage of great inflection gives way to the phase of advanced civilization. In the advanced stage, languages lose their inflection and become governed by an analytical syntax and morphology, a phase which Coetzee characterizes (apropos of *Dusklands*), as 'a more complacently colonial science of language' (*DP*, 144). These reflections on the protean nature of language and its unsuitability for the scientific ideal thus have a direct relationship to the colonial project, in which a false conviction of certitude might be expressed in a pseudo-scientific, non-inflected language.

The convictions of Empire and its agent Joll are usefully approached with these ideas about language in mind. Indeed, it is through a reductive perception of language that Joll attempts to exercise control, as this conversation with the magistrate makes clear:

'How do you ever know when a man has told you the truth?'

'There is a certain tone,' Joll says. 'A certain tone enters the voice of a man who is telling the truth. Training and experience teach us to recognize that tone.'

'The tone of truth! Can you pick up this tone in everyday speech? Can you hear whether I am telling the truth?' . . .

'No, you misunderstand me. I am speaking only of a special situation now, I am speaking of a situation in which I am probing for the truth, in which I have to exert pressure to find it. First I get lies, you see – this is what happens – first lies, then pressure, then more lies, then more pressure, then the break, then more pressure, then the truth. That is how you get the truth.'

Pain is truth; all else is subject to doubt. (*WB*, 5)

The irony of the magistrate's 'misunderstanding' is that he implies Joll must have an ear remarkably sensitive to linguistic inflection. The reverse, of course, is the case: the tone of truth is the uniform note of pain to which all victims can be reduced, if Joll's textbook procedure for torture is pursued. Just as the colonizer does damage to indigenous languages, so does Joll reduce all inflection to the single tone of pain/truth. His role as torturer thus has also this figurative connotation, representative of linguistic imperialism.

In a similar spirit, the magistrate's bellows of pain when strung from a tree are jokingly dismissed as calls for help in barbarian language (he is a suspected collaborator) (*WB*, 121). By Joll's logic, of course, this would make the barbarian language the language of truth, since it is heard, here, as the tone of pain: an intentional irony perhaps. It may be more important to note the inconsistency of the Empire position (for the magistrate is ridiculed from this position): pain in this episode has no meaning for Empire (it does not have the currency it would have in the enclosed chamber in which truth is extracted) and so, unless the suffering is to be acknowledged, this pain must be dismissed as Other.

Some of Colonel Joll's early prisoners, in his expeditions against the barbarians, turn out to be fisherfolk, arrested by soldiers who could not understand their language. This episode – apparently a farcical display in which suspicions are sustained only by virtue of military incompetence – also falls in line with the logic of Empire which effectively designates the Other (especially as denoted by language) as automatically guilty (*WB*, 18). The issue of language is one important area in which the magistrate is partly implicated in the Empire's perspective. His relationship with the barbarian girl, for example, is dogged by the lack of a common language. They have to make do with a makeshift mode of communication, susceptible to misunderstanding because it has 'no nuances', and is thus an emulation of the non-inflected analytical language of colonialism (*WB*, 40). On the expedition to return the barbarian girl to her people, the magistrate hears her talking animatedly with the other men in the expedition. She is fluent in the pidgin language of the frontier – witty, young and attractive, he realizes (*WB*, 63). He regrets not discovering how to communicate with her, not having asked her to teach him the language in their time together (*WB*, 71–2). This regret at not intensifying their bond through a shared understanding of a language and its nuances also associates the magistrate with the convictions of Empire. His lack of interest in the girl's language has ensured she has remained an intransigent Other, an alien to his own norms. The magistrate's treatment of the young barbarian is consequently ambivalent throughout, since his desire for, and control of, her links him, in particular, to the torturers he struggles to understand.

Early on in the novel, in fact, the magistrate recognizes an affinity between himself and the girl's torturers (*WB*, 27); this stems from a shared fascination with the girl's body as object, and much of the magistrate's career has to do with trying to grow beyond – and distinguish himself from – the impulses of the abuser. It is significant that sexual intercourse occurs between them only on the expedition to return her to her own people – at a time, that is, when she is about to become free of Empire's control, and can make her own choices.[13] This does not denote an enduring new plane of contact, however; their lovemaking 'peters out' at the next attempt (*WB*, 63–4, 66).

Indeed, the theme of sexuality is not used to explore the grounds of some kind of utopian physical bond. Its primary connotation has to do with broader issues of control and discourse, with the male desire for penetration consistently indicative of the kind of assertiveness the magistrate is learning to grow beyond. When the young barbarian woman becomes a fixture in his room, the magistrate finds himself drawn to the inn/brothel, to the room of a regular partner, whom he describes as 'bird-like'. In a key scene, the magistrate returns from the arms of his bird-woman to the sleeping barbarian, and attempts to make sense of his mysterious desire for her, in comparison with the straightforward physical desire he has just consummated:

There is no link I can define between her womanhood and my desire. I cannot even say for sure that I desire her. All this erotic behaviour of mine is indirect: I prowl about her, touching her face, caressing her body, without entering her or finding the urge to do so. I have just come from the bed of a woman for whom, in the year I have known her, I have not for a moment had to interrogate my desire: to desire her has meant to enfold her and enter her, to pierce her surface and stir the quiet of her interior into an ecstatic storm; then to retreat, to subside, to wait for desire to reconstitute itself. But with this woman it is as if there is no interior, only a surface across which I hunt back and forth seeking entry. Is this how her torturers felt hunting their secret, whatever they thought it was? For the first time I feel a dry pity for them: how natural a mistake to believe you can burn or tear or hack your way into the secret body of the other! (*WB*, 43)

The expression of phallic desire as an imposition on the Other is used consistently, and is an analogue for related topics. The magistrate's account of sexual relations with the bird-woman is entirely congruous with the analytical complacency of Empire, oblivious to the actual nuances of another culture (yet desirous of its exotic alterity). Just as scientific language projects its own hidden structures onto the mysterious observable universe, and just as the colonizer makes his colony conform to his own template, so does the magistrate's phallic possession involve the subjugation of a foreign body to the repetitive pattern of his own (unquestioned) desire. The barbarian girl, however, gives him pause for thought: this is a foreign body he cannot immediately comprehend. He realizes the desire to possess the 'interior' of the girl is a 'mistake', which, effectively, would involve a projection of his own schema – the marking of her surface that her torturers had attempted. In effect, the girl is established as a text which, it seems, must be approached in an appropriate manner. This issue is raised a few pages earlier when the magistrate indicates that he cannot relinquish the girl until he has interpreted the marks on her body (*WB*, 31). The symbolic terms are shifted slightly, here, since the torturers' marks are now part of the girl's own mystery, and not merely a sign of imperial imposition. This, however, serves to enrich the figurative dimension rather than to dilute it, since the girl's identity, which the magistrate struggles to understand on its own terms, is a complex one, formed by different forces (including the force of the colonizer).

The motif of the girl as text is central to the novel, because it links the treatment of individual experience and repression directly to broader questions of discourse and power. In this connection, Attwell sees a significance in the difference between the magistrate's relationship with the girl at the inn, and the barbarian girl. The difference, he feels, corresponds to Barthes' distinction between readerly and writerly texts, since 'the "bird-woman" is readerly, giving herself over to the agency of the Magistrate', whereas 'the barbarian girl is writerly, admitting no access to an imagined, fecund essence'.[14] It might be appropriate, initially, to place emphasis on what kind of a reader the magistrate is in each case, rather than on what kind of text each woman resembles: the agency of the 'reader' in the analogy is the point at issue. The girl's torturers try to make her into a readerly text, submissive to their own agenda, and this is why they leave their mark on her. For the magistrate, the evidence of this mistreatment, the mark of the readerly reader, gives him pause. In this sense, the decipherment of the marks is also an understanding of the dubious impulse of which they are a testimony, one he is coming to terms with in himself.

The acknowledgement of the barbarian girl as a writerly text deftly politicizes the novel's tendency to allude to theoretical ideas, and provides a direct link with the wooden slips bearing an ancient script which the magistrate has discovered in an archaeological dig near to the settlement. There are 256 of these slips – a 'perfect' number – on which are painted characters of an unknown script, perhaps belonging to a previous outpost of civilization (*WB*, 15–16). One of the magistrate's preoccupations is to try and understand the script contained on the slips, much as he tries to interpret the marks on the girl. Again, the lesson the magistrate must learn is to resist the need to impose a single meaning on this phenomenon, a point which becomes clear when Colonel Joll questions him about the slips. In the paranoid mind of Empire, these ancient relics may represent a contemporary hidden code, through which the magistrate communicates with the enemy. There is a contemporary resonance in this paranoia, suggestive of the effects of the South African regime's repression of the sources of African identity which might issue in a modern political mobilization: the concealment and misrepresentation of the traces of history is, of course, a seminal feature of apartheid mythology.[15] In response to Joll's request for a translation, the magistrate obliges, even though, looking at the slips, he has no idea in which direction they should be read, or, indeed, what any of the characters mean. The magistrate's translation session ends with a sarcastic lesson for the impassive Joll in the mutability of language:

'Now let us see what the next one says. See, there is only a single character. It is the barbarian character *war*, but it has other senses too. It can stand for *vengeance*, and, if you turn it upside down like this, it can be made to read *justice*. There is no knowing which sense is intended. That is part of barbarian cunning.

'It is the same with the rest of these slips.' I plunge my good hand into the chest and stir. 'They form an allegory. They can be read in many orders. Further, each single slip can be read in many ways. Together they can be read as a domestic journal, or they can be read as a plan of war, or they can be turned on their sides and read as a history of the last years of the Empire – the old Empire, I mean.' (*WB*, 112)

The lessons here are multifarious, the main one lying in the fluidity of language, the nuances of which are missed in a reductive analytical view. The message is that a pursuit of the truth might well result in an arbitrary representation in which 'war', 'justice' and 'vengeance' are interchangeable terms. In this spirit, that which is resistant to a single interpretation can be dismissed as elusive 'cunning'. The idea that the slips could form an allegory of the end of the old Empire has a particular resonance. Joll, in investigating the slips as a possible arcane barbarian code, misreads their potential much as the Empire is eventually undone by failing to recognize the nature of the 'barbarians' as Other: the imposition of a false template of warfare means that the Empire forces are depleted without ever facing their designated enemy face to face. Even when Joll dismisses the significance of the slips, *this* allegorical prognostication – of the catastrophic misreading of the Other – resonates: realizing his inability to decipher them according to his own schema, he demeans them by dismissing them as gambling sticks (*WB*, 113). Significantly, it is an old-style allegory, a one-to-one correspondence, which is undermined through the elusiveness of the slips. It is in such moments that the novel performs a formal 'decolonization' of the allegorizing impulse itself, which, in a basic manifestation (as Stephen Slemon suggests), is to set a literary text 'against a pre-existing master code'.[16] The parallel with the allegorizing impulse in imperialism is clear, revealed in the magistrate's exposure of Joll's expectations.

By the end of the novel the slips appear to have been accepted as barbarian artefacts, though initially this was by no means clear. They were excavated at a site that appears to have been populated by an earlier outpost for defence against the barbarians. This makes not just the meaning of the slips, but their provenance as well, ambiguous, thereby raising a host of difficult questions about the radical indeterminacy of discourse and the sources of power.[17]

It is the question of history which, ultimately, gives shape to the treatment of power. The definition of history, indeed, is a fundamental issue in *Waiting for the Barbarians*, and what the novel finally achieves is a pointed application of the idea that history can be variously constructed, that it is a field for contestation. The magistrate approaches the question of history in different ways as the novel progresses, and, on occasions, his concerns mirror the larger metafictional gestures of the work – by which I mean Coetzee's investigation of how fiction colludes with certain ideas of history. As in *In the Heart of the Country*, a main concern here is literary pastoral. This novel conforms to a basic convention of literary pastoral in that its action spans just one year. Attwell is right to point out that the structure of the single seasonal cycle emerges as a 'flagrantly formal, conventionalized device' in the context of this novel: the 'poetic-symbolic correspondences' between the natural cycle and events in the novel – for example the signs of spring which appear after the magistrate's expedition to return the barbarian girl – are marked up as misleading signposts in a novel which is radically dystopian.[18] Like recent human geographers, Coetzee is concerned with how socialization can be imposed on individuals through the ordering of time and space: the seasonal cycle is the most obvious temporal pattern which can be overlaid on historical experience as a normalizing device.[19] Here, the arrival of Joll's men, and the talk of the barbarian threat, coincides with winter: there is scope for the seasonal pattern of endurance and hardship to legitimize Empire's totalitarian operations. The magistrate is himself alert to (and complicitous with) the control of spatio-temporal practices: he remembers how his own administration, twenty years earlier, had moved a barbarian 'shambles' – a kind of shantytown – from the market-place to the town's outskirts (*WB*, 120).

The recognition of such social manipulation, with its attendant shaping of history, is part of a broader learning curve, which is 'realized' as a consequence of the magistrate's failed objective to write the history of his experiences. In the final pages, when he sits down to attempt the task, he finds himself beginning a pastoral celebration of existence in his 'oasis', the very myth that Magda clings to at the end of the previous novel. The magistrate, however, instantly dismisses this history as 'devious' and 'reprehensible', and considers the disappointment he would feel were the poplar slips bearing the unknown script found to yield nothing more. The magistrate's problem is in the conception and function of history. He wants to escape the history that Empire has imposed, and feels that such freedom must involve living outside history (*WB*, 154). Yet this desire to escape can also be read as a need to recast history – or to reimagine it – in a form which liberates it from hierarchical control.

The terms of this problem are set out in this passage: 'Empire has created the time of history. Empire has located its existence not in the smooth recurrent spinning time of the cycle of the seasons but in the jagged rise and fall, of beginning and end, of catastrophe' (*WB*, 133). The recourse to pastoral – to the seasonal cycle – is an incomplete reaction to Empire, to its end-oriented, teleological version of history, here presented as inevitably confrontational, apocalyptic. We remember, in any case, that the magistrate has also displayed faith in the teleological version of history, as, for example, when he claims to Joll that Joll's barbarities will be brought to light in historical records, and his stand will thus be exonerated. Joll indicates that no such history will be written (*WB*, 114). The magistrate has no recourse to history as a linear version of 'truth', because this is merely an instrument of ideological control. The same misperception about history is manifest in the magistrate's earlier (also abortive) attempt to begin a history. At this time, he associates his failure to make his mark upon the 'empty white paper' with his failure to possess the young barbarian woman sexually. The familiar identification of pen and phallus associates the control of linear history with imposed phallocentric desire; and, just as the magistrate's 'impotence' should be given a positive cast, so, too, should his inability to write a teleological account of events. His realization that pastoral is escape, and that the slips, like the uninterpretable barbarian girl, may present another kind of hope suggests that 'history' needs to be reimagined, rather than escaped from.[20]

The history that is finally offered as an alternative is a history of personal growth, presented obliquely through a sequence of dreams. This 'history' avoids linear forms – it does not appear in the form of a testament, or a memoir, or a confession (*WB*,

58) – as well as circular explanations: the logic of the dreams is accretive, progressive. It is these dreams which present a coherent narrative of individual commitment, and personal involvement in the construction of history.

The dream sequence affords also a progression beyond the limiting effects of the novel's use of the simultaneous narrative present: James Phelan shows how the dominance of this mode, which gives the impression that the magistrate is 'telling as he is living', effectively 'puts teleology beyond his control'. If there is a positive underpinning to this lack of control, in an ethical sense, the practical consequence of this narrative style, in Phelan's account, is to implicate the reader in 'the magistrate's own lack of perspective' and, by extension, in his complicity. While accepting, perhaps, this description of how, technically, the reader is drawn in to the theme of complicity, we may need also to understand how the text leads us out of the imprisoning present moment; this is done most arrestingly through the dream patterning.[21]

The first dream occurs early on and sets a scene which the magistrate will revisit and reconstruct and amplify as the novel goes on. Initially, however, the dream is ambiguous: the earth is covered with snow; the source of light is diffuse; and the magistrate progresses into the square of the settlement and comes upon a group of children building a snowcastle. All but one of the children disappear: the remaining figure is older – perhaps not a child – and the dream ends with the magistrate, standing behind her, trying in vain to imagine the face beneath her peaked hood, as she moulds the snow (*WB*, 9–10). The ambiguity of the girl in the dream – and the magistrate's response to her – clearly connects her with the young barbarian woman. In the face of the uncertainty, the magistrate displays the dubious need to order the experience through self-projection. When the scene is repeated, his attention is focused once more on a single figure (this time definitely a child) whose face is blank, without features, and to whom he holds out a coin (*WB*, 37). The logic of this dream is to expiate (as the coin suggests) the ambivalence of the magistrate's earlier 'reading' of the scene: the figure is a child, the earlier hint of sexual availability expunged; the face is still resistant to the expectations and projections of the onlooker's gaze.

In the next recurrence of the dream, now that the speculation has been expunged, the figure is clearly the barbarian girl, as a child: the magistrate is surprised by her smiling face, which he had feared to see. The detail in this dream is the major development: the snow fort the girl is building is actually a replica of the magistrate's walled town, though the model is empty of people. The magistrate – unable to make himself heard in dream-impotence – wants to tell her to put people in the square (*WB*, 52–3). The empty model of the town is both a forewarning of the town's demise, the flight of its inhabitants, and a figurative demonstration of the vacant human centre of the outpost of Empire.

In a later dream, the girl is attending not to a snow- or sandcastle, as the magistrate initially surmises, but to a clay oven she has built in the desert, from which she extracts – and then holds out in offering – a freshly baked loaf. The magistrate awakes just as he is about to embrace the girl in gratitude (*WB*, 109). The placing of this dream is important, as it occurs just after the magistrate's public beating, before his torture. The scene has now become a basic image of community, a kind of vision of basic human endurance – the baking of bread in the desert – in the face of difficult odds. The magistrate's gratitude is for a beacon of hope concerning a system which is quite apart from his own projections and desires. The novel ends with an echo of the dream when the magistrate watches some children building a snowman in the square. He resists the urge to interfere in their efforts (he feels that they should add some arms), and finally judges that they have built 'not a bad snowman'. The magistrate attaches no positive significance to the scene, and his narrative ends with a resonant tone of apparent resignation: 'this is not the scene I dreamed of. Like much else nowadays I leave it feeling stupid, like a man who has lost his way long ago but presses on along a road that may lead nowhere' (*WB*, 156). But these are words which the logic of the sequence calls into question. The scene *is* an echo of the dream scene, and, more importantly, it is an 'actual' scene in the world of the novel, in which the magistrate refrains from projecting his own scheme. In losing his way in the linear scheme of things (the road metaphor is pointed) he has advanced to a level where his subconscious works its own mythology.[22] The dream sequence amounts to an accreted narrative of sublimation and human advancement which belies the negativity of the final 'nowhere' of the novel, and which is validated by an appeal to a mimetic moment in which the lessons drawn from the dream-visions can be 'actualized' for the character: the magistrate awakes into a new present in which the traces of Empire are eradicated from his identity.

CHAPTER 5

Gardening as resistance: 'Life and Times of Michael K'

The title of Coetzee's fourth novel, *Life and Times of Michael K* (1983), announces a challenge. It alludes directly to a tradition of thinking about individual identity in relation to history – 'The Life and Times' – which is represented in a variety of genres, including the historical novel and the *Bildungsroman*, as well as non-fictional modes such as the political memoir. *Life and Times of Michael K* proclaims itself as having an involvement with this tradition in which the individual life is held to interact intimately with social and political development. The challenge is that the novel ironically undermines the association by presenting the life of an anti-hero who resists all obvious contact with the social and political milieu.

Despite this dynamic, there is some sense of political urgency in the conception of this novel when set against the vagueness – in the time and setting – of its predecessor, *Waiting for the Barbarians* (even though there are strategic reasons for that elusiveness): the new novel is set in modern South Africa, at a time of revolution. Neither is this merely future projection. The scenes of *Michael K* evoke the social breakdown of post-Soweto South Africa in the 1980s, just as the novel's themes represent governing fears and concerns of the time.[1] The operations of Umkhonto we Sizwe (the military wing of the ANC) are of especial significance. The most dramatic action, in a campaign of strategic bombings, was the attack against the SASOL oil-from-coal plants in June 1980, part of a series of acts of symbolic resistance which are representative of the historical background evoked through the setting of guerilla warfare in the novel. (Later operations targeted the Koeberg nuclear power station (1982) and Air Force headquarters in Pretoria (1983).)[2] In short, the novel, in the manner typical of the *œuvre*, is constructed in such a way that it simultaneously alludes to, and withdraws from, its context.

The story of Michael K is the story of a simple, non-white South African suffering the indignities and deprivations of apartheid, hardships intensified by the social disintegration of civil war. K resigns from his position as Gardener working for the City of Cape Town (he is to be laid off anyway) and sets off on a quest with his ailing mother, Anna, to find the farm near Prince Albert where she had grown up. The permits to allow them to travel by train do not arrive, so K constructs a barrow to carry his mother, but her health worsens on the journey, and she dies in hospital in Stellenbosch. K is aimless for a while, but then decides to continue the journey from Stellenbosch, carrying now a suitcase with his mother's effects, and her ashes. K is forced to work briefly on a labour gang on a railway, but eventually he arrives at a farm in the Prince Albert district, which may be the one his mother had described. Here he buries his mother's ashes, and begins to cultivate some patches of land, making this deserted white man's farm his own, in a minimal way.

Soon, however, Michael K's proprietorship is disturbed by the arrival of the grandson of the Visagies (the family that owns the farm): the grandson, an army deserter, is returning to the place he associates with safety from his childhood, a return which offers a rich and ironic parallel with Michael K's fulfilment of his mother's dream of return. Driven away by the Visagie grandson, K is picked up by the authorities and, after a stay in hospital, is taken to Jakkalsdrif camp in which unemployed workers are interned as a labour pool. K escapes and returns to the Prince Albert farm to cultivate a new crop of pumpkins and melons.[3] This time his task of cultivation is disrupted by the arrival of a small revolutionary force from the mountains, though K remains undetected. The idyll is finally destroyed by the arrival of soldiers in pursuit of the revolutionaries: they apprehend K as a suspected collaborator, and blow up the farmhouse, bearing K away with his plundered crop.

K is now interned in the Kenilworth camp, and section 2 of the novel is narrated by the camp's medical officer. The section is brief, but has a great importance to the generation of meaning. The medical officer is driven to try and interpret the elusive Michael K, to make him 'yield' his significance, in a metafictional gesture which implicates both author and reader. In the final, very brief section K, having escaped once more, returns to the Cape, and his mother's former residence at Sea Point. He encounters a group of survivors (two prostitutes and their pimp), whose philosophy of self-help in the scene of civil breakdown is set against K's minimalist philosophy of survival which is summarized in a lyrical close, in which K's perspective is made to emerge.

In the name Michael K there is, on the face of it, a direct reference to Josef K, the protagonist of Kafka's *The Trial*. This, together with various other allusions, suggests a shared theme of alienation, though there may be limits to how such connections assist in the interpretation of Coetzee's novel. Coetzee has said, even in the context of acknowledging the influence of Kafka, 'there is no monopoly on the letter K' (*DP*, 199). The most significant aspect of the link in *Michael K* may stem from the issue of minimal subsistence: Dovey indicates a connection between Kafka's treatment of 'fasting' (in works like 'A Hunger Artist'), and Michael K's function in representing 'that which *eludes* representation'.[4] Yet, in Coetzee's treatment, the theme is given a self-reflexive poststructuralist grounding (and ungrounding) which takes it beyond a simple comparison with sources in Kafka.

The problem the novel sets is the significance of K, a pointed challenge which disappoints certain set assumptions about social change and political commitment. A clue to this revisionism, as I have suggested, is already apparent in the title where the definite article has been dropped. Coetzee has expressed the view that 'The Life' implies an account of a life now over (and so, logically, available for recapitulation) whereas 'Life' on its own is not committed one way or the other, and this indicates the effect the novel has of interrogating the significance of the individual life.[5] So, despite the urgency of the setting, this apparently noncommittal element, this lack of temporal specificity, has been seen to detach the book from its context, and lend it the air of a fable or parable. This feature of the book has attracted the disapprobation of critics seeking a different kind of commitment. Sheila Roberts, in a piece published in 1984, comments on the lack of political edge of the novel, suggesting that its fabulistic nature distances it 'from the life of the ordinary reader', especially 'conservative white South Africans' who will not be prompted 'to change their ways or their political thinking'. This is not, however, offered as 'a literary judgement'.[6] Indeed, a literary judgement, based on the novel's concern with different types of discourse, would necessarily be less dismissive. Such an approach suggests an impact even – perhaps especially – on conservative white South Africans. Gallagher shows how a revision of Afrikaner mythology may produce the kind of impact Roberts denies. She shows, for example, how the Jakkalsdrif camp brings to mind actual relocation camps in which blacks, evicted from white areas, were interned. At the same time, however – and this is where the lack of specificity is productive – Jakkalsdrif would bring to the mind of the Afrikaner the British concentration camps of the Anglo-Boer war, an ironic association that is very effective in Gallagher's reading:

The implication of this part of Michael K's story is practically blasphemous to the Afrikaner mind. The suffering of the homeless and abandoned at Jakkalsdrif is equated with the holy suffering of the Boer women and children at the hands of the cruel British administrators. This juxtaposition not only highlights the ironic turn of events in South African history but also elevates the suffering of the black majority to its own mythic level.[7]

The ironic association effectively invalidates the Afrikaner mythology, which is supplanted through the writing of Coetzee's alternative myth of black suffering. (This is not to deny the suffering of Afrikaners in the Anglo-Boer war, but to question the relevance of this to contemporary South Africa: the mythology is false, in Gallagher's reading, in contributing to a false sense of justification and proprietorship in modern Afrikaner identity.) The important point for Coetzee's strategy is that the question of the control of discourse is itself politicized. Beyond this, the politicization of discourse is linked to the central colonial issue of the control of space, which is a dominant theme in the novel, as we shall see.

Michael K appears to be what the apartheid administration would classify as 'coloured': indeed, when he is arrested in Prince Albert, the charge sheet describes him as 'CM', or coloured male (*MK*, 70).[8] This detail, however, does not alter the general sense of K's elusiveness, a quality which calls into question attempts to classify and interpret him. This resistance of interpellation appears, at times, to constitute an apolitical withdrawal, as when K tells the medical officer that he is not in the war (*MK*, 138). Yet a number of critics have drawn attention to the positive significance of this elusiveness, even where K seems unable to take decisive action to help himself. Sarah Dove Heider, for example, shows that Michael K's lack of ambition and engagement is 'part of his withdrawing from the societal machines that attempt to engage him'.[9] This kind of challenge can be shown to have a very specific relevance. In an interview with Dick Penner, Coetzee indicates a pointed strategy of resistance in the elusiveness of the novel's conception: the exclusion of explicit racial reference is a way of resisting the classifications of apartheid, specifically the Population Registration Act (1950) (which required the population to be classified by race).[10]

Attwell properly points out that Coetzee's reluctance to represent mass resistance or to project a utopian future has very much to do with his ongoing interrogation of positions of authority.[11] The result, taken on its own terms, is a novel which, far from eschewing the question of engagement, is elusive precisely because of its political responsibility, its self-evaluation. There is an obvious parallel with Derridean notions of textuality in the elusiveness of Michael K, a character who eludes final meanings and whose story challenges the power of interpretation.[12] The association, however, is already rooted in a precise political context, and this ensures that the novel's presentations of the issue of textuality are never merely abstractions.

It is possible, however, to miss the complexity here. The motif of textuality may appear to validate K's elusiveness unequivocally, but the issue is more ambiguous than this, for another aspect of K's elusiveness is his silence, a sign of disenfranchisement as well as resistance. At the beginning of the novel, we learn that the infant K had learned to be quiet while watching his mother polishing floors: his language acquisition is expressed in the negative, the cultivation of silence in the face of oppression (*MK*, 4). The same reticence is displayed when K's resuscitation of the farm is interrupted by the arrival of the Visagie grandson, and K is reduced to a helpless speechlessness, a silence which offers no resistance to another significant dispossession (*MK*, 60). Where issues of material advantage are concerned, K's silence and compliance assist in his oppression. It is significant that discussing his dead mother is something K finds difficult, a silence which indicates a struggle to understand and articulate emotions for which he has no cultural referent (*MK*, 79, 139). Even so, K does offer a bitter account of his mother's exploited life to the medical officer, an outburst which implies an emerging political ethic (*MK*, 136). And, at the end of the novel, K's lyrical rationale of his gardening philosophy is an articulation of a moral high ground which redresses the loss of the farm, in theory at least. In this connection, the novel appears to draw an implicit distinction between 'text events' – the exploitation and death of Anna K; the loss and destruction of the farm – and the rationale of conduct. Where K's silences collude in the oppressive text events, he does ultimately find a voice to challenge these elements of oppression. The presentation of events, and the notion of K's development, are features which indicate a lingering realism in the novel, an effort to convey elements of typical historical action alongside the developing personal engagement of an individual in history. These elements of realism are contained within the novel's larger metafictional frame.

The narrative stances of the novel have a direct bearing on these questions of development and fictional mode. There is a principle of what Coetzee has termed 'limited omniscience' in the novel, a third-person narrative in which the extent of the narrator's knowledge about Michael K's story is unclear.[13] In fact, an important impetus of the novel is to raise doubts about this knowledge; but there is still a convention of realism which suggests appropriation in the narrative mediation of sections 1 and 3, akin, perhaps, to the medical officer's overt attempts at appropriation in section 2. Derek Wright considers the novel in this way:

In *Michael K* . . . the black protagonist's thoughts, in the fashion of realistic fiction are laid open to us as if of their own accord, although in fact by the white author who then has to resort to internal stratagems within the novel's realistic frame, such as making the white doctor unable to prize open K's mouth . . . The reflexive metafiction of *Foe* is the logical next stage on from this, totally abandoning the token psychological realism of *Michael K* and, with it, the attempt to write from a non-white perspective . . . *Michael K* marks the end of a phase in Coetzee's writing: realism has also gone to ground, the imperial text to earth.[14]

In this reading, Coetzee's attempt to speak for a non-white protagonist is seen as merely a staging-post on the way to a more sophisticated form of postmodernist expression in which no such attempt is made. For Wright, the more complex reflexiveness of *Foe* renders that novel 'capable of subverting its own ethnocentricity', where, in contrast, the lingering realism of *Michael K* goes hand in hand with a paternal ethno-centrism.[15] (With the benefit of hindsight, after the publication of subsequent novels, the phases that Wright detects seem less clearly defined.)

A similar complaint to Wright's emerges from Nadine Gordimer's review. Gordimer recognizes the stature and importance of Coetzee's novel, but discerns in it an important historical exclusion which can be traced to the question of narrative stance. Coetzee, she feels, 'does not recognize what the victims, seeing themselves as victims no longer, have done, are doing, and believe they must do for themselves'. A Lukács-ian principle is used to explain this flaw: 'The organicism that George Lukács defines as the integral relation between private and social destiny is distorted here more than is allowed for by

the subjectivity that is in every writer. The exclusion is a central
one that may eat out the heart of the work's unity of art and
life.'[16] What Gordimer is looking for, in addition to Lukácsian
typicality in the character, is the unifying principle of narration
that Lukács presents as an integral feature of realist writing.
Such narrative is characterized by a governing ideological
perspective, from which a coherent presentation of the historical moment may emerge.[17] There are several assumptions
here which *Michael K* explicitly challenges (as do many of
Gordimer's own novels, in fact). In the Lukácsian conception of
realism an ordered narrative framework makes sense of historical contradiction, offering an interpretive vantage-point,
which is both necessary and blameless. What Coetzee does in
Michael K is attempt to retain something of this vantage-point
whilst simultaneously questioning its validity, and this self-
conscious double stance may offer a more precise description of
the novel's 'lingering realism', an element which may now
appear in a more positive light, as a kind of *revitalized* realism.

To see how this attempt at revitalization operates, we need
to consider how the novel's action is framed through the use of
narrative stance. The third-person narrator of sections 1 and 3,
following the principle of 'limited omniscience', is very cautious
in offering interpretations of K. This caution indicates a refusal
to impose a unifying framework, at least not without questioning the validity of such an imposition. There is one
portentous pronouncement when K lays his mother's ashes to
rest on the farm: here we are told that this act begins 'his life as
a cultivator', a statement which conjoins filial duty, social
continuity and cultivation, thus discovering a persuasive interpretative frame (*MK*, 59). Such a pronouncement, however, is
quite atypical of the narrator's cautious stance. This caution is
thrown into relief – and given greater significance – by
comparison with the probing of the medical officer in section 2,
whose constant desire is to make K 'yield' his story (*MK*, 152).[18]
The latent violence of this need associates the medical officer
with those similar protagonists in the other novels, especially
those ambiguous figures in the hierarchy of power, like the
magistrate in *Waiting for the Barbarians* and Susan Barton in *Foe*.

Heider speaks of how the medical officer 'badgers K with words, his torture-machines of meaning', reminding us of Coetzee's continuing concern with the wielding of power through language.[19] There is an often-voiced critical view that the medical officer's section is superfluous, offering an explicit interpretation of K's meaning which is already apparent.[20] Yet the function of this section is dependent upon this jarring note, this sense of overstatement which validates the third-person narrator, less desirous of appropriating K's story. The comparison also has the effect of expiating guilt for traces of this impulse in the narrative stance. In the final section, moreover, K's thoughts emerge from the narrative, without signs of third-person interference: there are moments where his thoughts are presented in the manner of first-person monologues, especially in the crucial final pages where the use of free indirect discourse is pushed to its limits (*MK*, 182–4).

The significance of K's dominance at the novel's close is bestowed by the gardening motif, which has various connotations. Derek Wright considers the activities of Michael K as gardener in the context of ideas of the land in white South African literature, 'mythologies or mystiques which automatically exclude the non-Afrikaner'. For a while, Michael K 'achieves the Afrikaner's . . . pastoral ideal' with the crucial difference that he feels no need to anthropomorphize, to construct a mythology justifying his own presence: he is at one with the Karoo landscape, and its 'refusal of human meanings'. For Wright, Coetzee is concerned 'to found a new myth of the land' with Michael K 'less a man than a spirit of ecological endurance'. In this reading, Coetzee creates a myth which is 'primarily ecological, not political', because 'the mythological drift of the novel – although it is problematic for a white writer to use a black figure to say it – is that the land is to be returned not to the blacks but to itself'.[21] In an earlier version of this article, less critical of the novel, Wright puts the case differently, suggesting that 'a mystical–ecological meaning exists alongside, perhaps even emerges from the political one: the land is to be returned not only to the blacks but to itself, and these two things could conceivably be the same'.[22]

The fact that a critic can present the same idea in opposed ways is intriguing, and suggests the difficulties associated with thinking about ecology in relation to literature. We are in the habit of seeing evocations of the natural as divorced from the social world. This (perhaps mistaken) emphasis means that ideas about nature can have intrinsic value, but without any necessary connection to political questions. It is in this spirit that Attwell acknowledges an ethical significance in the presentation of gardening as cultivation, but wonders also if Coetzee uses gardening 'as merely the convenient, structural opposite of power'.[23] It is possible, however, that Wright was initially correct in suggesting that the ecological meaning emerges from the political. A decisive scene in this connection is the one in which K decides not to make himself known to the guerillas camping on the farm: it is a choice between joining in the war, or staying where he is and tending his crop. K chooses the latter, and has his own political justification for doing so:

K knew that he would not crawl out and stand up and cross from darkness into firelight to announce himself. He even knew the reason why: because enough men had gone off to war saying the time for gardening was when the war was over; whereas there must be men to stay behind and keep gardening alive, or at least the idea of gardening; because once that cord was broken, the earth would grow hard and forget her children. (*MK*, 109)

This rationale implies that K affiliates himself with the guerillas. It is not that K is explicitly thinking of producing supplies for the revolutionary forces – in interview Coetzee has slightly misremembered the scene as suggesting this (*DP*, 207) – but that his gardening work is seen as of a piece with their efforts. The significance of K as cultivator has also a broader significance, here: the idea of gardening is associated with human subsistence generally, and with a notion of human community based on reciprocity with the land. If this is ecological mysticism, it has also a political foundation with both a specific and a generalized meaning.[24]

The challenge to the Afrikaner rural idyll contained in K's career as gardener suggests, already, of course, an ideological dimension which also offers an intervention in the question of social collapse in 1980s South Africa. Gallagher, acknowledging that the presentation of the gardening theme is a revision of the enduring South African myth of a return to the land, suggests this is a demystification in which the garden is proposed 'as a millennial alternative to the cataclysm of the camps'.[25] In this sense, *Michael K* is a highly politicized novel, at once an account of – and a parable about – the control of social space.

Set against gardening, incarceration is the novel's counter-motif, the exercise of discipline through institutions. K's life as a cultivator, indeed, is only possible when he escapes the camps. Coetzee is careful to associate, very much in the tradition of Foucault, the identification between different kinds of institution in the process of socialization. The Jakkalsdrif labour camp is obviously Foucauldian, an anti-nomadic device to harness the utility of a homeless multiplicity.[26] Similarly, the Kenilworth camp serves the nation's disciplinary needs quite transparently. At one point we discover that the notion of 'rehabilitation' has been deemed no longer serviceable, and that the Kenilworth camp is to be redefined as an 'internment' camp. The former designation has become superfluous, since the latter can serve the purpose of providing a labour force just as well (*MK*, 153–4). Here is the refinement of a disciplinary practice for a particular end, which also exposes the spuriousness (the false notion of rehabilitation) of its original presentation. Perhaps more important is the association made between the camps and the less obvious disciplinary institutions, schools and hospitals. K was educated in a special school for 'afflicted and unfortunate children', evidently designed to produce docile and useful workers (*MK*, 4): K, himself, draws the obvious parallel with the Jakkalsdrif camp (*MK*, 74). Hospitals, also, figure significantly in the novel. K is taken to hospital briefly, while in police custody, before arriving at Jakkalsdrif. His mother, of course, dies in hospital in Stellenbosch, an event which K presents as an integral part of her lifetime of institutionalized exploitation (*MK*, 136). As the novel closes, there is an extended passage in which K is made to articulate his situation. His own first-person monologue effectively takes over the narrative in this passage which makes the camps a focus of his story:

There is nothing to be ashamed of in being simple. They were locking up simpletons before they locked up anybody else. Now they have camps for children whose parents run away, camps for people who kick and foam at the mouth, camps for people with big heads and people with little heads, camps for people with no visible means of support, camps for people chased off the land, camps for people they find living in storm-water drains, camps for street girls, camps for people who can't add two and two, camps for people who forget their papers at home, camps for people who live in the mountains and blow up bridges in the night. Perhaps the truth is that it is enough to be out of the camps, out of all the camps at the same time. Perhaps that is enough of an achievement, for the time being. How many people are there left who are neither locked up nor standing guard at the gate? I have escaped the camps. (*MK*, 182)

The camp motif is here revealed as the basis of the novel's allegorical intervention, and this element of allegory, as is typical of Coetzee, is refigured, as it crosses over to a literal connection. It approaches a description of the actual social context, and so operates to *blur* rather than to *maintain* the distinction between two parallel planes of signification.

The level of allegory that is sustained more diligently is the allegory of ideas. The simple man is heroic in his challenge to disciplinary practices, because he is the archetypal deviant, the primary target for incarceration. K's elusiveness thus establishes a utopian zone – in a theoretical sense – which is beyond the control of discipline. And even this vantage-point, for all its richness in abstract and theoretical terms, also brings a literal connection to mind. Indeed, questions of spatial control in relation to apartheid South Africa must inevitably do this, for this was a regime based on 'zoning', on the control of social space. K thus becomes a symbol of geo-political defiance, resistant to spatial control as well as classification, and this is perhaps the most radical kind of challenge that can be presented to the colonial regime in general, and the apartheid regime in particular.

The allegorical resonances in the novel bring together the various areas of significance: the idea of gardening; the geo-political challenge; K's elusiveness. The role of K as cultivator, and his care of plots on the Visagie farm appear to form an allegory of repossession. This is suggested by a number of parallels. The farm, which K takes to be the farm of his mother's memories, is a subject of nostalgia for the Visagie grandson too: he recounts memories of Christmas feasting to the uninterested K (*MK*, 61). Excess and flamboyant indulgence are at the heart of this white man's nostalgia, the mirror-image of K's modest and secretive cultivation of his pumpkin patch. The parallel becomes explicit on K's return to the farmhouse after his internment at the Jakkalsdrif camp. As he stands in the house, listening for sounds of occupancy, we read that 'the very heart of the grandson, if there were a grandson and he were alive, beat in time with his own' (*MK*, 98). Here, the narrator makes another rare intervention, underscoring this important structural parallel. It is in K's own reported thoughts, however, that the idea is represented most explicitly: K wonders if the grandson, like himself, has dug a hole in the veld in which to hide, 'living a life parallel to his own' (*MK*, 103). The point of making the association this obvious is ambivalent. It supplies a neat binary opposition – a frame of meaning – against which K's significance can be initially tested. In this way, his reluctance to inhabit the farmhouse, or to try and rival the epoch it represents, suggests a contrary ethos (*MK*, 98, 104). K represents a new era of subsistence 'gardening' rather than accumulation and 'farming'. The mirror-parallel thus indicates a new myth of repossession in which a communal impulse supplants an acquisitive one.

The terms of this opposition, however, are made suspect, complicating the notion of a too-simple allegory of utopia through revolution. K's elusiveness casts doubt on his place in this frame of meaning with its neat oppositions of gardening/farming, subsistence/accumulation. When K's crop is purloined by soldiers, his pump destroyed, and the Visagie farmhouse blown up, the site of this opposition is effaced from the novel. K retains the identity of potential cultivator – his packet of seeds remains his most treasured possession – but this identity is shown, implicitly, to require a different frame of meaning, independent of the Afrikaner farm, which, as the site of possibility, becomes the positive term in an opposition where it should be the negative one.

The opposition, however, retains its presence in the generation of meaning, and this pointed ambivalence achieves two things simultaneously: it shows a self-consciousness in the composition which makes us question the terms of the allegory; and, as we do so, we necessarily interrogate the external referents for these terms. This chain of interrogation leads to a realization that the space in which K's experiment as cultivator can endure does not exist, either in expectations of the novel at this time, or in the particular terrain alluded to. This self-cancelling aspect of K's story gives it its most pointed significance.

The deconstructive principle I am tracing is one in which a frame of meaning based on a binary opposition is reversed and then undermined.[27] This gesture inevitably calls into question the framework of interpretation and the hegemony it involves. As with the gardening/farming, subsistence/accumulation homology, the reversal undermines the basis of the comparison, and the hegemony implied in it. If the mythic story of Michael K is self-cancelling in this respect, so is the allegory of *Michael K*, the novel. Just as K eludes interpretation, so does the novel. The effect of this, in the reading offered here, is not to obfuscate, but to elucidate more clearly the hegemonies that are involved in the reading exchange. Interpretive assumptions are themselves held up to question, just as the function and definition of allegory is self-consciously examined.

As I have mentioned, *Michael K* appears, at certain points, to allude to ideas drawn from Derridean deconstruction.[28] It seems that this is the connotation of the medical officer's overt attempt to allegorize in his imaginary address to K:

Your stay in the camp was merely an allegory, if you know that word. It was an allegory – speaking at the highest level – of how scandalously, how outrageously a meaning can take up residence in a system without becoming a term in it. (*MK*, 166)

If this is an allusion to the idea of an infinitely deferred meaning, it has also the effect, once more, of calling the idea of allegory into question. This is so because the impulses of the medical officer are suspect and are overlaid on the novel's own allegorical structure. This self-consciousness demands that we

examine the very basis of the novel's metaphoricalness. It is as
if the term 'allegory' itself has been placed 'under erasure', the
Derridean procedure by which terms are crossed through: this
indicates a profound provisionality which underscores the
inadequacy of terms which yet remain necessary to the thinking
through of an idea.

Another Derridean association is suggested in K's care for
his pumpkins and melons, grown from seed: this is a parallel of
Derrida's version of textuality as 'dissemination', characterized
by Gayatri Spivak as 'a sowing that does not produce plants,
but is simply infinitely repeated. A semination that is not
*in*semination but *dis*semination, seed spilled in vain, an emission
that cannot return to its origin in the father.'[29] K does refer to
his crop collectively as his children (*MK*, 63, 101, 111, 118), and
is denied a proper harvest. Late in the novel, the pimp, picking
K's pocket, takes his packet of seeds, and casts them away. K is
able to recover half of them, but abandons the rest, scattered in
a barren shady spot (*MK*, 177). At an immediate level, the
parallel suggests that K's story (and by extension Coetzee's
novel) can be taken to illustrate a principle of textual free play,
divorced from an originating meaning or author, and this
properly locates the novel's significance in the realm of discourse. At this level of intervention, however, the novel brings
out a more radical implication by deconstructing the figure of
dissemination itself. K, for example, also sees his pumpkins and
melons as his brothers and sisters, already undermining his role
as metaphorical father-originator (*MK*, 113). This disruption of
the figure applies also to K's thoughts about his own genealogy,
and the paradox of parenthood:

When my mother was dying in hospital, he thought, when she knew
her end was coming, it was not me she looked to but someone who
stood behind me: her mother or the ghost of her mother. To me she
was a woman but to herself she was still a child calling to her mother
to hold her hand and help her. And her own mother, in the secret life
we do not see, was a child too. I come from a line of children without
end.
He tried to imagine a figure standing alone at the head of the line,
a woman in a shapeless grey dress who came from no mother; but

when he had to think of the silence in which she lived, the silence of time before the beginning, his mind baulked. (*MK*, 117)

The burial by K of his mother's remains at the farm automatically associates her with his crop, an association strengthened, here, by a parallel blurring of the parent/child dichotomy. K's (failed) attempt to think back to a moment of origin in his family tree is a pointed demonstration of the hankering after origins which Derrida sees as a seminal flaw in Western metaphysics; but K finds this silence unimaginable, much as Derrida finds nothing outside the text. In Coetzee's use of this figure, a consciously constructed idea of community emerges, in which a human collective (and the means of its subsistence) is presented as a given, a primary factor. This is not an ahistorical gesture, but a figure of discourse in which a deconstructive principle is used to alert us to the dangers of a myth of origins; in the South African context, this unavoidably invokes an Afrikaner myth of origins, and its manipulation of racial histories.

These allusions to theoretical ideas, however, have a 'surface' quality to them; they are not embedded in the writing. This is not deconstruction-as-fiction, for K's rationale for his life has its own, alternative dynamic. One effect of the final brief section of the novel is to draw a comparison between the medical officer's insistent attempts to interpret K, and his own rationale for his behaviour, presented through indirect free discourse. The medical officer's narrative expresses understanding of his oppressive urge, which he is nevertheless unable to resist. In an imagined final address to the fleeing K, he acknowledges his position as 'persecutor, madman, bloodhound, policeman', but the pursuit of meaning has now become his *raison d'être* (*MK*, 167, 165). His view of K's story as an allegory of elusive meaning thus offers a corrective to his own impulses. (His interpretation is 'correct', here, however, and this does justify him, partially.) In this regard K's final reported thoughts are clearly privileged: the novel ends with his own imagined return to the farm, and the improvised use of a teaspoon to draw water from the damaged well (*MK*, 183–4).

Yet this image of the most minimal existence openly confronts us with the organizing influence of the author: a narrative circle is closed, since it was a teaspoon with which the infant, hare-lipped K was fed, again by way of improvisation (*MK*, 3). The rhetorical force of this narrative loop is to stress the resistance of K, through the persisting motif (the teaspoon) of his bare survival. The minimalism and simplicity of this circle appears to overshadow the fretful exegetical efforts of the medical officer, an effect which also diverts attention from the sense of authorial intrusion. K's mere presence – his *being* – bestows his significance.

In interview, Coetzee has suggested that K is a figure of *being* rather than of *becoming*.[30] However, this does begin to problematize the novel's theoretical self-consciousness. An essential feature of the deconstructive principle represented by K is, as we have seen, an invalidation of origins prior to the principle of textuality. In Derrida's rereading of Heidegger, this is presented as a challenge to the idea of 'Being' as a state of existence prior to all knowledge.[31] The validation of being in the story of Michael K now appears to undo elements of the novel's deconstructive principle, since being becomes primary. This also offers validation to the medical officer's reading of K, and how his body baulked, where his will is made to acquiesce: again simple being is his ultimate resistance (*MK*, 163).

What Coetzee appears to be doing is installing a further level of metafictionality, a deconstruction of the novel's evocation of deconstruction. The contradiction implies a reversion to a simpler idea of reference where the presence of K represents the existence of the people he symbolizes. Being, in this sense, is a gestural bridge to the novel's social referent. It was the sheer presence of non-white South Africans as a majority that finally undermined the spatial ordering of apartheid, and it is this political necessity that K's resistance of the camps symbolizes quite directly. The urgency of the politics finally anchors the book as allegory, resulting in a mixture of modes where an idea of representation is placed in a dialectical interaction with an evocation of purer textuality.

In Coetzee's quest for an ethical lyricism, there are intriguing affinities with the project of Heidegger, which surface most noticeably in this presentation of Michael K as a figure of being rather than of becoming. There is a parallel in the idea that 'authenticity is to be found in the authentic man's silent resolve to be true to himself and to the possibilities of his own historicity'. Allen Thiher is here talking about Heidegger's project in *Being and Time*, but the description serves equally well as an account of Michael K's discovery of the grounds for his authenticity.[32] His silence and his elusiveness ultimately give way to an authentic philosophy of subsistence, a projected celebration of being which is also a recuperation of personal history – the historicity K asserts through his appropriation of his mother's nostalgia for the past. This sense of temporality – a combination of past possibilities and future projection, eschewing the limitations of the now – corresponds with Heidegger's conception of the interaction of timescales in personal history.[33]

A further affinity, concerning the role of fiction, is suggested in Michael K's identification with the earth. K's at-oneness with the earth, which becomes a kind of fusion in the repeated suggestion that he is a sort of burrowing creature, offers a deliberate gesture of materiality. This materialism might be interpreted as an aspect of Coetzee's ongoing project to resuscitate a kind of realism, or reinvigorated bridge between world and text.

Helpful here is Thiher's discussion of Heidegger's 'exploration of . . . the nature of tools', significant because 'tools or equipment apparently occupy a half-way place between works of art and natural things. Thus an investigation of the nature of "toolness" might shed light on the nature of the artwork.' Heidegger's example of a tool is a pair of peasant shoes in a painting by Van Gogh, which 'reveal the pairing of earth and world'. Heidegger's famous reading of this painting stresses how the shoes contain the call of the earth, the sense of ripening grain, while also evoking the sense of the peasant woman's world, her patterns of life: the boots – a tool of the *earth* – enjoy also the protection of the peasant woman's *world*.[34]

Heidegger's interpretation of the Van Gogh painting is

designed to show how 'in the work of art, there exists an opening between earth and world that allows truth to take place', where 'the earth is the essential materiality of the work – sounds, stone, paint, words, or the earth – that in its "strife" with a world gives rise to that openness in which truth occurs. Or, rather, the world of the work *is* that openness in which truth takes place.'[35]

There is a sense of slippage in this interpretation, and the model of the artwork it implies – between the evocation of materiality and the Real, for instance – but this is the kind of bold gesture that *Life and Times of Michael K* also (knowingly) makes. Indeed, it is the tension between different understandings of materiality, emphasized in Michael K's fusion with the earth, which gives the novel its resonance. The idea of openness in the artwork, the disclosure of 'truth', is a haunted possibility in Coetzee's work, never entirely relinquished, never left unproblematized. The ethic of Michael K's gardening tips the balance in favour of the possibility of such disclosure in which an idea of earth, of 'thingness', can be accepted as embedded in the text, much as it is embedded in K's fanciful projection of a future minimal subsistence.

CHAPTER 6

The maze of doubting: 'Foe'

If the ambivalences of *Michael K* finally point, unavoidably, to the South African context, the same gestural bridge is built in *Foe* (1986), with a sense of still greater poignancy. Here, underlying Coetzee's preoccupation with textuality and the function of literature, is the problem of the silencing and mutilation of the colonial Other.

Foe is Coetzee's most obviously metafictional text, a postcolonial reworking of *Robinson Crusoe* (which also contains allusions to other works by Defoe). The manner in which this unavoidable self-consciousness unfolds makes the book amenable to contemporary academic concerns. However, there is no sense of this novel being 'unavailable' to a general readership, even if its literariness is still more pronounced than in the earlier novels: there is no impediment to the narrative as story, or disengagement from the possibilities of intervention.[1]

Foe exemplifies Helen Tiffin's conception of postcolonial literatures in which the principle of decolonization is 'process, not arrival', involving 'an ongoing dialectic between hegemonic centrist systems and peripheral subversion of them'. This hybridity is productive where space is available for 'counter-discursive strategies', but the question of balance in these hybridized cultural models is delicate: 'unless their stress is on counter-discursive fields of activity, such models run the risk of becoming colonisers in their turn'. For Tiffin, *Foe* succeeds in 'writing back', not just 'to an English canonical text, but to the whole of the discursive field within which such a text operated and continues to operate in post-colonial worlds':

Robinson Crusoe was part of the process of 'fixing' relations between Europe and its 'others', of establishing patterns of reading alterity at the same time as it inscribed the 'fixity' of that alterity, naturalizing 'difference' within its own cognitive codes. But the function of such a canonical text at the colonial periphery also becomes an important part of material imperial practice, in that, through educational and critical institutions, it continually displays and repeats for the other, the original capture of his/her alterity and the processes of its annihilation, marginalization, or naturalization as if this were axiomatic, culturally ungrounded, 'universal', natural.[2]

Tiffin's analysis carries authority here because, with hindsight, we can see *Robinson Crusoe* not just as a canonical English text – Defoe is the father of the English novel in conventional accounts – but as an embodiment of the great myth of Western imperialism, an enthusiastic narrative of the project of 'civilizing' virgin territories and indigenous peoples, even against all odds. There is a sense of historical placing in the way Coetzee writes back to Defoe. He makes a strong association between this example of English literature and the moment of colonialism which is his concern: *Robinson Crusoe* was published in 1719, at the time of early Dutch settlement in South Africa. (The Dutch East India Company established a settlement at Cape Town in 1652; 'The Narrative of Jacobus Coetzee' is set in 1760, and 1761–2.) However, Coetzee's response to Defoe is complex. He has spoken of *Foe* as a tribute to eighteenth-century prose style, indicating that he is after something more responsive than a simple pastiche of his models (*DP*, 146). As a writer, he is sensitive to Defoe's technical achievements and innovations; he also uses the process of literary allusion to focus a sophisticated consideration of the issue of canonicity. In this connection, he is also undertaking an ambivalent writing back to Ian Watt, and his classic work, *The Rise of the Novel*, which establishes Defoe's formative role in the history of the genre.

The allusions to Defoe's work are complex and paradoxical, raising productively rich and various questions about power and textuality. There is a series of three intertextual references, effectively embedded within each other, from *Robinson Crusoe* to *Roxana* (1724) to the short story/anecdote 'A True Revelation of

the Apparition of One Mrs Veal' (1706). The most immediate
of these is the most apparent: the 'reworking' of *Crusoe*.

In *Foe*, Susan Barton is the intermediary of Cruso's story
(Coetzee omits the 'e'), seeking out Foe (as Defoe was originally
called) as the wordsmith who can record the story. The
imaginative premise is thus literary–historical, positing a
moment before *Crusoe* is written in order to speculate on the
omissions, silences and pointed constructions involved at the
notional moment of the 'fathering' of the novel as a genre.
There are some immediate ironies in the reversal of details,
and this suggests a straightforward critique of Defoe's artifice.
Superficially, Defoe's technique as a writer of fiction is to
conceal artifice and to appeal to verisimilitude. Indeed, the
title-page of the first edition of *Crusoe* effaces the author and
announces the book as the autobiographical account of its
protagonist. Coetzee alerts us to the implausibility of *Crusoe* by
reversing particular details. Where Defoe's Crusoe is the
archetypal imperialist, governed by economic self-aggrandise-
ment, Coetzee's Cruso is concerned merely with subsistence
and sterile work. Accordingly, Cruso feels no need for tools (*F*,
32), whereas Crusoe makes repeated trips to his wrecked ship
to make substantial finds, including a chest of tools, guns,
ammunition, canvas, food, spirits, cable, iron, razors, scissors,
knives, forks, a hammock, gold and silver.[3] In Coetzee's novel,
it is Foe who is preoccupied with the guns and tools that Cruso
does not have (but which do appear in *Crusoe*) (*F*, 53, 55, 83).
The reversals are systematic: Cruso, unlike his literary model,
makes no table or chair, no lamp or candle (*F*, 16, 82, 27); he
has no desire to keep a journal or to build a boat (*F*, 16–17, 13);
and he has no seed to sow, but occupies himself building barren
terraces for planting (*F*, 33–4). At a basic comparative level of
interpretation, this highlights the fissures in Defoe's novel: the
enthusiasm for the means of economic spatial control, for
example, drives the inventory of Crusoe's resources, stretching
credulity and exposing the authorial artifice 'concealed' in the
autobiographical conceit. Yet this goes beyond an insistence on
the artificiality of text as text. The conceit of Coetzee's novel is
to present Cruso's story as Defoe's *Ur*-text, more substantial,

more plausible than *Crusoe*. Of course, the premise is already circular, since *Foe* depends on the textual 'substantiality' of *Crusoe*; but this appeal to verisimilitude echoes through much of the text, even though, paradoxically, it is already recontained within a densely allusive work which insists on the primacy of textuality.

The question of 'truth' in competing versions of the Crusoe story is focused, in *Foe*, not on Cruso himself, but on the marginalized figures, Susan Barton and Friday. In the case of Susan Barton, this complicates the Defoe connection, as she is a version of the eponymous heroine of *Roxana* (whose first name is also Susan). If we lay this second transtextual reference over the first, we find a number of interpretive problems lying in wait. Following the premise that Susan Barton's story of the island is the *Ur*-text of *Crusoe*, we must conclude that she is effaced from this text of Defoe's, and placed in another (*Roxana*). In this sense, the novel represents a repression of female experience which is rechannelled according to the desires of the patriarchal author: *Crusoe* remains a myth of the male pioneering spirit, while the challenge which Susan represents is reinscribed, in *Roxana*, as a challenge to codes of economic subjugation and sexual fidelity in marriage (a challenge ultimately condemned in that novel's moral scheme). *Foe* invites us to speculate about Defoe's novels along these lines, and the issue of how stories are constructed and who controls them recurs throughout the text.

The possibility that Susan Barton is subject to the authorial manipulations of Foe is raised overtly through a sustained echo of the daughter episode at the end of *Roxana*, where Roxana is dogged by one of her abandoned children, now grown up and claiming kinship. *Roxana* ends with the strong implication that the faithful maid Amy, in an act of deluded loyalty, murders the daughter, leaving her mistress in a state of misery and repentance at the novel's close (though these are only briefly evoked). In *Foe*, Susan Barton is dogged by the return of a daughter she believes cannot be hers. She puts the appearance of the daughter down to Foe's invention, though here the intertextual circularity wilfully disrupts any remaining credulity in different

ontological levels: previously the reading experience has permitted a certain credulity in the historical moment before the
writing of *Crusoe* and *Roxana* (even if the circularity of the
allusion must ultimately refute this), and Susan Barton's assertion to the 'daughter' that 'there are no stories of daughters
searching for mothers' reinforces such credulity (if *Roxana* is yet
to be written) (*F,* 77). But the possibility of this premise
achieving authority depends on the psychological coherence of
Susan who, when confronted with the 'daughter' and the maid
Amy, becomes uncertain about the question of maternity (*F,*
132). Indeed, she now becomes conflated with the fictional
model, behaving much as Roxana does when confronted, in
public, with the daughter she is intent on denying: Roxana's
perturbation is echoed in Susan Barton's dizziness and breath-
lessness (*F,* 129, 131).

The main paradox of Susan Barton, however, is that she can
be shown to resemble Foe. Their tussle for control of the island
story, with its apparent feminist challenge to the author-father,
collapses when the desires of Susan Barton are seen to emulate
those of Foe. She reflects, for example, on what a disappointment Cruso will be to the world, how his tale will not shape up
as an adventurer's tale of genuine interest (*F,* 34). In this she
anticipates Foe's preoccupation with the means of embellishing
Cruso's tale, and even his desire to impose a formulaic
narrative principle on her tale (*F,* 117). There is a hierarchy of
control in this connection, it is true, but there is much stress on
her longings and desires (*F,* 36, 51) and this serves to emphasize
her complicity since desire is associated with narrative control
(*F,* 131). In connection with Friday the assertion of such desire is
described as shaping his identity (*F,* 121).

In the affinity between Foe and Susan Barton there may be a
further allusion to, and critique of, Defoe. If Susan/Roxana, as
the fictional creation of Defoe, can be identified with the
author, Coetzee may be implying an imposition of Defoe's own
desires onto Roxana. (*Roxana* can certainly be read as a contradictory text which punishes its female protagonist for embody-
ing paradoxical male desires for sexual freedom combined with
material success and social stability.) The possibility of this kind

of inversion and affinity is suggested in an echo of Conrad's *Heart of Darkness*, when Barton speaks of Foe as 'my intended, the one alone intended to tell my true story' (*F,* 126). In Conrad's tale, the intended is Kurtz's fiancée, in effect a representative of the colonial female who is simultaneously innocent of, yet in complicity with the colonial project. This inversion makes the author-figure the complicitous one, rather than the colonial female, thus blurring the different roles, implying an ambivalence that is shared by Barton and Foe (and Coetzee too).

The metafictional dimension of the affinity between Susan Barton and Foe becomes clear as the third section ends. Confronted with the daughter, Barton expresses doubts about her identity: 'now I am full of doubt. Nothing is left to me but doubt. I am doubt itself. Who is speaking me? Am I a phantom too? To what order do I belong? And you: who are you?' (*F,* 133). The self-conscious ontological uncertainty of the character, familiar in postmodernist writing, is given a metafictional richness. Barton draws the authorial figure, Foe, into this philosophical speculation on (in)substantiality, and he describes his own 'maze of doubting' (*F,* 135). It is in this episode that explicit reference is made to another text by Defoe, 'A True Revelation of the Apparition of One Mrs Veal'. This is Defoe's rendering of an account of the visit of Mrs Veal to her old friend Mrs Bargrave. (Coetzee calls her Barfield.) Mrs Veal is anxious to make amends to Mrs Bargrave, to rekindle their friendship, having lost touch with her, and she is anxious, also, that Mrs Bargrave write to her (Mrs Veal's) brother concerning the bequeathing of minor items of jewellery and gold. Mrs Bargrave subsequently discovers that Mrs Veal had died the day before the visit. Much of Defoe's version – which draws on four accounts of this purportedly true event – is given over to countering doubts concerning its credibility. The insistence on truth, of course, conflicts with the selective amalgamation of different versions in the interest of narrative impact. In this, Defoe's version of the anecdote is typical of his novelistic method, geared to the concealment of narrative artifice.[4]

'A True Revelation of the Apparition of One Mrs Veal' is first

alluded to in section 2 of *Foe*, when Barton and Friday are in
Foe's lodgings. Barton reads from a book containing the story –
a realized text in the world of *Foe* – trying to persuade Friday of
the attraction for a 'humble person' of being made famous
through the written record (*F*, 58). This enticement represents a
misplaced attempt to unlock Friday's history, an attempt
summarized in Barton's 'hope that if I make the air around
him thick with words, memories will be reborn in him which
died under Cruso's rule' (*F*, 59). This observation stems from
the use of Defoe's story as an enticement to fame, if accepted at
face value; and this mistaken view of narrative – as documen-
tary realism – is implicitly condemned in the imprisoning figure
of discourse, 'the air thick with words' around Friday, which
signifies colonial silencing.

The second allusion to the Defoe story is redemptive, and
provides a context for the novel's deliberations on ghosts,
phantoms and insubstantiality. It is when Barton has reminded
Foe of the anecdote of the apparition of Mrs Veal that he
explains his own maze of doubting, indicating how he shares
Susan's doubts about identity. It is through the *dismissal* of the
narrative artifice of the story, in other words, that representations of author and character are united at the same plane of
ontological uncertainty, an equality figured most clearly in their
sexual union (*F*, 139–40).

The irony is quite deliberate that 'A True Revelation of the
Apparition of One Mrs. Veal', Defoe's first attempt at fiction, is
the only one of Defoe's texts alluded to that is extant in the
notional time-frame of *Foe*. A slight text, a fictional conceit
written to lend validity to the idea of ghosts, has more
substance in Coetzee's novel than *Crusoe* or *Roxana*. The embed-
ding of this self-cancelling text within the novel, through a
double allusion which progressively challenges the validity of its
narrative premise, is a complex intertextual gesture. It is a
gesture which obviously repudiates a straightforward realism,
but which also uncovers an affinity between the narrative
operations of *Foe* and those of Defoe's novels.

The allegorical analogues of the novel are revealed in the
ambivalent manner typical of Coetzee, and Friday's function in

the text is a prominent factor in this. The obvious allegorical connotation of his silence is to represent the repression of South Africa's black majority. Yet this basic level of correspondence has to be supplemented if Friday's silence is perceived to have a positive significance.

It is possible to discern traces of several contemporary political parallels. It has often been remarked that Coetzee's Friday is pointedly black, whereas Defoe's is tawny, distinct from 'the Negroes': the change appears to reinforce a sense of the novel as an allegory of modern South Africa. Pursuing this allegorical dimension, Robert Post sees (for example) Cruso's territorialism as emblematic of Afrikaner expansionism. Similarly, Post suggests that, since Cruso's attitude appears to embody the recalcitrance of the Afrikaner government, so his fever may symbolize the 'diseased' nature of the administration.[5] However, this kind of association is embedded in the writing without being offered on the basis of a one-to-one correspondence. Responding to this element of ambivalence, Gayatri Spivak reports, concerning the issue of the two Fridays' racial difference, 'I ask my students to note it, not to make it the tool to an unproductive closure.'[6]

A similar association is denoted in the reading of Susan Barton as fulfilling an 'allegorical role representing white South African liberals'.[7] At its broadest level, this is connoted by the manner in which she desires to facilitate the telling of Friday's story, by giving him the 'gift' of language, and by merging her own desire to have the island story told on her own account with the imperative to record Friday's history. There are moments when she offers recognizably liberal formulations, such as this account of life on the island:

It seemed to me that all things were possible on the island, all tyrannies and cruelties, though in small; and if, in despite of what was possible, we lived at peace with one another, surely this was proof that certain laws unknown to us held sway, or else that we had been following the promptings of our hearts all this time, and our hearts had not betrayed us. (*F,* 37)

This quasi-mystical conviction in the faithfulness of the human 'heart', as a corrective to the inhuman impulse, announces a *laissez-faire* attitude which is exposed as pointedly inadequate if, at one level, the island is an allegorical representation of modern South Africa where, in the 1980s, the tyrannies and cruelties of civil war are averted, not by a fundamental human ethic, but by brutal state control. The novel, however, resists the systematic allegory which it partially evokes, and, accordingly, the significance of Barton's complicity is extended. She comes to occupy a different margin to Friday, the position of the half-colonized in *Foe*. (In this she reveals some affinity with Magda in *In the Heart of the Country*.)

There are scenes in section 2, when Barton and Friday are travelling to Bristol, where the two are united as social pariahs, refused service in an inn on the road to Windsor, and insulted outside a church in Marlborough (*F*, 102, 108). Barton's experience in the social margin is partial, and she, as the half-colonized, confirms Friday as the genuine Other through her responses to him. She experiences revulsion at Friday when she learns he has no tongue. Her horror at this mutilation – at the *fact* of it rather than the circumstances – inevitably has a dubious metaphorical connotation, since this mutilation is, in various ways, a figure for colonial repression (*F*, 24). In her response to Friday's other 'mutilation' – his possible castration – the ambivalence of her attitude is aptly captured. This is her account of what she witnesses as Friday spins in his whirling dance:

In the dance nothing was still and yet everything was still. The whirling robe was a scarlet bell settled upon Friday's shoulders and enclosing him; Friday was the dark pillar at its centre. What had been hidden from me was revealed. I saw; or, I should say, my eyes were open to what was present to them.

I saw and believed I had seen, though afterwards I remembered Thomas, who also saw, but could not be brought to believe till he had put his hand in the wound. (*F*, 119–20)

This, in fact, is the only suggestion of the other mutilation, the possible castration, an absence presented as a presence ('my eyes were open to what was present to them'). The possibility is given credence as an explanation of Friday's lack of sexual desire, over which there is speculation elsewhere in the novel (*F*, 86); but this *literal* explanation of an indeterminate *symbolic*

detail has an evident weakness. The reference to doubting
Thomas supplies a further obfuscation. Thomas doubted the
truth of the resurrection until he had touched the wounds on
the living Jesus.[8] The idea of a wound supports the sense of a
mutilation, but the association with the resurrection, where the
wounds are 'overcome', as it were, makes the account still less
determinate. Barton is unable to capture or describe the Other,
and this inability, of course, is a tacit feature of the book's
larger narrative strategy. In a sense, Friday's possible double-
mutilation achieves a mythic status which cannot be adequately
addressed in a discourse other than his own.

In this sense, Friday's silence presents an irreducible duality.
It is a silence which is a resistance to, yet also the product of,
the dominant discourse. Derek Attridge, in a fine essay, shows
how *Foe* links the question of literary canonization with cultural
exclusion. The novel aligns itself with a defining Western
literary myth, yet also undermines the association by exposing
the silences – in terms of gender and race – upon which the
myth depends. There is, however, no easy solution to these
silencing structures, and so 'the novel refuses to endorse any
simple call for the granting of a voice within the existing
sociocultural discourses; such a gesture would leave the silencing mechanisms, and their repressive human effects, un-
touched'.[9] Here we arrive at an apparent double-bind which
must render Friday's story unavailable, unless it is to be
appropriated and misrepresented. The novel does, however,
attempt to progress beyond this impasse.

In Ina Gräbe's view, Friday's ' "untouchability" derives from
a double mutilation that puts him outside and above the
contemporary discourses of psychoanalysis and feminism', and
this indicates 'the need for a different means of communication', posited in the text by the evocation of 'deconstruction
as a possible strategy for creative writing'.[10] The text's elusiveness in the face of interpretive schemata may oblige us also to
question this last formulation, and the intellectual affiliation it
might imply. Even so, there is an explicit challenge to notional
conventions in fictional representation. Brian Macaskill and
Jeanne Colleran write perceptively of Friday's subversiveness,

as 'a character inscribed within this text, but not quite assimilated by it': this inscription is 'a textual gesture that operates
outside the level of character representation' by taking 'a stance
below or at least against the possibility of such representation'.[11] This is also a consciously new approach to writing the
Other, a progression from the third-person mediation presented in *Michael K.*

Coetzee does, however, adopt strategies to gesture towards
the revealing of Friday's story. An important episode concerns
Friday's enigmatic writing: Susan Barton's attempts to teach
Friday to write founder in the presence of this resistant pupil;
but he discovers his own mark, his own written 'language'
when unattended:

While Foe and I spoke, Friday had settled himself on his mat with the
slate. Glancing over his shoulder, I saw he was filling it with a design
of, as it seemed, leaves and flowers. But when I came closer I saw the
leaves were eyes, open eyes, each set upon a human foot: row upon
row of eyes upon feet: walking eyes.

I reached out to take the slate, to show it to Foe, but Friday held
tight to it. 'Give! Give me the slate, Friday!' I commanded. Where-
upon, instead of obeying me, Friday put three fingers into his mouth
and wet them with spittle and rubbed the slate clean. (*F,* 147)

This is a powerful scene which insists on an effort of interpretation, which must still remain indeterminate. There are various
ways of interpreting Friday's 'writing': for Gräbe, the writing of
the walking eyes 'probably refers to his roaming of the English
countryside in the company of his would-be "mistress" and
suggests that he might have his own particular focalization of
"voyages" undertaken under the guise of some assumed
"worthy" objective, like trying to undo the injustices of slave-
hood or exploring the concept of a different kind of voyage as a
metaphor for writing, for instance'.[12] This reading is thorough
in the links it makes between Friday's experiences, and the idea
of decolonization as both an historical and a textual process.
For Gayatri Spivak, the emphasis is on the resistance of
meaning, while for Hena Maes-Jelinek – who speculates that
the eyes might signify the stare of Friday's victimized people –
it is the history of repression that resonates.[13] This, I think, is

powerfully suggested in the row upon row of open, walking eyes, which convey not only the displacement of the enslaved and the colonized, but also the sense of bearing witness. There is a brooding, latent violence in this, an implication of impatience and necessity in the prescription for historical revision.

The problem of the silencing/enabling of voice/writing reaches a culmination in the final section of the novel, where a new narrating persona appears, an 'authorial' voice supplying an ultimate frame to this metafiction. This is the novel's boldest gesture, supplanting Susan Barton, the female narrator of the previous sections, and installing an apparently 'higher' omniscient position. In the Genettean model Ina Gräbe uses to discuss this, the final section represents the most self-conscious diegetic level, so that the appearance of a voice representing Coetzee permits the author to occupy the 'privileged position of the ultimate focalizer of the previous three levels'. This also demands of the reader 'a reassessment of the entire foregoing enterprise'.[14]

Whether or not one agrees that this new narrator represents Coetzee, there is an authority attached to this level which has proved contentious. In Kirsten Holst Petersen's reading, the displacement of Susan Barton's perspective is telling, indicating Coetzee's desire 'to show that there is no special insight to be gained from a woman's point of view or woman's writing'. Petersen accordingly concludes that Coetzee himself is the 'foe', to 'those of us who search for the place and role of a female view of literature and history'.[15]

The novel, however, avoids this kind of competing claim. Barton is already established in the position of the half-colonized: her position is not, finally, to promote the claims of woman's writing, since Friday is the genuine Other of this text. Moreover, the authority that is established in the final section is claimed only to be relinquished. Indeed, the effect of the final section is to offer a compromise rather than an authorial imposition. The crucial moment in this section occurs when the author/narrator 'dives' into the wreck in an attempt to release Friday's story. The necessity of this task has been signalled in the previous section where Foe, in conversation with Barton, indicates the imperative to 'make Friday's silence speak, as well as the silence surrounding Friday'. In response, Barton asks 'who will dive into the wreck? On the island I told Cruso it should be Friday . . . But if Friday cannot tell us what he sees, is Friday in my story any more than a figuring (or prefiguring) of another diver?' (*F,* 142). The familiar deliberate merging of the figurative and the literal is evident here: that which is discussed by characters in the novel, themselves drawn from different ontological planes, is both a symbolic and an 'actual' problem (in the world of the text). The discussion anticipates the culminating 'event' in the novel's final metafictional frame. Who this diver should be – the submarine archaeologist of revisionist colonial history – is signalled as a problem: is Friday, himself unable to fulfil this role, a figuring or prefiguring of the diver? It is only if he *pre*figures the role that the actual diver will be in his mould, the Other recouped from the margin. Consequently, when an authorial-narrator, apparently standing for Coetzee, performs the dive, we perceive this to be less than ideal.

Section 4 actually comprises two attempts by this new narrator to make Friday's silence speak. In the first, the narrator enters Foe's lodgings, ascends to his room to find a dead couple, apparently Susan Barton and Foe, in bed, with the barely alive Friday in the alcove. The scene offers a clear metaphor for the post-colonial moment, with Friday outlasting the late-colonizers who have struggled unsuccessfully to release his voice. The narrator, pressing close, hears 'the sounds of the island' issuing from his mouth (*F,* 154). But what is heard here is unsatisfactory. The association of Friday merely with the sounds of the island can be seen as a continuing marginalization, a stereotypical identification of the 'native' with 'native culture' which is in tune with the original presentation of the Nationalist government's 'homeland' policy.

The inadequacy of the first attempt is tacitly acknowledged by the presence of a second (*F,* 155–7), and the existence of two attempts itself implies the unsuitability of this narrator to the task. Nevertheless, this version supplements the first and represents a partial progression. Approaching Defoe's house a second time, the narrator observes a commemorative plaque on the wall announcing '*Daniel Defoe, Author*', a detail which places us in the literary–historical present, from which the cultural project of the novel as a genre is being examined. In Foe's room, the narrator this time scarcely casts a glance at 'the couple', but, concentrating on Friday, observes a detail previously undetected, 'a scar like a necklace, left by a rope or chain'. The detail evokes the history of colonial slavery and subjugation, the mark of Friday's identity, together with his mutilation(s). (The violence and unrest in 1980s South Africa is also evoked in an association which implies the continuity of black African suffering, where the colonial past produces the repression – and also the factional violence – of an uncertain political interregnum.)

At this point, the novel makes its boldest metafictional gesture. The narrator, in Foe's chamber, finds the manuscript of Susan Barton's account of her island experiences. He begins to read the words with which *Foe* opens, and then slips 'overboard', into Barton's text and into the water above the shipwreck, finding himself surrounded by the petals Barton witnesses Friday casting on the water (*F,* 31–2, 87). It is here that the narrator 'dives' down to a wrecked ship which seems to conflate three different ships: Cruso's wreck (it is located off his island); the ship from which Barton is originally set adrift (she is found with 'her captain'); and the vessel which rescues her (and Friday, who is on board as well). She and the captain have become bloated corpses, and once more the only signs of life come from Friday, as the narrator urges him to speak. Friday's response constitutes the novel's powerful lyrical close:

I tug his woolly hair, finger the chain about his throat. 'Friday', I say, I try to say, kneeling over him, sinking hands and knees into the ooze, 'what is this ship?'

But this is not a place of words. Each syllable, as it comes out, is caught and filled with water and diffused. This is a place where bodies are their own signs. It is the home of Friday.

He turns and turns till he lies at full length, his face to my face. The skin is tight across his bones, his lips are drawn back. I pass a fingernail across his teeth, trying to find a way in.

His mouth opens. From inside him comes a slow stream, without breath, without interruption. It flows up through his body and out upon me; it passes through the cabin, through the wreck; washing the cliffs and shores of the island, it runs northward and southward to the ends of the earth. Soft and cold, dark and unending, it beats against my eyelids, against the skin of my face. (*F*, 157)

The narrator begins by asking an ambiguous question – 'what is this ship?' – which underscores the concentration of impressions in the passage. The question may be taken to mean '*which* ship is this?', while also alerting attention to the strange nature of the vessel, and what it represents. The merging of details makes it unnecessary to differentiate ship from ship: this composite vessel is a distillation of the mechanics of colonization, the ironic 'home' of Friday, where a mutilated and (now) chained body, being its 'own sign', bears the marks – and bespeaks the history – of the colonial Other. The 'voicing' of Friday's silence is an extraordinary literary gesture. This 'slow stream' is uninterrupted, indicating its irresistible historical necessity. It also challenges the narrator, who lets it beat against his eyes, his face. It is an unvoiced history which is acknowledged, a silence with a moral compulsion that, itself, silences the authorial figure who is obliged to cease his narrative in its presence. The novel ends by gesturing towards a post-colonial utopia, through the symbolic release of Friday's 'unending' history, filling first the island, and then the earth itself. In the face of this enormous implication, the complicitous author willingly chooses silence.

It is the metafictional quality of the novel – its allusiveness and self-consciousness – which validates and justifies its intervention. Helen Tiffin sees Coetzee's texts as 'meta-counter-discursive' – a special category of the counter-discursive post-colonial text – and this emphasis on textuality is the basis of their cultural and political involvement. Even so, there is something provisional, and deliberately so, about the counter-discursive gesture in *Foe*. It is this provisionality which enables the novel to eschew the danger of a new colonization. *Foe* does not 'overturn or invert the dominant in order to become dominant' in its turn, 'but to question the foundations of the

Mrs Curren – as squeezing her life's breath out of her in a symbolic embrace at the very end (*AI*, 181). There *is* a frame-breaking gesture in this moment of closure, but it is not entirely inconsistent with the voice of a narrator dependent on pain-killing drugs, moving on from hallucinatory dreams to death; and the idea that Vercueil is an angel is one of hers, and one that she dismisses early on (*AI*, 12). Indeed, his function in the novel, as Mrs Curren's ideal confessor, depends on his prosaic function as social outcast, with no gift of redemption to bestow. Or, perhaps, the 'redemption' he offers is unconventional, based on the apparent nullity – the undefinable otherness – he embodies.[3] In general, Mrs Curren's narrative is explicit about its potential metaphorical dimension, and this has the effect of reducing the validity of this dimension, and concentrating attention on the mimetic plane.

The narrator's formative experiences revolve around the deaths of two black boys. Bheki, the fifteen-year-old son of her maid, Florence, and his friend John, are both shot by police in the course of the narrative. Mrs Curren sees the dead Bheki when she has driven Florence into the Guguletu township to look for him. In this crucial scene, she is rebuffed by both the black community, and the security forces, and her words of incipient moral growth are dismissed or ridiculed. Later, John is shot at Mrs Curren's house, in Florence's quarters, where he is hiding from the police. As Mrs Curren's understanding of the evils surrounding her grows, she comes to see her own role in the political structure more clearly. This is not to suggest that there is a process of total reversal and enlightenment: she is disgusted by the activities of the regime at the outset, so her progression has more to do with a new sense of urgency in the face of brutal first-hand experience. Even so, this progression is not uncomplicated. She retains certain liberal notions, but where she does not entirely relinquish entrenched ideas – most notably about childhood – she does relinquish all sense of her own authority, and this is the crucial point. Mrs Curren's advancement is based on her increasing sense of her own insignificance, which becomes a kind of atonement for her complicity with the dying colonial order. In accordance with

ontologies and epistemological systems which would see such binary structures as inescapable'.[16]

Part of this provisionality, in another paradox, is also a partial turning away from the extreme self-consciousness, the stress on textuality. The novel does expose the dangers of a naive perception of realism – principally through its interrogation of Defoe – and there is a convincing (and in my view successful) attempt to associate important poststructuralist insights, having implications about power and discourse, with the post-colonial moment. There is also, however, the typical Coetzean counter-movement in which appeal is made for the immediacy of a transparent realism that is already acknowledged, in one sense, to be lost forever. The gesture, however, is more than mere nostalgia: it appeals for an informed acceptance of substantiality, a knowingly poststructuralist suspension of disbelief which will allow intervention through empathy. Coetzee acknowledges the possibility of the sterility of language games, through Foe's warning to Susan: 'you must ask yourself, Susan: as it was a slaver's stratagem to rob Friday of his tongue, may it not be a slaver's stratagem to hold him in subjection while we cavil over words in a dispute we know to be endless?' (*F*, 150). This is a clear acknowledgement of the danger of the new colonization to which postcolonial theorists like Helen Tiffin are sensitive. Foe's words here alert us, in particular, to the possible complicity of poststructuralism, caricatured as a 'cavil over words', a 'dispute we know to be endless'. A circular theorizing about discourse, even in the interests of decolonization, may be seen as another 'slaver's stratagem'.

Yet there is no *rejection* of the privileging of textuality. In fact, Foe turns out to be markedly in alignment with Coetzee's position. In arguing that 'writing is not doomed to be the shadow of speech', he is made to articulate a recognizably poststructuralist opinion concerning the primacy of writing (*F*, 142). Here, Foe comes to occupy an anachronistic position, closer to Coetzee than to Defoe. This affinity is especially significant where Foe is giving his account of the doubts which haunt him in his writing:

In a life of writing books, I have often, believe me, been lost in the maze of doubting. The trick I have learned is to plant a sign or marker in the ground where I stand, so that in my future wanderings I shall have something to return to, and not get worse lost than I am. Having planted it, I press on; the more often I come back to the mark (which is a sign to myself of my blindness and incapacity), the more certainly I know I am lost, yet the more I am heartened too, to have found my way back. (*F*, 135–6)

Foe's maze of doubting is an apt metaphor for the provisional postcolonial position. As with other areas of postmodernism, such a position can be represented as a process of decentring succeeded by an informed recentring, where the colonizer is decentred and the colonized Other is redeemed from the margins. The provisional recentring, in this model, locates the position of the complicitous author needing to write about – without writing for – the Other. It is in this sense that Gayatri Spivak suggests that the book situates 'the politics of over-determination as aporia':

Perhaps that is the novel's message: the impossible politics of over-determination (mothering, authoring, giving voice to the native 'in' the text; a white male South African writer engaging in such inscriptions 'outside' the text) should not be regularized into a blithe continuity, where the European redoes the primitive's project in herself. It can, however, lead to a scrupulously differentiated politics, dependent on 'where you are'.[17]

This is a transitional model of decolonization in which, so *Foe* suggests, the need for a false centre is recognized as a sign of blindness and incapacity, yet its value comes out of its negativity: the redemptive value of a sign acknowledging the false (but, for now, necessary) authority of the writer. If the way out of this maze cannot yet be found, this provisional recentring within the maze establishes the certainty of losing the way. This locale in the maze of doubting produces a genuine meta-counter-discursiveness. It is the position of Coetzee refusing to write for Friday.

CHAPTER 7

A true confession: 'Age of Iron'

The projected silencing of the post-colonizer at the end signalled by an anticipated post-colonial history, conti leitmotif of relinquishment that runs through the no quence, and which becomes the dominant feature in *Age* (1990). This novel takes the form of a letter narrated elderly Mrs Curren, and notionally addressed to her da in the United States.[1] Mrs Curren, a retired classics le begins writing on the day she is diagnosed as suffering terminal bone cancer. The dynamic of the novel is t personal dissolution involving Mrs Curren's relinquishm all personal investment in life in South Africa, a mov which is necessary to generate a reverse process, the g acquisition of political enlightenment. The novel is t paradoxical, inverse novel of personal development, a cedure which depends upon the self's acceptance of it unimportance.[2]

On the day that Mrs Curren is given her bleak diagnos is 'adopted' by an alcoholic down-and-out named Vercue impassive shadowy character (his race is not mentioned accompanies her – without offering her comfort or succ on her path to death and semi-enlightenment. He even agrees to take responsibility for posting the letter which the novel to the US after Mrs Curren's death, thoug unreliability makes him an improbable messenger. The that Vercueil may represent an angel of death to Mrs C introduces an allegorical dimension to the novel, but one v is clearly held at the level of ideas, even within the world text. However, he is described – by an apparently disembd

this dissolution of self, she rejects an egotistical plan to set fire to herself in front of the parliament buildings, a dramatic protest designed to link private and public realms in a way that does not register appropriately her own unimportance.

The dates Coetzee gives for the composition of this novel are 1986–9, defining years in the anti-apartheid struggle. The scenes of township violence evoke the Cape Town unrest of 1986, and this would appear to be the date of the novel's setting.[4] The wave of nationwide unrest in the mid-1980s was a dramatic response to the government's 'total strategy', involving ideological as well as repressive control. One important element of this strategy was a tinkering with the constitution on a principle of 'divide and rule'. A new parliament was created with three chambers: one each for whites, 'coloureds' and Indians. This attempt to isolate the black majority was scuppered by a massive boycott by the new Indian and 'coloured' voters. This principle of non-white solidarity and non-cooperation is a key to the struggle of the 1980s, and to the protests described in *Age of Iron*.

The project of black resistance – to present the black majority as ungovernable in the face of the regime's 'total strategy' – found a focus in the activities of an increasingly militant youth, and in a new wave of school boycotts. 'Liberation before education' was a keynote phrase of this action, one which characterizes Bheki's attitude in the novel (*AI*, 62). The wave of boycotts, commencing in 1983, gathered pace through 1984 and 1985, becoming more widespread. The consensus amongst different community groups over this action took a strategic turn in 1986, a turn of some importance to Coetzee's novel. The National Education Crisis Committee (NECC), consisting of political and community groups, as well as parents and students, suspended the boycott in December 1985, and decided not to renew it in March 1986, issuing a call for a 'people's education' instead. This debate about appropriate strategy on the education issue is one which the novel takes up.

A state of emergency from July 1985 to early 1986 was followed by a still more vigorous nationwide State of Emergency which extended from June 1986 to 1990. Detention and torture, with school pupils often the victims, were familiar features of this period. Governmental control of media was another essential part of the ideological struggle, registered clearly in Mrs Curren's reactions to TV and newspaper coverage of politics (*AI*, 9, 36, 49, 165). The fostering of vigilante groups to destabilize black opposition was another tactic employed by the security forces at this time. One such group was the 'Witdoeke', named after their white headbands, infamous for destroying shacks in Cape Town squatter camps in May and June 1986; these actions were apparently facilitated by the collusion of the police. In her trip to Guguletu, where the 'Witdoeke' are explicitly mentioned, Mrs Curren witnesses a representation of one of these events.[5]

Alongside this element of *imitative* representation, the novel displays the familiar self-consciousness about literary modes, as, for instance, when Mrs Curren feels as if she were living in an allegory (*AI*, 84); indeed, there is an allegorical dimension to her complicity and demise, a suggestion that she stands for the nation as a whole, the cancer within mirroring the metaphorical social cancer without. It is more accurate, however, to say that the idea of such an allegory (which occurs to the character herself (*AI*, 59)) functions as merely one idea in a text which cultivates the mode of realism more than it does that of indirect allegory. It might seem more accurate to talk of her development as having a typical rather than an allegorical function; or, rather, it is the sense of typicality which dominates. In this respect, Coetzee's most immediately engaged novel reveals a surprising affinity with Nadine Gordimer's *Burger's Daughter*, in which the life of the central character, Rosa Burger, runs in parallel with the history of modern South Africa; Rosa becomes representative of white South Africa both in her complicity and in her final position as a political subversive, a stance which, so the novel implies, is required of all the people in her situation. However, the novel takes this notion of typicality in new directions, into a confessional realm beyond the Lukácsian model.

At the most straightforward level, Mrs Curren's relinquishment of desire, of love for her land (*AI*, 111), is evidently a required typical response. A particularly powerful image emphasizes this necessary acceptance of decolonization. After the death of Bheki, in one of her confessions to Vercueil, Mrs Curren says:

Now that child is buried and we walk upon him. Let me tell you, when I walk upon this land, this South Africa, I have a gathering feeling of walking upon black faces. They are dead but their spirit has not left them. They lie there heavy and obdurate, waiting for my feet to pass, waiting for me to go, waiting to be raised up again. Millions of figures of pig-iron floating under the skin of the earth. The age of iron waiting to return. (*AI*, 115)

The age of iron, in this connection, is the age of political transition, of decolonization, produced as a necessity by the manifest evidence of repression. This is at one with Coetzee's ongoing preoccupation with the physical evidence of repression as the basis of the history of the Other. It also suggests an interesting appropriation by Coetzee of the motif of the buried black man. In his discussion of Gordimer's *The Conservationist*, he casts doubt on the validity of the symbol of ownership of the land, contained in the motif of the resurfacing corpse. If the ghost of the pastoral cannot be laid so easily (*WW*, 81), he has nevertheless used the same motif towards that end, in a steely image which redoubles a sense of white complicity.

The political context of the novel is precisely evoked. This includes references to the Schools' boycott (*AI*, 34, 62), as well as to media censorship. Mrs Curren is keenly aware of the ideological control of the media, an awareness which issues in an explicit condemnation of the Afrikaner heritage in this passage where she is watching television, with Vercueil observing through the window:

The curtains behind me were open. At a certain moment I became aware of him, the man whose name I do not know, watching over my shoulder through the glass. So I turned up the sound, enough for, if not the words, then the cadences to reach him, the slow, truculent Afrikaans rhythms with their deadening closes, like a hammer beating a post into the ground. Together, blow after blow, we listened. The disgrace of the life one lives under them: to open a newspaper, to switch on the television, like kneeling and being urinated on. Under them: under their meaty bellies, their full bladders. 'Your days are numbered', I used to whisper once upon a time, to them who will now outlast me. (*AI*, 9)

This passage is remarkable in that it yokes together the characteristic Coetzee tendency towards lyricism with a sense of transparent reference: the direct condemnation of the regime is astonishingly blunt, conveyed through an insulting image of visceral brutishness. The sense of explicit outrage encapsulates Mrs Curren's desperate situation, and anticipates the direction of the novel.

This direction is mapped through competing ideas about childhood, a debate which supplies the background to the central themes – concerning Mrs Curren's uncertain personal development as well as the particular political referent. Her memories of feeling immortal as a child (*AI*, 14) set the tone for the essential contrast between her (more innocent) conception of childhood, and the stage of youth as activism which has supplanted childhood for the young blacks she meets, prepared to die for the cause. The fact that there is 'an air of child-lessness' about Vercueil places him clearly outside her initial frame of reference (*AI*, 10).

Early in the novel, addressing her daughter, Mrs Curren recounts her mother's childhood memories of Christmas holi-days, travelling from the Eastern Cape to the seaside at Plettenburg Bay, by ox-wagon. On this hundred-mile journey the family would camp by the roadside overnight, Mrs Curren's mother sleeping beneath the wagon, with her brothers and sisters, while the grandparents slept inside. The specific memory concerns sleeping at the top of a pass, watching the stars through the spokes of the wheels, and feeling that the stars were moving: or that, perhaps, the wagon was starting to roll down the mountainside. Not knowing whether to call out a warning, and choked with fear, Mrs Curren's mother would eventually fall into a sleep 'full of dreams of death', only to emerge into daylight to find everything as it was (*AI*, 15). This image of the colonizer's precariousness – the thought of the grandparents plunging to their death in their ox-wagon – is presented as a defining childhood memory. Mrs Curren later identifies strongly with this story, a story that has chosen *her*: 'it is there that I come from, it is there that I begin' (*AI*, 110). The acceptance of the story of childhood insecurity is also an acceptance of complicity.

The dream thus appears to be double-edged, contributing, on the one hand, to the elegiac tone of Mrs Curren's story; at the same time, however, the plunging ox-wagon of a child's nightmare, as a metaphor of decolonization, links Mrs Curren's sense of childhood to recent colonial history, and this disquieting association ensures she can never acquire moral authority in discussions of childhood. We may identify with her feeling that Bheki and John are merely children, unfitted for political struggle (*AI*, 61, 131), but the ex-schoolteacher Mr Thabane's contrasting term 'youth' is compelling. Mr Thabane respects the comradeship of the new youth, while Mrs Curren criticizes this 'mystique of death': again we may see some justice in this criticism, even while we sense its lack of historical authority, and this, ultimately, is the important thing. Responding to Florence's pride at the new generation of children, who are 'like iron', Mrs Curren considers the grounding of this age of iron:

Is it truly a time out of time, heaved up out of the earth, misbegotten, monstrous? What, after all, gave birth to the age of iron but the age of granite? Did we not have Voortrekkers, generation after generation of Voortrekkers, grim-faced, tight-lipped Afrikaner children, marching, singing their patriotic hymns, saluting their flag, vowing to die for their fatherland? ... Are there not still white zealots preaching the old regime of discipline, work, obedience, self-sacrifice, a regime of death, to children some too young to tie their own shoelaces? (*AI*, 46–7)

The age of iron may be a time out of joint, producing distortions, but it is not 'a time out of time', without a context: Mrs Curren understands that it is the history of colonialism – specifically the ideology of Afrikaner Nationalism – which has called into being this new time. Significantly, the formation of this ideology involves a manipulation of childhood more sinister than the comradeship of the new black youth which begins to appear now, as a justified response.

In another image which reverses preconceptions about child-hood, Mrs Curren considers she was stolen, as a baby, from the cradle, and replaced by a doll, to live a doll's life (*AI*, 100–1). In a family photograph from 1918, she wonders whether to interpret the gesture of her infant self, reaching towards the camera, as an imposter's attempt to prevent the camera from revealing the truth about the 'doll-folk' (*AI*, 101–3). Again the metaphor implies a personal loss, yet also points at a falsity and a moral vacuity in Mrs Curren's heritage, the legacy of the colonizers, the doll-folk.

There remains a sense of lamentation for the loss of child-hood innocence, and this partly accounts for the novel's elegiac tone. This is complicated, however, because Mrs Curren's relinquishment of this idea of childhood is also a necessary part of her political progression. This ambivalence is aptly conveyed in the episode of the scavenging children. After the shooting of John in the servant quarters of her house, Mrs Curren flees and spends the night sleeping rough under a flyover. She is disturbed by three small boys – ten years old or younger – who, finding no valuables about her person, force her mouth open with a wooden stick, looking for gold teeth (*AI*, 144–5, 147). Mrs Curren, fleeing from the brutal shooting of one 'child', is confronted with the cruelty-in-poverty of three smaller chil-dren: the carelessness for herself, the relinquishment of her own bodily desires, coincides with the continued discrediting of her idea of the 'child'.

Mrs Curren's revised perception of the child's role is encap-sulated in her haunted response to the shooting of John, the boy she disliked personally. The fourth section of the novel ends with her identification with John's final moments, alone in the annexe, waiting to fire his single gestural shot as the door opens onto his death. This is 'a hovering time, but not eternity. *A Time being*, a suspension, before the return of the time in which the door bursts open and we face, first he, then I, the great white glare' (*AI*, 160). The brave anticipation of John acquires a symbolic significance for her, which is fitted to her own political transition: this 'hovering time' is a personal interregnum, before the interregnum of political engagement.

It is a taking stock, an acceptance of 'the great white glare' which will need to be faced as the apartheid regime musters its brutal resistance to the final movements of decolonization.

The focus, however, is on the personal dissolution. The novel begins on the day that Mrs Curren has been informed that her cancer is terminal, news which, she writes, 'was mine, for me, mine only, not to be refused. It was for me to take in my arms and fold to my chest and take home, without headshaking, without tears' (*AI*, 3). This emphasis on embracing the damaging truth establishes a principle of facing up to difficult self-knowledge. The paradox of finding succour in that which is damaging to the self is the novel's dominant mood, and one which seeks to assert a new kind of narrative authority based on self-effacement: Mrs Curren becomes an authoritative narrator because, having lost all stake in life, she has no other kind of authority left. Even so, much of her narrative has to do with the *process* of relinquishing personal authority which is matched by an inverse accumulation of narrative authority.

In accordance with this process, there are several indications that Mrs Curren's perceptions are changing. In response to Vercueil's suggestion that she is like iron herself, Mrs Curren feels something break inside her (*AI*, 68). Similarly, after seeing the dead boys, including Bheki, in Guguletu, she implies that her eyes have been opened permanently to some hitherto concealed truth (*AI*, 95). These suggestions of awakening, however, are tempered by a certain intransigence in Mrs Curren's attitude: her remonstration with Mr Thabane over the issue of comradeship shows that she does not fully relinquish outmoded ideas. But the question of relinquishment has to do with Mrs Curren's sense of her own irrelevance, and not simply with her personal awakening. This becomes clear when she mulls over her telephone call with Mr Thabane in a later 'confession' to Vercueil. She has not changed her mind, but has come to realize that her opinions are irrelevant: 'now I ask myself: What right have I to opinions about comradeship or anything else? What right have I to wish Bheki and his friend had kept out of trouble? To have opinions in a vacuum, opinions that touch no one, is, it seems to me, nothing' (*AI*,

148). Here, out of this negative, emerges the most positive feature of Mrs Curren's narrative. The purpose of the fictional project is suggested if one sets the achievement of the novel against the problems discussed by Coetzee in his essay, 'Confession and Double Thoughts: Tolstoy, Rousseau, Dostoevsky' (1985). A main concern of the essay is with how the confessional mode is tainted by self-deception. Mixed motives involving self-interest and self-congratulation account for the pattern of 'double thought', 'the malaise that renders confession powerless to tell the truth and come to an end' (*DP*, 282). The (apparently unattainable) 'end of confession is to tell the truth to and for oneself' (*DP*, 291), and the narrative logic of *Age of Iron* is to reveal a narrator who reaches out as far as possible towards this confessional end.

The authority of secular confession, for Coetzee, depends upon the willingness of the confessant to confront that which is worst within himself (*DP*, 263). However, the disease of self-consciousness, the movement of double thought, is always apt to uncover a hidden motive, thereby invalidating the 'truth' of a confession which, thus, cannot be brought to an end. Coetzee considers the death of Ippolit, in Dostoevsky's *The Idiot*, and Ippolit's claim that, because he is dying of tuberculosis, his confession will be genuine: the claim is that imprisoning self-consciousness can be transcended, and a revelation of truth can occur, in the unique moment before death (*DP*, 284). Ippolit's claim to truth, however, is doubtful. The prognosis of death is suspect, and his confessors, who refuse to accept Ippolit's sincerity, or the seriousness of his vow to kill himself, taint the understanding of his motives, destroying the possibility of truth in the confession (*DP*, 285–6). Even the suicide of Kirilov in *Demons* – he is the Dostoevsky character who comes closest to achieving a guarantee of truth through death – is complicated by the inaccessibility of his consciousness (*DP*, 288). From these examples, Coetzee argues that, in the confessional mode, wilful acts cannot force the revelation of truth, not even through the willing of the final moment of one's death, since this too may be tainted by double thought (*DP*, 287).

Mrs Curren's situation, dying, alone, makes self-interest

irrelevant. Her abandonment of the plan to commit suicide publicly is a refusal of the wilful act in which the final moment is tainted by the suspicion of double thought. The motive of self-justification might appear to figure significantly in this letter to her daughter, to be delivered after her death. But indications are given that this is primarily a confession by and for the self. Of course, there has to be a notional auditor for a confession to occur, and this function is fulfilled by the absent daughter, as well as by the unresponsive Vercueil, and (because this is an aspect of the reading experience) by the distanced reader; but there is no listener to engage in explicit dialogue. Indeed, one of Mrs Curren's moral imperatives is to do without the comfort of such a confessor: at the outset she realizes that she must 'resist the craving to share my death', and the extremity of that desire indicates that progressing towards the purity of untainted confession will be part of her development. This does raise the question of why she is writing to her daughter, but she poses and answers this question herself: 'To whom this writing then? The answer: to you but not to you; to me; to you in me' (*AI*, 5). The letter, in other words, is a confession for the self, but expresses the mother's affinity with the daughter, eschewing the taint of accusation or self-absorption. There is something of a paradox here, but this has to do with the conceit of the novel in establishing the circumstances for a 'true' confession which may be logically impossible. In effect, a special kind of limited 'dialogue' emerges in which the mother is interrogated by the absent daughter, who becomes a theoretical, or phantom, confessor. Vercueil, who elicits some key confessional moments, is a stooge confessor, in his taciturnity. Ultimately, however, the reader occupies the role of a distanced confessor, the necessary auditor for the conceit to work.

Mrs Curren's 'first confession' (*AI*, 124–5) concerns her inability to love John, a failure redressed after his shooting, and her understanding of its significance. That haunted response to John's final moments – a scene which is symbolic of a desired heroic confrontation with the apartheid regime – now reveals a double significance: it denotes Mrs Curren's acceptance of the exigencies of the age of iron (the irrelevance of childhood), but it also revises the perception of authority in the moment before death. Where, in Coetzee's argument, such authority is impossible to verify for the confessant in secular confession (exemplified in Dostoevsky's works), here we may perceive a new conjuncture. Mrs Curren, as confessant, is *in sympathy* with the authoritative moment before death experienced by *another*. This sympathy already installs a validity beyond the imprisoning self-consciousness of double thought, since the idea of the final moment, of courageous authority, is based on the example of another. In this 'hovering time' before the confrontation with 'the great white glare' the self is alone with the self to acknowledge the irrelevance of self-motivation (*AI*, 160). The paradoxical result of such reflection is to produce a moment of political solidarity, beyond the imprisoned self.

The most important confessional scene involves Mrs Curren talking aloud in the presence of Vercueil, coming to terms with the irrelevance of her ideas. Vercueil makes no response and shows no sign of having heard, and Mrs Curren, ostensibly recounting the episode to her daughter, asks: 'Is a true confession still true if it is not heard? Do you hear me, or have I put you to sleep too?' (*AI*, 151). In Coetzee's conception of the end of confession, Mrs Curren's is true *because* it is not directly heard: the truth, the self-knowledge, is produced by Vercueil's uselessness as a confessor and his likely unreliability as a messenger. The delivery of the letter is, thus, neither part of the narrative design, nor cultivated as a possibility which qualifies the reception of the text. His name underscores this enigmatic role: Mrs Curren confuses his name with 'verkuil' ('verkul' in Afrikaans means 'to cheat') and with the (Afrikaans) word 'verskuil' which means to hide or conceal. These associations reinforce his position as Other, unfitted to any scheme of atonement she may set out with. Yet if he 'cheats' or obscures expectations of the confessor's role, this completes the double negative – the double negation – of the problematic confessional mode. Because Vercueil does not respond as confessor (within the text the confession remains for the self) he cannot elicit or encourage double thought from her.

The process of relinquishment I am tracing produces moments in *Age of Iron* which acquire greater poignancy through allusions to the earlier novels, *Michael K* in particular, and to developing themes in the *œuvre*. In Mrs Curren's process of abnegation, there does seem to be a resolution, in one sense, of the colonizer's role. Mrs Curren's interpretation of snapshots from the family album implicitly suggests that a particular construction of childhood glosses over the truth of colonialism. We have seen how the doll motif, through the inversion of innocent childhood play, suggests the invalidity of the colonizer's position, through the generations. Describing the eerie photograph of herself, Mrs Curren wonders 'does my mother hold me back from striking the camera to the ground because I, in my doll's way, know that it will see what the eye cannot: that I am not there? And does my mother know this because she too is not there?' (*AI*, 102). The theme of ontological doubt in the post-colonizing persona appears to reach a culmination, here. In *Dusklands*, violence inflicted on the Other supplies the means by which Jacobus Coetzee, the archetypal colonizer, confirms his sense of being, the tangibility of his existence. Part of Mrs Curren's process of renunciation is to think through this inherited ontological doubt, and grasp its validity. In this sense, the novel, tracing the demise of Mrs Curren as reluctant colonizer, enacts this intangibility. In another photograph, Mrs Curren's reading of the image's margins takes the decentring dynamic further:

We were photographed, that day, in a garden. There are flowers behind us that look like hollyhocks; to our left is a bed of melons . . . Who laid the melon-seeds in their warm, moist bed? Was it my grandfather who got up at four in the icy morning to open the sluice and lead water into the garden? If not he, then whose was the garden rightfully? Who are the ghosts and who the presences? Who, outside the picture, leaning on their rakes, leaning on their spades, waiting to get back to work, lean also against the edge of the rectangle, bending it, bursting it in? (*AI*, 102)

Mrs Curren asks explicitly that which *Michael K* had posed implicitly through its narrative: the ghosts and presences outside the picture, the true gardeners – tenders of melon-beds;

preservers of seed – are the moral 'owners' or true guardians of the garden, just as Michael K's nurturing redeems the forsaken Visagie farm. Later, thinking of John, Mrs Curren sheds tears for the garden boys of South Africa (feeling John was destined to be one of their number, in other circumstances) (*AI*, 138): this clearly associates the gardening theme with the question of political struggle, just as does Michael K's choice between gardening and joining the guerilla band.

The perception of Vercueil as Other is also enhanced by references to the earlier novels. At one point he begins to dance to the radio in a way which baffles Mrs Curren, much as Friday's dancing baffles Susan Barton (*AI*, 166). More significant is the disfigurement of his hand, which obliges us to associate him with both Friday and Michael K. When Mrs Curren manages to elicit something of his life story, in the manner of the author-narrator trying to make Friday 'speak' at the end of *Foe*, the circumstances of the disfigurement form the significant episode (*AI*, 170–1); and when Mrs Curren faces the police interrogation over the harbouring of John, she holds Vercueil's disfigured hand, momentarily, when confronted by the detective's questioning (*AI*, 157). The gesture is important, not just because Mrs Curren aligns herself with Vercueil's own history, but, more significantly, because of what the disfigurement of the Other has come to symbolize more generally in Coetzee's work. This is not Vercueil's sole, or even main, function in the novel, but this detail corresponds to the idea that disfigurement and mutilation becomes strangely positive as the history – the literal mark or text – of colonialism.

Towards the end of *Foe*, the character Foe employs the metaphor of 'a maze of doubting' to explain the provisionality of his sense of himself as a writer, a position which corresponds to that occupied by postcolonial writers like Coetzee. In Foe's maze of doubting, succour is found in returning to the starting-point, as a confirmation of the certainty of being lost (*F*, 135–6). Something of this paradoxical affirmation characterizes Mrs Curren's progression towards a 'true' confessional writing style, made specific to her case, as her own maze-metaphor indicates:

I am written out, bled dry, and still I go on. This letter has become a maze, and I a dog in the maze, scurrying up and down the branches and tunnels, scratching and whining at the same old places, tiring, tired. Why do I not call for help, call to God? Because God cannot help me. God is looking for me but he cannot reach me. God is another dog in another maze. I smell God and God smells me. I am the bitch in her time, God the male. God smells me, he can think of nothing else but finding me and taking me. Up and down the branches he bounds, scratching at the mesh. But he is lost as I am lost. (*AI*, 126)

Mrs Curren's writing is a secular maze – distinct from the maze in which God might be found – and this emphasis on the secular equivalent of absolution is an essential feature of Coetzee's interest in the end of confession (*DP*, 252). Such a Godless maze, in which one can only be the unattainable victim of the Deity, is the appropriate metaphor for the notionally untainted confession – logically impossible, but produced by narrative artifice – in which the self is alone with the self, without comfort or pity.

This sense of closure seems entirely appropriate to Coetzee's last novel written and set within the apartheid era. If heroism is needed in this historical juncture, as Mrs Curren suggests (*AI*, 151), then it may be that Coetzee tries to bestow on her 'the status of the confessant as a hero of the labyrinth' (*DP*, 263), able to bring self-doubting to an end. But here, any sense of an abstract pursuit of the secular equivalent of absolution becomes hazy, a secondary matter: the focus is on the political ethics of a particular time and place. The literary project, of developing the confessional mode, is precisely structured by the political context. Mrs Curren's letter – the novel's very structure – is itself demanded by the *situation* of the absent daughter, living a self-imposed political exile (*AI*, 68): the dilemma and the style of the novel are *determined by* this ordering frame, and the 'truth' that emerges is consequently relative, not transcendent. It is Mrs Curren's own truth about this time and place (*AI*, 119), the authority of which is dependent on the sense of contingency, of the hovering time of interregnum.

CHAPTER 8

Producing the demon: 'The Master of Petersburg'

In *The Master of Petersburg* (1994), Coetzee offers a complex deliberation on authorship, rivalled in metafictional complexity only by *Foe* among the earlier novels. But, whereas *Foe* locates a precise moment of postcolonial writing, in ambivalent relationship to the Western literary canon, *The Master of Petersburg* makes a gesture to extend the broader questions about authorship and responsibility, and the directions for the postmodernist novel, questions which here stem from problems in Dostoevsky's poetics.

The protagonist of Coetzee's novel is Fyodor Dostoevsky himself. The novel opens in October 1869 with the return of this 'Dostoevsky' to St Petersburg, following a self-imposed exile in Dresden (he has been avoiding creditors). He returns, travelling on a false passport, to collect the papers and belongings of his stepson Pavel, who has died in mysterious circumstances. The papers, which include a terrorist hit-list, are in the hands of the Tsarist police, with whom Dostoevsky becomes embroiled. He takes up residence in Pavel's former lodgings, eventually commencing an affair with the landlady, whilst becoming fascinated with her adolescent daughter (who had loved Pavel).

There is, as Zinovy Zinik observes, a wilful manipulation of the biographical data: the real Dostoevsky was survived by his stepson, and this significant change signals the novel's preoccupation with the dilemma of 'fathering' and authorship.[1] There is also, however, a dependence on actual resonances. At the heart of the novel's narrative development is Nechaev, a real historical figure, a nihilist and revolutionary, associated with the murder of a fellow student, Ivanov, who had left Nechaev's group and could have become an informer. The ideological confrontation, in *The Master of Petersburg*, between 'Dostoevsky' and Nechaev is decisive in the presentation of the authorial role.

As with *Foe*, Coetzee posits a time before the composition of a significant European novel. The killing of Ivanov occurred in November 1869, and was the event which set the deliberations in train for Dostoevsky's novel *The Devils* or *The Possessed* (now also translated as *Demons*.)[2] In Coetzee's novel, there is a character called Ivanov who is murdered in November 1869, possibly by Nechaev, and this is one of many semi-correspondences and allusions in a complex pastiche. But, where *Foe* combined sustained references to several of Defoe's works, *The Master of Petersburg* narrows its focus. There are references to characters and themes in several works by Dostoevsky, but the novel becomes, in one sense, an extended treatment of the chapter 'At Tikhon's', originally suppressed from *Demons*, and which often appears as an appendix in modern editions.[3] In this sense, Coetzee's *Ur*-text is almost a non-text, redeemed from a liminal margin of the European novel.

In Dostoevsky's novel, the demons are consuming ideas which dictate the behaviour of the characters, driving them to desperate and wicked acts in the pursuit, for example, of freedom through revolutionary activities. The 'sin' here, as presented in *Demons*, seems to be the assertion of human autonomy – implicitly a rebellion against God – an autonomy expressed most fully in Stavrogin.[4] Coetzee's appropriation of the idea of being 'possessed' has a secular basis, but draws on the Dostoevskyan critique of ideological conditioning. The focus for this issue is the manipulation of Coetzee's 'Dostoevsky' by Nechaev: when he is tricked by Nechaev into making a statement about his son's death (in which he implicates Nechaev) he realizes that it is his name only that Nechaev wishes to exploit to foment agitation (*MP*, 203). The recognition of this 'trap' occurs at the end of the sixteenth chapter, which comprises a crucial exchange between the two. Nechaev gains the upper hand, already trapping 'Dostoevsky' by virtue of an uncomplicated surety he cannot match:

As if sensing his weakness, Nechaev pounces, worrying him like a dog. 'Eighteen centuries have passed since God's age, nearly nineteen! We are on the brink of a new age where we are free to think any thought. There is nothing we can't think! . . . You must know it – it's what Raskolnikov said in your own book before he fell ill!'

'You are mad, you don't know how to read,' he mutters. But he has lost, and he knows it. He has lost because, in this debate, he does not believe himself. And he does not believe himself because he has lost. Everything is collapsing: logic, reason. He stares at Nechaev and sees only a crystal winking in the light of the desert, self-enclosed, impregnable. (*MP*, 201–2)

Raskolnikov, the murderous hero–villain of *Crime and Punishment*, is an exemplary figure of Dostoevskyan doubleness; he is self-divided, at once horrifying and fascinating, and is clearly misread by Nechaev here. 'Dostoevsky', however, feels himself helpless to oppose this misappropriation of Raskolnikov in the name of liberating autonomy. John Bayley, in his review of the novel, interprets this passage to show that 'Nechaev has got him, because whatever truth the writer utters can be twisted by the terrorists to their own purposes and the author will necessarily collude with the terrorists just by writing for them and about them.'[5] Revolutionary fervour, as the idea-demon, produces explanations which traduce other texts, collapsing complexity, different accents, into a flat, utilitarian monologism. At one level, this suggests the kind of contemporary commentary by Coetzee which Zinovy Zinik has detected: 'considering that Nechaev and his followers have been an inspiration for so many political figures with terrorist tendencies, from Lenin to Gerry Adams, not to mention certain ANC leaders, it is tempting to see in Coetzee's work an obvious parable of present-day world politics'.[6] This is not a possibility which the novel entirely denies, though 'Dostoevsky's' remark that 'I don't speak in parables' seems more in tune with the multi-layered effect of the novel (*MP*, 183): what is offered is a deliberation about the responsibilities of representation, one element of which suggests a contemporary parallel.

The image of Nechaev as a crystal winking in the desert conveys the enticement of reductive lucidity (enticing where the alternative is a complexity which gives rise to a barren undecidability), as well as a clear warning about his autonomy. The image is focalized by 'Dostoevsky', and this belies his sense of having lost the argument: he retains the writer's vision, the ability to present an oblique counter to the monolithic idea-demon.

Other issues, familiar in Coetzee's ongoing defence of narrative fiction, are attached to this confrontation. Immediately before the argument's culmination, the two have discussed the function of words, the idea of authorship, and the construction of history. 'Dostoevsky' argues for the responsibility borne by the author of ideas, whereas Nechaev aligns himself with a vertiginous freedom in which history can be accelerated:

You keep talking about the inside's of people's minds. History is made in the streets. And don't tell me I am talking *thoughts* right now. That is just another clever debating trick, the kind of thing they confuse students with. I'm not talking thoughts, and even if I am, it doesn't matter. I can think one thing at one minute and another thing at another and it won't matter a pin as long as I *act*. (*MP*, 200)

Nechaev associates words with actions and repudiates an emphasis on textuality in the construction of ideas. This invokes the debate about 'realism', and the rivalry between the novel and history which is continually present in Coetzee. Nechaev's irrationalism here presents the underlying illogicality of putting the novel at the service of history – for example, in a transparent portrayal of a radical agenda. Without paying attention to the construction of ideas, to textuality, the fabric of one's project collapses, ideas become inconsequential, even contradictory. Yet if this is a parody of the revolutionary position, it is used to focus the responsibilities of the author, rather than to comment on the psyche of the activist: if Dostoevsky parodies the Nechaevites in *Demons*, Coetzee subverts that parody into a debate about writing. The political dimension to this debate is underscored by a simultaneous evocation of censorship, and the distortions it produces. In chapter 16, Nechaev is condemned by a colleague for watching over 'Dostoevsky' as he composes his statement. 'Writers have their own rules', says this other man: 'they can't work with people looking over their shoulders'. 'Then they should learn new rules', replies Nechaev: 'Privacy is a luxury we can do without. People don't need privacy' (*MP,* 198). The invocation of censorship implicitly identifies two poles of influence for the writer to resist. The argument is already shifting from a radical-versus-writer confrontation to a more complex model of the course the writer must chart in order to negotiate the Scylla of ideological utility and the Charybdis of state control.

In his essay 'Breyten Breytenbach and the Censor' (1991), Coetzee considers questions of dialogue and demonization which have an interesting bearing on his thinking in this novel. Coetzee shows how the Bakhtinian notion of hidden contestatory dialogue has a special relevance to Breytenbach's prison poetry in which the voice of the censor/oppressor/persecutor is present, and is spoken against. There is a self-interrogation in this kind of writing in which the self is dissolved. Coetzee argues that, in interrogation and torture, the suffering of the victim produces a loss of integrity, a sense that the victim takes on some of the persecutor's own degradation. The result is a doubling of self, of 'interrogator and revolutionary, criminal and victim, colonizer and colonized, even censor and writer'. The idea of mirror-image confrontation provokes Coetzee to pose a crucial set of questions concerning the white policeman and the black revolutionary, 'enemies brought together in the mirror':

Is the mirror the place, then, where history is transcended? Does the dialogue with the mirror-self shade into dialogue between the selves in the mirror? And can the dialogue with the mirror be trusted to proceed peaceably, or will it degenerate into hysterical confrontation and self-accusation?

The questions are posed rather than answered, and the essay concludes with a consideration of the problems of secular confession, its endless self-reflection signalling that 'getting to the real self is a life's task', a process of living with the demons within one, a process not best served by a simple denunciation or demonization of the oppressor.[7] This essay has a direct relevance to the direction of the novel sequence, and not just to Coetzee's achievement in *The Master of Petersburg.* The familiar postmodernist dissolution of the subject-position, of the boundaries of self, is rooted here in the moment in which the colonized recognizes being contaminated by the colonizer who is simultaneously confronted. It is a moment of doubling which is essential in the process of decolonization, because the given of colonial history can be arrested, as the materials for its supplanting are assembled: this, it seems, is the transcendence of which Coetzee speaks. But the moment is potentially catastrophic, too, supplying an alternative route to a disabling self-accusation. The censor/writer confrontation, which includes a self-confrontation with the internalized demon-voices, is thus a new figure for the moment of postcolonial writing as it is manifested in Coetzee's work. Significantly, it also elides the resisting writer (white or black) with the oppressed Other more generally.[8]

This question of voice and contamination puts a new angle on the exploration of the narrating self conducted in *Age of Iron*. We have seen that, in 'Confession and Double Thoughts: Tolstoy, Rousseau, Dostoevsky', Coetzee considers how, in *Demons*, Dostoevsky takes his 'last steps in the exploration of the limits of secular confession' (*DP*, 287). *Age of Iron* tries to progress beyond these limits through a carefully constructed narrative situation; in *The Master of Petersburg*, however, the limits are confronted through a more sustained intertextual gesture. Coetzee's discussion of *Demons* culminates in his consideration of the suppressed chapter 'At Tikhon's', in which Stavrogin makes his confession to the monk Tikhon, or rather hands over his confession – for it is in the form of a printed document – for Tikhon to read. This chapter was apparently deemed too salacious and was cut from the work as originally published. At the heart of Stavrogin's confession is the apparent seduction of his landlady's fourteen-year-old daughter, and his refusal to intervene when he senses the guilt and despair which result in her suicide. Indeed, suspecting that this girl, Matryosha, is about to take her life, he deliberately waits long enough for the deed to be completed before confirming her death for himself. Among the other crimes he confesses, committed out of boredom or indifference, is his marriage to the mad and disabled Marya Lebyatkin, as a dark and self-destructive joke.

Coetzee stresses the role of the confessor, and the duality of the exchange: Tikhon interrogates Stavrogin to discover his motivation to confess, while, at the same time, Stavrogin assesses Tikhon's credentials as confessor. In that Tikhon assumes the role of self-interrogator in first-person confession, the chapter is illustrative of the Dostoevskyan view that, as Coetzee has it, 'the self cannot tell the truth of itself to itself and come to rest without the possibility of self-deception'. The episode forms part of 'a sequence of texts in which Dostoevsky explores the impasses of secular confession, pointing finally to the sacrament of confession as the only road to self-truth' (*DP*, 289, 291).

It may be, however, that, by exteriorizing the internal dialogue of first-person confession, Dostoevsky has already opened a way beyond the impasse, a solution stemming from the dialogic style, even if the possibility of genuine dialogue is refused. Tikhon detects already the anticipation of the receiver in the style of Stavrogin's confession, an implicit dialogue, written 'as if you purposely want to portray yourself as coarser than your heart would wish'. In Tikhon's analysis, this suggests the possibility that Stavrogin already challenges – hates even – those who might hear his confession, complicating his impulse to repentance. Tikhon goes on to suggest that Stavrogin's need to confess betrays, instead of humility, a desire for martyrdom, a desire which he exhorts him to relinquish by giving up the intention of publishing his printed confession. This double-bind is an important aspect of the 'trap' Stavrogin fears is being set for him.[9]

In the light of the above, it is interesting to recall that Bakhtin's analysis of *Demons*, in *Problems of Dostoevsky's Poetics*, concentrates on Stavrogin's confession, anticipating Coetzee's analysis in several respects. In Bakhtin's reading, Tikhon's role is to highlight the dialogue opened up – and simultaneously refused – in Stavrogin's account, dominated by the effort to ignore the listener.[10] The wilful, and circular monologism this implies is, effectively, undermined by the position of Tikhon.

A way of explaining this position, and an explanation that chimes with Coetzee's interest, is offered by Gary Saul Morson and Caryl Emerson, who view the Dostoevsky book as important in the conception and demonstration of polyphony. They show how, for Bakhtin, an initial obstacle to the polyphonic novel, and to genuine dialogue in the novel, is the author's 'surplus of vision', his or her knowledge about a character's psyche, fate and so on, which makes it impossible for author and character to exist on the same plane, or to engage in dialogue. However, the partial authorial renunciation of a position of superior knowledge ('surplus of meaning') creates the space of relative independence for character, a space enhanced by what Morson and Emerson have dubbed the 'addressive surplus'. This is the surplus of 'the good listener', which represents an invitation to the Other to grow, realize his or her capacity for change. One manifestation of the authorial use of the addressive surplus is the creation of characters – such as Tikhon – able to unleash this surplus and its opening-out tendency.[11]

Elsewhere Morson points out how the ambiguity of Stavrogin's confession in 'At Tikhon's' is further complicated by its existence in different versions: in one version, Stavrogin withholds the page of his confession that concerns the actual seduction from Tikhon, and then denies that it happened.[12] It is clear, however, that, in composing his essay on confession and double thought, Coetzee follows the reading in which the sexual crime is assumed to have occurred (*DP*, 288). Even so, there is a further resonance for *The Master of Petersburg* in the doubts about the suppressed chapter. With the circumstances of Stavrogin's culpability intact, the chapter seems a logical part of the narrative, supplying an important psychological explanation for Stavrogin's haunted sense of guilt. Its suppression, however, makes it both part, and yet not part, of the novel. The existence of different versions of the episode adds another twist to this model of receding textual substantiality; Morson observes that 'reading across several variants, one may have the strange experience of an absent absence'.[13]

The issues raised in the chapter of Stavrogin's confession, and the uncertainties of its production and reception, are appropriated to Coetzee's own project in *The Master of Petersburg*. What he does is to focus questions of polyphony, the addressive surplus, and the nature of narrative knowledge, through a deliberation on authorial responsibility. This is achieved through a mergence of Dostoevskyan motifs with his own, a process which culminates in the final chapter. In this concluding section, 'Dostoevsky' confronts the loss of his stepson Pavel, and the question of how he can write through and beyond the experience by 'betraying' his sense of parental protectiveness. This betrayal is a figure for authorial relinquishment of control – or surplus meaning – signalled emphatically by the refusal to pursue sentiment or personal interest.

The chapter is called 'Stavrogin', underscoring an association between Pavel and Dostoevsky's anti-hero, though here we are asked to imagine the author of *Demons* confronted by an hallucination of Pavel/Stavrogin to parallel the demon/hallucination seen by Stavrogin in the corner of his study in *Demons*. For this 'Dostoevsky', his Other, facing him across the writing-table, is an enigma. The identity of the phantasm is uncertain, though various possibilities are considered, then dismissed: it could be the son Pavel; the terrorist Nechaev; a demon; even Christ. Ultimately, this featureless statue, which might be the Pavel of the future, becomes the author's responsibility, to father and be fathered by (*MP*, 238–42). This image of simultaneous authorial responsibility and capitulation – of composition as partial self-effacement – is the goal of Coetzee's project, both its form and its content.

Yet, before we can consider the implications of this, there is a further dimension of metafictional 'nesting' to consider. The entire novel extends the scenario of the 'At Tikhon's' chapter in *Demons*, where Stavrogin recounts his sin against the child Matryosha, his landlady's daughter. In *The Master of Petersburg*, it is 'Dostoevsky' who takes rooms in Petersburg and becomes fascinated with his landlady's daughter (also Matryosha). The author-figure is already implicated, in other words, in the idea-demon that the actual Dostoevsky will project onto Stavrogin. The evocation of 'At Tikhon's' is repeated, as the final Chinese-box, in the last chapter of Coetzee's novel, where 'Dostoevsky' is seen to set about writing (in Pavel's empty diary) variations of scenes described in Stavrogin's confession. The first is the induction of a girl into vicarious sexual experience as voyeur

(*MP*, 242–5); the second is the account of courting Maria Lebyatkin, out of boredom, as a joke (*MP*, 247–9). (A version of this episode has already been recounted as part of Pavel's history (*MP*, 72–4).) It is clear that the gesture Coetzee offers through this extended reference to the 'At Tikhon's' chapter is irreducibly ambivalent. The predatory sexuality of 'Dostoevsky' raises important doubts about authorial power and 'the dance of the pen' (*MP*, 236). Yet this may also be seen as a figure for the taint of the colonizer, and so implicitly redemptive, just as the 'betrayal' of Pavel can be interpreted as a figure for the relinquishment of authorial surplus meaning, and the facilitation of a future dialogue. Perhaps most importantly, the gesture 'recuperates' a suppressed, liminal site of the European novel, bringing to attention an object of censorship. And, if this has a positive momentum, so too may the ambivalences of Coetzee's chapter itself, now appearing to be representative of the divided identity necessarily produced by the effects of censorship. In Coetzee's case, we can conceive of censorship broadly to incorporate the prescriptive, normative criticism of his oblique productions as a writer in South Africa.

In the first brief scene, Pavel's behaviour is governed by an idea-demon with a parallel in another Dostoevsky character, the exploitative Svidrigailov in *Crime and Punishment*, whose attitude is remembered here. In this scene, Pavel and his lover are heard, or watched through a crack in the door, by his landlady's daughter:

'Do that again,' the girl will whisper.
'Do what?'
'That!' she whispers, flushed with desire.
'First say the words,' he says, and makes her say them. 'Louder,' he says. Saying the words excites the girl unbearably.
He remembers Svidrigailov: 'Women like to be humiliated.'
He thinks of all of this as *creating a taste* in the child, as one creates a taste for unnatural foods, oysters or sweetbreads.
He asks himself why he does it. The answer he gives himself is: History is coming to an end; the old account-books will soon be thrown into the fire; in this dead time between old and new, all things are permitted. He does not believe his answer particularly, does not disbelieve it. It serves. (*MP*, 244)

In this fictional projection by his father, Pavel is associated with the dubious 'freedoms' of Svidrigailov (who has a taste for young girls), and is also made to articulate a perception of history which conforms with the views of Nechaev that we have already seen. Nechaev had used the attitude of Raskolnikov, in *Crime and Punishment*, to validate a revolutionary acceleration of history unhampered by ethical restraints on thoughts. The lack of complexity in Nechaev's understanding of 'history' results in an ahistorical monologism, a point reinforced here. An effect of 'Dostoevsky's' dispute with Nechaev is to make an implicit appeal for a complex understanding of history as competing texts (*MP*, 200–2). His re-creation of the argument, in this fiction within the fiction, underscores the need for this textual understanding of history, as he is at last empowered, in the process of composition, to criticize implicitly Nechaev's position. The idea of the end of History is here presented as a denial of different interpretive layers – the old account-books thrown into the fire – releasing an 'unnatural' influence, which is random, without ethical content, detached from authorial conviction.

An allusion to *Foe* is contained in the drowning motif, which is the image which haunts 'Dostoevsky's' imaginary reconstruction of Pavel's demise. The death is presented as a metaphorical drowning/silencing in successive versions, and these evoke the treatment of Friday's silence in the final section of *Foe*. In the third chapter, 'Dostoevsky' dreams of swimming underwater, searching for Pavel, calling for him, only to find each syllable of his cry 'replaced by a syllable of water'. When he finds Pavel he touches the face with a kiss that might also be a bite (*MP*, 17–18). The ambivalence in this loving gesture, which is perhaps also predatory, is repeated in a later dream which follows a pleasureless, insensate love-making between 'Dostoevsky' and Anna: at the point of climax he is described plunging into sleep, as if into a lake, to be met by a drowning Pavel, calling out 'in a strangled rush of words' (*MP*, 56). A baffling desire, without apparent meaning, is once more associated with the death of Pavel, and the anguish of drowning/silencing. (The episode repeats itself (*MP*, 58).) Coetzee is taking an intriguing step in extending the image of Friday's silence – a metaphor for colonial repression and misperception of the Other – into a realm with a double significance, evoking not only the repression of the Other, but equally and simultaneously silencing as a perennial problem of 'authoring' a fiction.

Indeed, in the final chapter a complex manoeuvre is performed: here, the fictional Dostoevsky projects onto an imagined 'future' Pavel the demonic doubleness that will inform *Demons*, and in which the author figure is already implicated. This bespeaks, as we have seen, a great effort to renounce authorial surplus meaning, or rigid control, most difficult to achieve in the face of the claims of sentiment or duty. Beyond this – and this is where our particular interest lies – the Other that is Pavel/Stavrogin becomes emblematic of the kind of postcolonial representation that is Coetzee's hallmark. This figure has the significance, for Coetzee's work, that 'Mrs Brown' had for Virginia Woolf. The quest for the inner life of Mrs Brown – the stranger in the train carriage travelling 'from one age of English literature to the next', is emblematic of the problem of representing identity in modernist fiction.[14] The phantasm which haunts the end of *The Master of Petersburg* conjoins the problems of representing identity in this branch of postcolonial literature, where the European literary canon remains a decisive presence. The demon which possesses the post-colonizer, but which must be produced, is irreducibly double, the self and the Other, a split literary and historical identity.

In his excellent essay on *Foe* and the politics of canonization, Derek Attridge demonstrates how Coetzee's allusiveness produces a coherent politics of textuality. This is achieved precisely through the claim to an ambivalent relationship with, rather than a direct challenge to, the canon. This ambivalence in the novels helps us to conceive of 'a mode of fiction which expose[s] the ideological basis of canonization, which dr[aws] attention to its own relation to the existing canon, which thematize[s] the role of race, class and gender in the processes of cultural acceptance and exclusion, and which, while speaking from a marginal location, addresse[s] the question of

marginality'. This formulation links the various questions of
literary and theoretical self-consciousness raised by Coetzee's
novels, and suggests an ethical grounding in such a fictional
process which 'would have to be seen as engaged in an
attempt to break the silence in which so many are caught,
even if it did so by literary means that have traditionally been
celebrated as characterising canonic art'. If this is the *process*,
Attridge offers a speculative ending to his essay, concerning
the point of arrival:

> If I may end with a Utopian thought . . . it would be that the
> canonization – however partial and uneven – of Coetzee's novels,
> along with other texts . . . that question the very processes of
> canonicity itself, will slowly transform the ideology and the institu-
> tions from which the canon derives its power, so that new and
> presently unimaginable ways of finding a voice, and new ways of
> hearing such voices, come into being.[15]

This explains, very appropriately, the ethical grounding of
Coetzee's work, where the stress on textuality also concerns the
identities of both self and Other, and the need to renegotiate
these identities. This aspect of the literature of the post-
colonizer explains how the projection of abnegation can be
seen as a responsible confrontation with the present moment.

Attridge also offers a dialectical understanding of canonicity
which is appropriate to this latest novel in which the idea of
'mastery', suggesting the literary masters of the Western tradition, is used to locate this site of authorial ambivalence and
transition. In correspondence with Coetzee, Philip R. Wood
suggests that Coetzee's work, in keeping with the ' "postmodern" turn', avoids notions of mastery or totality. Coetzee
declines the invitation to define his achievement, if 'mastery' is
an inappropriate term, but this exchange, dating from 1991,
has a resonance for Coetzee's usage of the idea of mastery in
this novel.[16] The title announces that Coetzee's 'Dostoevsky' is
'The Master', though, clearly, a cultivated ambiguity comes to
surround the notion of mastery assigned to the authorial
position. A key exchange occurs between 'Dostoevsky' and the
landlady Anna, where he is trying to enlist her help in some
kind of resurrection of Pavel's memory:

'You are an artist, a master,' she says. 'It is for you, not for me, to bring him back to life.'

Master. It is a word he associates with metal – with the tempering of swords, the casting of bells. A master blacksmith, a foundry-master. *Master of life*: strange term. But he is prepared to reflect on it. He will give a home to any word, no matter how strange, no matter how stray, if there is a chance it is an anagram for Pavel.

'I am far from being a master,' he says. 'There is a crack running through me. What can one do with a cracked bell? A cracked bell cannot be mended.'

What he says is true. Yet at the same time he recalls that one of the bells of the Cathedral of the Trinity in Sergiyev is cracked, and has been from before Catherine's time. It has never been removed and melted down. It sounds over the town every day. The people call it St Sergius's wooden leg. (*MP*, 140–1)

The passage indicates that 'Dostoevsky', like the image of the cracked bell that is still good, is both master (where it is expedient) and not-master. This duality is established elsewhere: Pavel's writing includes an undercutting ridicule of his father as master (*MP*, 218), though the novel shows him as the ultimate victor in his struggle with Nechaev for mastery (*MP*, 190).[17]

How might one summarize the sense of profound provisionality that emerges from Coetzee's novels, and which is signalled, especially, in the authorial figure of *The Master of Petersburg*? The focus in this literature is on the identity of the post-colonizing self, and in this sense the surrounding silences of the Other cannot be fully approached.[18] This means that a way of figuring the intermediary nature of Coetzee's postcolonialism – as it is manifested in his treatment of voice – is through a carefully tailored application of dialogism.

Coetzee has spoken of the dialogic nature of writing as 'a matter of awakening the countervoices in oneself and embarking upon speech with them'. This observation acquires great significance when Coetzee continues: 'it is some measure of a writer's seriousness whether he does evoke/invoke those countervoices in himself'. The context of this discussion is an explanation by Coetzee of his dissatisfaction with the interview procedure which, in his experience, tends towards 'a monologic ideal' (*DP*, 65). In suggesting that monologism is antipathetic to the writer's objectives, Coetzee affiliates himself with the Bakhtinian moment. This familiar correspondence between his creativity and contemporary literary theory locates another point where theory and praxis coincide: Coetzee indicates that a measure of a writer's significance – 'seriousness' he calls it – is dependent upon the writer allowing the conflict of discourses which have produced him or her to generate contestation in his or her work.[19] This is not to imply that Coetzee's novels are paragons of heteroglot diversity. This would be quite inappropriate to the transitional site of decolonization from which he writes, a site which, as we have seen, produces certain kinds of restricted contestation, and certain silences too.

In the essay on voice and censorship in Breyten Breytenbach, we find a further indication of the kind of limited dialogism that is relevant to Coetzee. He quotes from Bakhtin's work on Dostoevsky, with particular reference to the notion of 'hidden dialogue' as something which is found, as Bakhtin writes, 'when there is no access to one's own personal "ultimate" word', so that 'every thought, feeling, experience must be refracted through the medium of someone else's discourse, someone else's style, [or, in the continuation of the passage, which Coetzee omits] someone else's manner, with which it cannot immediately be merged without reservation, without distance, without refraction'.[20] Coetzee's focus is precise: the particularity of South African censorship and Breytenbach's position, writing 'for' the censor whilst in prison, a constraint which results in a particular manifestation of that 'hidden contestatory dialogue'.[21]

This problem of authority/voice, which emerges as a defining feature of Coetzee's first seven novels (though without the immediacy of Breytenbach's suffering), is a particular site, specific to the dilemma of the white writer in South Africa. This specific relevance is underscored in Coetzee's essay, 'Into the Dark Chamber' (1986), in which state brutality is shown to delimit narrative possibility. In this essay (discussed earlier in chapter 4), Coetzee argues that 'relations in the torture room provide a metaphor, bare and extreme, for relations between authoritarianism and its victims' (*DP,* 363). The challenge for the novelist is how to write about the dark chamber of torture – which in one sense 'is the origin of novelistic fantasy per se' – without reproducing the brutalities of the state. This is very much a formal problem, because it indicates that, in extreme contexts, an effective disabling of the novelist's imaginative facilities occurs. A new kind of authority has to be established as a consequence, the authority to find new terms in which to imagine torture and death (*DP,* 364). In miniature, this is the dilemma of the post-colonizer as writer, a position encapsulated in a scene from Nadine Gordimer's *Burger's Daughter.* Coetzee discusses this scene (which recalls Raskolnikov's nightmare, in *Crime and Punishment,* of a mare beaten to death by peasants) in which Rosa Burger comes across a black peasant family on a donkey-cart ahead on the road. The (male) driver is whipping the animal, with a terrified woman and child looking on. Rosa feels herself powerless to intervene, since to do so – by reporting them from her position of white authority – would be to confirm the status quo. For her, the episode crystallizes an understanding of her complicity with the system, and this sense of helplessness reaffirms her decision to leave South Africa.[22]

In Coetzee's reading, the scene of the driver and the donkey locked in violence/suffering belongs to a dehumanized world which Rosa cannot break into. The problem of progressing beyond this impasse – the focus of Gordimer's novel of discovered political commitment – is offered by Coetzee as emblematic of the writer's dilemma in South Africa:

What Rosa suffers and waits for is a time when humanity will be restored across the face of society, and therefore when all human acts, including the flogging of an animal, will be returned to the ambit of moral judgement. In such a society it will once again be *meaningful* for the gaze of the author, the gaze of authority and authoritative judgement, to be turned upon scenes of torture. When the choice is no longer limited to *either* looking on in horrified fascination as the blows fall *or* turning one's eyes away, then the novel can once again take as its province the whole of life, and even the torture chamber can be accorded a place in the design. (*DP,* 368)

Even if Coetzee makes direct attempts to confront this problem (as in the treatment of torture in *Waiting for the Barbarians*), there is a more general sense in which the paradox identified here is not resolvable. Indeed, this is as close as one might expect to get to a political rationale for the realization of style in Coetzee's novels: he implicitly justifies the production of an oblique mode of expression which avoids complicity through representation, but which also gestures towards a different mode fitted to a different time.

This formal crossroads reveals various points of significance. It embodies the appropriately provisional position of the white writer in South Africa, needing to establish a position of qualified authority. Arguably, this model of a recentred post-colonialism takes its real significance by virtue of its specificity and its sense of impermanence: in the case of Coetzee, we can see what the otherwise abstract model of literary decoloniz-ation means for one historical and political nexus. This example of decolonization as process hints at a future destina-tion, a new juncture, and a new literary model.

Coetzee's work thus suggests that postcolonialism as a critical field will need to be reformulated as the processes it maps progress. This already indicates Coetzee's broader significance in twentieth-century literature. We can conceive the model of postcolonialism as transitional to be an *extended* moment of great significance in world history, an economic decolonization involving movement towards a post-industrial world not yet in evidence. In this sense, Coetzee's formal project might be expected to speak to, and encapsulate, the contradictory experiences of global development for some generations to come.

In any consideration of Coetzee, however, one is obliged to place emphasis on the issue of textuality, which we can now see clearly as a politicized matter. This is evident in Coetzee's discussion of Zbigniew Herbert and the censor, in which the notion of canonicity – and the literary classic – becomes a figure for creativity in the face of censorship. It is also a prescription that one might apply to Coetzee himself. In the opening chapter, reference was made to Coetzee's remarks on

Herbert and the European literary tradition: I end with a consideration of Coetzee's fuller discussion of Herbert, which emphasizes the distinctiveness of fictional discourse in Coetzee's conception.

'Interpretation', suggests Coetzee, is 'the road absolutists take to the truth behind poetry. The censor is a figure of the absolutist reader: he reads the poem in order to know what it *really* means, to know its truth' (*GO*, 161). This is a resolutely politicized understanding of the processes of criticism and literary creativity. Further, the arresting association between interpretation and censorship is revealing of Coetzee's own rationale as a writer. It reinforces the perception that his style is determined both by a particular political moment – the censored culture of apartheid South Africa – and the broader intellectual moment, with its emphasis on the world as text. The way in which these forces leave traces, and yet are elided, in Coetzee's novels is implied in the continuation of his analysis:

What the interpreter/censor desires from Herbert and looks for in him is second-order writing (metaphor, allegory) that will open itself to interpretation – to interpretation as belief in a heavenly abstract order of one or other variety, for instance. What he looks for is therefore a certain faith. But an underpinning, foundational faith in a second order of representation, a faith that by its nature would sanction some revelation of itself, however devious, some opening of itself to interpretation, is stubbornly not there. Herbert's fidelity remains to first-order language, the language of the flesh . . . The censor remains the emblematic tyrannical second-order reader, whether his tyranny is the tyranny of political absolutism or of rationalistic reduction. (*GO*, 161)

In the sense that all critical interpretation of literature may tend towards the detection of 'second-order' writing, this is a salutary warning for the student and the critic of Coetzee. What Coetzee says of Herbert may need modification, however, in his own case, since there is a sense of vacillation between 'first-' and 'second-order' language, rather than a sense of fidelity to the former. It is this – necessarily gestural – dynamic which results in a tension between metaphoric and metonymic modes, between literary self-consciousness, and realist illusion. If aspects of a celebration of 'first-order language, the language of the flesh' seems a retrograde stance in a postmodernist writer, we may be misled by our impression, since there is no simplistic appeal for an older kind of transparency of language in Coetzee: his wistfulness for the Real is, rather, an aspect of an informed, strategic recentring. Again, his comments on Herbert are apposite:

The body of Herbert's poetry rests on one great secret that the censor does not know: the secret of what makes a classic. Whatever popular opinion may say, whatever the classics themselves may claim, the classic does not belong to an ideal order, nor is it attained by adhering to one set of ideas or another. On the contrary, the classic is the human; or, at least, it is what survives of the human. (*GO*, 162)

In the face of certain kinds of adversity, whether it be censorship and political control, or the pressure for intellectual conformity, the idea of literariness can create an alternative expressive space, which is 'human', not in its appeal for universality, but in its claim to independence, non-conformity, alterity. The idea of heroism has become a recurring topic in Coetzee's work, and there may, indeed, be something heroic in his *own* evolving project to create alternative fictional spaces and an alternative site of creativity.[23]

Notes

I. THE WRITER'S PLACE: COETZEE AND POSTCOLONIAL LITERATURE

1 In avoiding the hyphen in 'postcolonial' (where a literary or cultural perspective is implied) I follow Elleke Boehmer's useful taxonomy which distinguishes between 'postcolonial literature' ('that which critically scrutinizes the colonial relationship') and the hyphenated term 'post-colonial' as a 'period term designating the post-Second World War era'. See *Colonial and Postcolonial Literature* (Oxford University Press, 1995), p. 3.

2 On Coetzee's boyhood, and bilingualism see Dick Penner, *Countries of the Mind* (Westport: Greenwood Press, 1989), p. 2. For Coetzee's own (perhaps over-modest) assessment of his language skills, and his work as a translator from Dutch, see *Doubling the Point*, p. 57.

3 In an interview, Coetzee indicates that he wrote 'most' of *Dusklands* in the USA (see 'J. M. Coetzee: Interview' (with Folke Rhedin, 1982), *Kunapipi*, 6 (1984), 1, 6–11 (9)). There is, however, some doubt concerning exactly how much was drafted before Coetzee's return to South Africa. On this point see Susan VanZanten Gallagher, *A Story of South Africa: J. M. Coetzee's Fiction in Context* (Cambridge, Mass.: Harvard University Press, 1991), p. 222.

4 Philip R. Wood, in the preamble to his interview-by-correspondence with Coetzee, has to 'trust that a question's going almost unanswered can be as interesting and revealing as a question that provokes a copious response'. (This has not been an uncommon experience for Coetzee's interviewers.) 'Aporias of the Postcolonial Subject: Correspondence with J. M. Coetzee', *South Atlantic Quarterly*, 93 (Winter 1994), 1, 181–95 (181). The interviews with David Attwell in *Doubling the Point*, conducted between 1989 and

1991, are especially valuable since, in Attwell, Coetzee has found an interlocutor he evidently likes and trusts.

5 David Attwell, *J. M. Coetzee: South Africa and the Politics of Writing* (Berkeley: University of California Press, 1993), pp. 118, 70.

6 'Black Earth, White Myth: Coetzee's *Michael K*', *Modern Fiction Studies*, 38 (1992), 2, 435–44 (443).

7 In *A Guest of Honour* (1970), Gordimer draws on Fanon's *The Wretched of the Earth* to help focus the presentation of neo-colonialism, and to chart the process of political enlightenment for the novel's protagonist, Colonel James Bray.

8 See G. W. F. Hegel, *Phenomenology of Spirit*, translated by A. V. Miller (Oxford University Press, 1977), pp. 116–17. On the influence of Hegel see especially Teresa Dovey, *The Novels of J. M. Coetzee: Lacanian Allegories* (Craighall: Donker, 1988), and David Attwell, *J. M. Coetzee*.

9 Ian Glenn, 'Nadine Gordimer, J. M. Coetzee, and the Politics of Interpretation', *South Atlantic Quarterly*, 93 (Winter 1994), 1, 11–32 (20).

10 Attwell, *J. M. Coetzee*, p. 11.

11 Georg Lukács, *The Meaning of Contemporary Realism*, translated by John and Necke Mander (London: Merlin, 1979), p. 122.

12 'The Idea of Gardening', *New York Review of Books*, 2 January 1984, 3–6 (6).

13 *The Black Interpreters* (Johannesburg: Ravan Press, 1973).

14 'Speaking: J. M. Coetzee' (Interview with Stephen Watson), *Speak*, 1 (1978), 3, 21–4 (24).

15 *A Story of South Africa*, p. 44.

16 'The Idea of Gardening', 6.

17 'Colonialism and the Novels of J. M. Coetzee', in *Critical Perspectives on J. M. Coetzee*, edited by Graham Huggan and Stephen Watson (London: Macmillan, 1996), pp. 13–36 (pp. 36, 22).

18 'The Novel Today', *Upstream*, 6 (1988), 1, 2–5 (3).

19 Ibid., 4.

20 Attwell, *J. M. Coetzee*, pp. 6, 109, 112, 117.

21 The relationship is a complex one, but I am agreeing, here, with Fredric Jameson that 'contemporary theory – or better still, theoretical discourse – is . . . itself very precisely a postmodernist phenomenon'. *Postmodernism, or, the Cultural Logic of Late Capitalism* (London: Verso, 1991), p. 12.

22 Simon During, 'Postmodernism or Post-colonialism Today', extract in *The Post-colonial Studies Reader*, edited by Bill Ashcroft, Gareth Griffiths and Helen Tiffin (London: Routledge, 1995), pp. 125–9 (125).

23 Kumkum Sangari, 'The Politics of the Possible', in *The Post-colonial Studies Reader*, pp. 143–7 (pp. 145–6, 147). See also Kwame Anthony Appiah's discussion of the postmodern and the postcolonial in *In My Father's House: Africa in the Philosophy of Culture* (London: Methuen, 1992), pp. 221–54 (extract printed in *The Post-colonial Studies Reader*, pp. 119–24). Appiah argues that Africa's postcolonial novelists appeal to 'an ethical universal' in the idea of Africa (and so beyond nationalist projects), an appeal which is not postmodernist, but which bespeaks a humanism which may be recoverable within postmodernism (pp. 246, 250–1).

24 Elleke Boehmer, *Colonial and Postcolonial Literature* (Oxford University Press, 1995), p. 244.

25 'Circling the Downspout of Empire', in *Past the Last Post: Theorizing Post-Colonialism and Post-Modernism*, edited by Ian Adam and Helen Tiffin (Hemel Hempstead: Harvester, 1991), pp. 167–89 (pp. 176, 182–3).

26 'The White Inuit Speaks: Contamination as Literary Strategy', in *Past the Last Post*, pp. 191–203 (pp. 191, 192).

27 'Postmodernism or Post-colonialism Today', p. 127.

28 For an overview of this question see Stephen Gray, *Southern African Literature: An Introduction* (Cape Town: David Philip, 1979).

29 'Game Hunting in *In the Heart of the Country*', in *Critical Perspectives on J. M. Coetzee*, pp. 120–37 (p. 136).

30 Helen Tiffin, 'Post-Colonial Literatures and Counter-Discourse', *Kunapipi*, 9 (1987), 3, 17–34 (17).

31 The international reception and celebration of white South African writers has sometimes reinforced the sense of privilege, producing a new source of guilt, another cause of their over-determined self-consciousness. On this point see Michael Chapman, *Southern African Literatures* (London: Longman, 1996), pp. 385–7.

32 'The White Inuit Speaks', p. 196.

33 Graham Huggan and Stephen Watson offer a more pessimistic interpretation of Coetzee's impact, arguing that his 'work possesses a disquieting vision, with those distinctly apocalyptic, even nihilistic overtones we usually take to be characteristic of the era of international modernism', *Critical Perspectives on J. M. Coetzee*, p. 5.

34 For an account of the senses of 'amalgamation, or dialectic, of break and continuation' that may be perceived in the prefix 'post', see Margaret A. Rose, *The Post-Modern and the Post-Industrial* (Cambridge University Press, 1991), p. 2. Brian McHale also indicates how the prefix 'post' may 'emphasize the element of

logical and historical *consequence* rather than sheer temporal *posteriority*'. See *Postmodernist Fiction* (1987; reprinted, London: Routledge, 1991), p. 5.

35 Michael Chapman, *Southern African Literatures*, pp. 389, 391.

36 Homi K. Bhabha, *The Location of Culture* (London: Routledge, 1994), p. 252.

37 An important theoretical work in this connection is Paul de Man, *Allegories of Reading: Figural Language in Rousseau, Nietzsche, Rilke, and Proust* (New Haven: Yale University Press, 1979). (Coetzee has referred to this work in his own criticism: see *Doubling the Point*, pp. 266–9.)

38 Fredric Jameson, *Postmodernism, or, the Cultural Logic of Late Capitalism*, pp. 167–8.

39 Stephen Slemon, 'Post-Colonial Allegory and the Transformation of History', *Journal of Commonwealth Literature*, 23 (1988), 1, 157–68 (158–60, 162, 163). See also, Slemon, 'Monuments of Empire: Allegory/Counter-Discourse/Post-Colonial Writing', *Kunapipi*, 9 (1987), 1–16.

40 'Nadine Gordimer, J. M. Coetzee, and the Politics of Interpretation', 26. In Teresa Dovey's study, Coetzee's 'strategy' is presented as '(Lacanian) psychoanalytic criticism-as-fiction', *The Novels of J. M. Coetzee*, p. 11.

41 'Nadine Gordimer, J. M. Coetzee, and the Politics of Interpretation', 24–6.

42 'Nabokov's *Pale Fire* and the Primacy of Art', *UCT Studies in English*, 5 (1974), 1–7.

43 'Introduction', *Critical Perspectives on J. M. Coetzee*, p. 6.

44 Jean Sévry, 'An Interview with J. M. Coetzee', *Commonwealth Essays and Studies*, 9 (Autumn 1986), 1, 1–7 (1).

45 Attwell, *J. M. Coetzee*, p. 10.

46 'Preface', *Critical Perspectives on J. M. Coetzee*, p. ix.

47 'Afterword', *Critical Perspectives on J. M. Coetzee*, p. 214.

2. WRITING VIOLENCE: *DUSKLANDS*

1 See, for example, Dick Penner's discussion of this in *Countries of the Mind*, pp. 31–2.

2 For an alternative view see Penner's argument that 'the two *nouvelles* do not really merge as one work, despite their shared themes', in *Countries of the Mind*, p. 52.

3 See Frank E. Armbruster, Raymond D. Gastil, Herman Kahn, William Pfaff and Edmund Stillman, *Can We Win in Vietnam? The American Dilemma* (London: Pall Mall Press, 1968). The quote

which supplies the epigraph is on p. 10. I quote from this source subsequently in the chapter. For further discussion of this source see Gallagher, *A Story of South Africa*, pp. 52–4; Attwell, *J. M. Coetzee*, pp. 40–3.

4 For a discussion of Coetzee's use of sources see Peter Knox-Shaw, '*Dusklands*: A Metaphysics of Violence', *Commonwealth Novel in English*, 2 (1983), 1, 65–81; see also Gallagher, *A Story of South Africa*, pp. 73–8, and Attwell, *J. M. Coetzee*, who shows how omissions and alterations to the actual deposition of Jacobus Coetsé intensify the sense of confrontation with the Other in the fiction (pp. 45–8). Coetzee's eighteenth-century journal sources are: *The Journals of Brink and Rhenius*, translated by E. E. Mossop (Cape Town: The Van Riebeeck Society, 1947), and *The Journal of Hendrik Jacob Wikar, and the Journals of Jacobus Coetsé Jansz, and Willem van Reenan*, translators A. W. van der Horst and E. E. Mossop (Cape Town: The Van Riebeeck Society, 1935).

5 Knox-Shaw, '*Dusklands*: A Metaphysics of Violence', 74; W. J. B. Wood, '*Dusklands* and "The Impregnable Stronghold of the Intellect"', *Theoria*, 54 (1980), 13–23 (22).

6 Knox-Shaw, '*Dusklands*: A Metaphysics of Violence', 72–3.

7 For a consideration of violence in relation to Coetzee's work see Rosemary Jane Jolly, *Colonization, Violence and Narration in White South African Writing* (Athens: Ohio University Press, 1996).

8 Gallagher has pointed to this association. See *A Story of South Africa*, p. 70.

9 In *Giving Offense*, Coetzee offers some sane and persuasive deliberations on the usually emotive subjects of the harms of pornography and the dangers of censorship; see, especially, chapters 1 and 4.

10 See, for example, *Postmodernism, or, the Cultural Logic of Late Capitalism*, pp. 44–5.

11 Pertinent in this connection is Coetzee's (1976) essay 'Captain America in American Mythology', in which ideas about national power, phallic assertion, patriarchal confusion and the pursuit of a worthy (evil) adversary are conjoined. See *Doubling the Point*, pp. 107–14.

12 On this point see Attwell, *J. M. Coetzee*, pp. 37–40.

13 For another account of the pornographic in *Dusklands* see Dovey, *The Novels of J. M. Coetzee*, pp. 115–19.

14 Coetzee's use of the name 'Adonis' may have been inspired by his reading of Alex La Guma. In his (1974) essay, 'Man's Fate in the Novels of Alex La Guma' (*Doubling the Point*, pp. 344–60), Coetzee discusses the novella *A Walk in the Night*, the central (black) protagonist in which is called Michael Adonis. This Adonis,

sacked from his job, accidentally kills a white man, a crime for which another black man is killed, while Michael Adonis descends into a gangland underworld. Coetzee's Adonis, like La Guma's, is evidently named ironically: the beautiful mythological youth, whose name means 'Lord', acts as a poignant disjunction. Yet, in the sense that the mythical Adonis is associated with the vegetative cycle, there may be something hopeful in Coetzee's use of the name, a distant evocation of a mythical resurrection and regeneration.

15 In Rosemary Jolly's reading, the solipsism of both Eugene Dawn and Jacobus Coetzee supplies another theoretical bench-mark, in that it tallies with the position of the Sadean hero, the 'individual who is incapable of accepting the paradox of mutual independence'. Jolly argues that both narratives, as part of a broader strategy, employ what are, in effect, 'disguised forms of the Sadean fantasy to justify and perpetuate patterns of racial and sexual domination in a colonial context'. See *Colonization, Violence and Narration in White South African Writing*, p. 115.

16 'Samuel Beckett's *Lessness*: An Exercise in Decomposition', *Computers and the Humanities*, 7 (1973), 4, 195–98.

17 Armbruster et. al., *Can We Win in Vietnam?*, pp. 28–31, 43.

18 Writers such as John Barth and Donald Barthelme were experimenting with the idea of 'textual games' in this period. A text with a strong affinity with this aspect of *Dusklands* is Donald Barthelme's short story 'Game', published in *City Life* (1970), while Coetzee was in the United States. This is a story of two military men in an underground bunker, whose duty is to turn separate keys simultaneously to launch a nuclear warhead. While they wait for the order, one of them plays jacks, while the other (the narrator) scratches descriptions of natural forms on the walls with a diamond. The 'madness' of the narrator, linked to the obsession with the jacks, is established through the repetition and permutation of words. See Barthelme, *Sixty Stories* (London: Secker and Warburg, 1989).

19 Coetzee was much exercised by the idea of a new dawn of historical hope – as a literary trope – in two essays he published in 1973–4. In the essay on *Lessness*, the dawn–dusk combination is a focus of Coetzee's interpretation, though it is limited by the sense of game-playing. (See 'Samuel Beckett's *Lessness*', 198.) In the La Guma essay, however, even though he is ultimately critical, Coetzee is sensitive to the association between children and dawn/sunlight, as indicative of hope in both *A Walk in the Night* and *In the Fog of the Season's End*. See *Doubling the Point*, pp. 352, 357.

3.THE WRONG KIND OF LOVE: *IN THE HEART OF THE COUNTRY*

1 The effect of this juxtaposition, which meant that the text 'conducted a dialogue between the two primary South African forms of discourse', is discussed in Gallagher, *A Story of South Africa*, p. 110. The novel was first published in the US under the title *From the Heart of the Country*.

2 For a discussion of the novel's publication history and initial reception see Josephine Dodd, 'Naming and Framing: Naturalization and Colonization in J. M. Coetzee's *In the Heart of the Country*', *World Literature Written in English*, 27 (1987), 2, 153–61.

3 Sheila Roberts, 'Cinderella's Mothers: J. M. Coetzee's *In the Heart of the Country*', *English in Africa*, 19 (1992), 1, 21–33 (21).

4 Dovey's chapter on the novel traces the direct echoes of psychoanalytic theory. See *The Novels of J. M. Coetzee*, pp. 149–207.

5 *A Story of South Africa*, p. 83.

6 Both Attwell and Penner alert us to the importance of rulebreaking and transgression in Magda's account. See, especially, Attwell, *J. M. Coetzee*, pp. 60–6, and Penner, *Countries of the Mind*, pp. 63–5.

7 *A Story of South Africa*, pp. 84–5. Gallagher develops her argument about the 'elevated' role of woman in the patriarchal – and hierarchical – foundation of Afrikaner identity through her chapter on the novel. See especially pp. 84–94.

8 *Countries of the Mind*, p. 61; Penner offers a summary of the variations in the readings of the novel as allegory, pp. 61–2.

9 Hena Maes-Jelinek, 'Ambivalent Clio: J. M. Coetzee's *In the Heart of the Country* and Wilson Harris's *Carnival*', *Journal of Commonwealth Literature*, 22 (1987), 1, 87–98 (90).

10 Fredric Jameson, *Postmodernism, or, the Cultural Logic of Late Capitalism*, pp. 167–8.

11 For Penner, this makes the novel quite distinct from the liberal tradition associated with Alan Paton and (for Penner) with the early novels of Nadine Gordimer. See *Countries of the Mind*, p. 66.

12 For a cogent and perceptive survey of Afrikaner mythology, and its (politically expedient) adaptability, see Leonard Thompson, *The Political Mythology of Apartheid* (New Haven: Yale University Press, 1985).

13 Magda's position is a variation of Robin Visel's description of the 'half-colonized' white settler woman: though oppressed by the patriarchal structures of white men, she is still part of the colonizing system. See 'A Half-Colonization: The Problem of

the White Colonial Woman Writer', *Kunapipi*, 10 (1988), 3, 39–45 (39).

14 *Countries of the Mind*, p. 56.

15 It is true that the opening description already raises doubts about the reliability of Magda's narrative, since she gives alternative (detailed) observations, and claims not to have seen what she describes.

16 For Coetzee's view on the difficulties in translating his work into film (and his criticism of *Dust*) see *Doubling the Point*, pp. 59–60.

17 *J. M. Coetzee*, p. 67.

18 *Countries of the Mind*, p. 67.

19 Dick Penner offers a longer list of authors, gathered from the observations of several critics. See *Countries of the Mind*, p. 69. See also Dodd, 'Naming and Framing', 158–60.

20 Ian Glenn, 'Game Hunting in *In the Heart of the Country*', in *Critical Perspectives on J. M. Coetzee*, edited by Huggan and Watson, pp. 120–37 (p. 125). Glenn also finds an invocation of Whitman and Joyce to add to the list of literary allusions (p. 128).

21 Gallagher, *A Story of South Africa*, p. 106. See also Dovey's chapter for a view on Coetzee's rewriting of South African pastoral: *The Novels of J. M. Coetzee*, pp. 149–207.

22 In an interview, Jean Sévry ponders the insect theme in the novels, speculating that 'maybe the insect represents the Other'. Coetzee's response is typically enigmatic: 'That is for you to say.' 'An Interview with J. M. Coetzee' (Jean Sévry), *Commonwealth Essays and Studies*, 9 (1986), 1, 1–7 (4).

23 For translations of Magda's responses see Penner, *Countries of the Mind*, pp. 70–1, and Gallagher, *A Story of South Africa*, p. 104.

24 Coetzee offers a cool dissection of the racist underpinnings of apartheid in his essay on Geoffrey Cronjé, one of its architects. The essay appears as the ninth chapter, 'Apartheid Thinking', in *Giving Offense*.

25 Caroline Rody, 'The Mad Colonial Daughter's Revolt: J. M. Coetzee's *In the Heart of the Country*', *South Atlantic Quarterly*, 93 (Winter 1994), 1, 157–80 (161).

26 Ibid., 165.

27 Dovey, *The Novels of J. M. Coetzee*, p. 23.

28 G. W. F. Hegel, *Phenomenology of Spirit*, translated by A. V. Miller (Oxford University Press, 1977), pp. 116–17.

29 Peter Strauss, 'Coetzee's Idylls: The Ending of *In the Heart of the Country*', in *Momentum: On Recent South African Writing*, edited by M. J. Daymond, J. U. Jacobs and Margaret Lenta (Pietermaritzburg: University of Natal Press, 1984), pp. 121–8 (pp. 127–8).

4. AN ETHICAL AWAKENING: *WAITING FOR THE BARBARIANS*

1 *J. M. Coetzee*, pp. 70, 72.
2 Minna Herman Maltz, 'Dual Voices and Diverse Traditions in Coetzee's *Waiting for the Barbarians*', *Unisa English Studies*, 28 (1990), 1, 22–32 (31).
3 C. P. Cavafy, *Collected Poems*, translated by Edmund Keeley and Philip Sherrard (London: Chatto & Windus, 1990), pp. 14–15.
4 For a discussion of this duality see Debra A. Castillo, 'The Composition of the Self in Coetzee's *Waiting for the Barbarians*', *Critique*, 27 (1986), 2, 78–90 (79).
5 Anne Waldron Neumann, 'Escaping the "Time of History"? Present Tense and the Occasion of Narration in J. M. Coetzee's *Waiting for the Barbarians*', *Journal of Narrative Technique*, 20 (1990), 1, 65–86 (81).
6 *J. M. Coetzee*, pp. 73–4.
7 See *A Story of South Africa*, chapter 5.
8 On this see Attwell, *J. M. Coetzee*, pp. 79–80.
9 Michael Valdez Moses talks of this 'virtuoso scene that rewrites Kafka's "In the Penal Colony" in the wake of Foucault's *Discipline and Punish*'. See 'The Mark of Empire: Writing, History, and Torture in Coetzee's *Waiting for the Barbarians*', *Kenyon Review*, 15 (1993), 1, 115–27 (121).
10 Franz Kafka, *The Complete Short Stories*, edited by Nahum N. Glatzer (London: Mandarin, 1992), pp. 144–5.
11 Ibid., pp. 150, 154.
12 Ibid., pp. 161, 166.
13 Rosemary Jolly suggests that 'the reunion of girl and territory is the turning point of the fiction: the narrator returns, resigned, to the settlement as prisoner – not agent – of the Empire'. See 'Territorial metaphor in Coetzee's *Waiting for the Barbarians*', *Ariel*, 20 (1989), 2, 69–79 (73).
14 *J. M. Coetzee*, p. 79.
15 For an overview of how the myth of settler 'discovery' in South African history has been overturned in recent historical and archaeological work see Nigel Worden, *The Making of Modern South Africa: Conquest, Segregation and Apartheid* (Oxford: Blackwell, 1994), pp. 5–7. If the novel's references to archaeology evoke this ideological confrontation, they have also a theoretical association: the resonance between the magistrate's archaeological pursuit of historical heritage, and Foucault's notion of archaeology seems deliberate. On this point see Attwell, *J. M. Coetzee*, p. 77.
16 'Post-Colonial Allegory and the Transformation of History', 162.

17 Coetzee, in tapping into poststructuralist ideas about language, is attempting to raise serious questions about power and discourse, though not all critics feel this is an appropriate route for such concerns. Lance Olsen, for example, sees in the novel an affinity with poststructuralist ideas about the instability of meanings, the enactment of which ideas results in a moral failure, 'a web of linguistic misfirings that disintegrate before anyone has heard, a field of blankness and a desolation that there has to be such blankness'. See 'The Presence of Absence: Coetzee's *Waiting for the Barbarians*', *Ariel*, 16 (1985), 2, 47–56 (49, 55–6).

18 *J. M. Coetzee*, p. 86.

19 See, for example, David Harvey, *The Condition of Postmodernity* (Oxford: Blackwell, 1990), pp. 211–25.

20 Michael Valdez Moses sees a straightforward opposition in the magistrate's attempt to escape from History, and return to nature, an 'anti-teleological version of a cyclical local "history" [which] turns out to be a conscious fabrication'. See 'The Mark of Empire', 124.

21 James Phelan, 'Present Tense Narration, Mimesis, the Narrative Norm, and the Positioning of the Reader in *Waiting for the Barbarians*', in *Understanding Narrative*, edited by James Phelan and Peter J. Rabinowitz (Columbus: Ohio State University Press, 1994), pp. 222–45 (pp. 234, 241).

22 In Dovey's reading of the dream sequence, emphasis is placed on the sense of impasse: she discerns a symptomatic exposure of liberal humanist novelistic discourse, the aporia of which is implied at the novel's close. See *The Novels of J. M. Coetzee*, pp. 208–64 (p. 257).

5. GARDENING AS RESISTANCE: *LIFE AND TIMES OF MICHAEL K*

1 On this issue see, especially, Gallagher's chapter on the novel (*A Story of South Africa*, pp. 136–65).

2 See John Pampallis, *Foundations of the New South Africa* (London: Zed Books, 1991), pp. 264–5.

3 Coetzee's own preference for 'a diet without flesh' evidently helps fashion the vegetarian ethos of Michael K. (See 'Meat Country', *Granta*, 52 (Winter 1995), 41–52 (43).)

4 *The Novels of J. M. Coetzee*, pp. 299–301 (p. 301).

5 Tony Morphet, 'Two Interviews with J. M. Coetzee, 1983 and 1987', *Northwestern University Triquarterly*, 69 (1987), 454–64 (454).

6 'A Questionable Future: The Vision of Revolution in White South

African Writing', *Journal of Contemporary African Studies*, 4 (1984–5), 1–2, 215–223 (221).

7 *A Story of South Africa*, pp. 154, 156.

8 Gallagher makes this observation: *A Story of South Africa*, p. 144.

9 Sarah Dove Heider, 'The Timeless Ecstasy of Michael K', in *Black/White Writing: Essays on South African Literature*, edited by Pauline Fletcher (Cranbury, NJ; Associated University Presses, 1993), pp. 83–98 (p. 86).

10 *Countries of the Mind*, p. 91.

11 *J. M. Coetzee*, p. 93.

12 See Attwell on this: *J. M. Coetzee*, p. 99.

13 See Penner, *Countries of the Mind*, p. 94.

14 'Black Earth, White Myth: Coetzee's *Michael K*', *Modern Fiction Studies*, 38 (1992), 2, 435–44 (443).

15 Ibid., 443.

16 'The Idea of Gardening', *New York Review of Books*, 2 January 1984, 3–6 (6).

17 See Lukács' essay 'Narrate or Describe?' in *Writer and Critic*, translated by Arthur Kahn (London: Merlin Press, 1978).

18 Mark D. Hawthorne argues that Michael K uses similes to describe himself – as does the narrator – whereas the medical officer moves instead between 'clinical description' and 'poetic trope'. The distinction indicates the medical officer's desire to interpret, as opposed to the narrator's distrust of language that may categorize. See 'A Storyteller Without Words: J. M. Coetzee's *Life and Times of Michael K*', *Commonwealth Novel in English*, 6 (1993), 1–2, 121–32 (127–8).

19 'The Timeless Ecstasy of Michael K', p. 89.

20 Gallagher offers a summary of such readings. See *A Story of South Africa*, pp. 164–5.

21 Derek Wright, 'Black Earth, White Myth', 2, 435–44.

22 'Chthonic Man: Landscape, History and Myth in Coetzee's *Life and Times of Michael K*', *New Literature Review*, 21 (Summer 1991), 1–15 (9).

23 *J. M. Coetzee*, pp. 96–7.

24 The significance of Michael K's occupation seems also to echo Voltaire's famous phrase from *Candide*: 'il faut cultiver notre jardin' – a call for defiance, rather than despair, in the face of the painful lessons of experience.

25 *A Story of South Africa*, p. 156.

26 Foucault discusses this principle in *Discipline and Punish*. A relevant extract can be found in *The Foucault Reader*, edited by Paul Rabinow (London: Penguin, 1991), p. 207.

27 In an important essay, Michael Marais shows how a deconstructive principle operates through the text, and is bound up with its metafictional gestures: this necessarily relates questions of hegemony to the reader's relationship to the text. See 'Languages of Power: A Story of Reading Coetzee's *Michael K*/Michael K', *English in Africa*, 16 (1989), 2, 31–48.

28 Attwell persuasively suggests that this aspect of the book is given 'a socially nuanced meaning'. See *J. M. Coetzee*, pp. 99–100.

29 Gayatri Spivak, 'Translator's Preface' to Jacques Derrida, *Of Grammatology* (Baltimore: Johns Hopkins University Press, 1976), p. lxv. (On this connection, see Dovey, *The Novels of J. M. Coetzee*, p. 295, and Attwell, *J. M. Coetzee*, p. 99.)

30 Tony Morphet, 'Two Interviews', 455.

31 On this topic see Gayatri Spivak, 'Translator's Preface'.

32 Allen Thiher, *Words in Reflection: Modern Language Theory and Postmodern Fiction* (University of Chicago Press, 1984), p. 44.

33 Martin Heidegger, *Being and Time*, translated by John Macquarrie and Edward Robinson (Oxford: Blackwell, 1962; reprinted 1995), pp. 370ff. For a gloss on this see Thiher, *Words in Reflection*, pp. 37, 39, and Dorothea Frede, 'The Question of Being: Heidegger's Project', in *The Cambridge Companion to Heidegger*, edited by Charles Guignon (Cambridge University Press, 1993), pp. 42–69 (p. 64).

In a contrary reading to mine, Michael Valdez Moses sees Michael K's 'primordial existential state' to take the situation of Rousseau's solitary walker as its main parallel. For Moses, the emphasis on the *present* in this state makes Heidegger's more complex temporality inapplicable. See 'Solitary Walkers: Rousseau and Coetzee's *Life and Times of Michael K*', *South Atlantic Quarterly*, 93 (Winter 1994), 1, 131–54 (147).

34 See Martin Heidegger, *Poetry, Language, Thought*, translated by Albert Hofstadter (New York: Harper & Row), pp. 33–4.

35 Thiher, *Words in Reflection*, pp. 48–50.

6. THE MAZE OF DOUBTING: *FOE*

1 For Gayatri Spivak, the novel's metafictional orientation serves to supplement rather than occlude more directly interventionist writing on South Africa: 'I should hope that my students would keep this duplicitous agent of active marginalizing – theory, our friend Foe – in mind as they read with informed sympathy interventionist writing . . . Mongane Serote's *To Every Birth Its Blood* is an example.' Gayatri Chakravorty Spivak, 'Theory in the

Margin: Coetzee's *Foe* Reading Defoe's *Crusoe/Roxana*', in *The Consequences of Theory*, edited by Jonathan Arac and Barbara Johnson (Baltimore: Johns Hopkins University Press, 1991), pp. 154–80 (p. 175).

2 Helen Tiffin, 'Post-Colonial Literatures and Counter-Discourse', *Kunapipi*, 9 (1987), 3, 17–34 (17, 20, 23).

3 See *Robinson Crusoe* (Harmondsworth: Penguin, 1982), pp. 69–81.

4 For the text of 'A True Revelation of the Apparition of One Mrs Veal', and a note on its composition, see *Selected Writings of Daniel Defoe*, edited by James T. Boulton (Cambridge University Press, 1975), pp. 132–41.

5 Robert M. Post, 'The Noise of Freedom: J. M. Coetzee's *Foe*', *Critique*, 30 (1989), 3, 143–54 (145–46).

6 Spivak, 'Theory in the Margin', p. 169.

7 Kirsten Holst Petersen, 'An Elaborate Dead End? A Feminist Reading of Coetzee's *Foe*', in *A Shaping of Connections: Commonwealth Literature Studies – Then and Now*, edited by Hena Maes-Jelinek, Kirsten Holst Petersen and Anna Rutherford (Sydney: Dangaroo Press, 1989), pp. 243–52 (p. 250).

8 The biblical reference is to the fourth gospel (John 20: 24–8).

9 Derek Attridge, 'Oppressive Silence: J. M. Coetzee's *Foe* and the Politics of the Canon', in *Decolonizing Tradition: New Views of Twentieth-Century 'British' Literary Canons*, edited by Karen R. Lawrence (Urbana: University of Illinois Press, 1992), pp. 212–38 (pp. 228, 235).

10 Ina Gräbe, 'Postmodernist Narrative Strategies in *Foe*', *Journal of Literary Studies*, 5 (1989), 2, 145–82 (175, 176).

11 Brian Macaskill and Jeanne Colleran, 'Reading History, Writing Heresy: The Resistance of Representation and the Representation of Resistance in Coetzee's *Foe*', *Contemporary Literature*, 33 (1992), 3, 432–57 (451).

12 'Postmodernist Narrative Strategies', p. 177.

13 Spivak wonders 'Are those walking eyes rebuses, hieroglyphs, ideograms, or is their secret that they hold no secret at all? Each scrupulous effort at decoding or deciphering will bring its own rewards; but there is a structural possibility that they are nothing. Even then it would be writing.' See 'Theory in the Margin', pp. 171–2. See also Hena Maes-Jelinek, 'The Muse's Progress: "Infinite Rehearsal" in J. M. Coetzee's *Foe*', in *A Shaping of Connections: Commonwealth Literature Studies – Then and Now* (Sydney: Dangaroo Press, 1989), pp. 232–42 (p. 238).

14 'Postmodernist Narrative Strategies', 150.

15 Petersen, 'An Elaborate Dead End?', p. 251.

16 Tiffin, 'Post-Colonial Literatures', 31–2.
17 Spivak, 'Theory in the Margin', pp. 174–75.

7. A TRUE CONFESSION: *AGE OF IRON*

1 Coetzee speaks of his protagonist as 'Elizabeth Curren' (*Doubling the Point*, pp. 250, 340), and we do discover, in addition to her surname, that her initials are 'E. C.'. However, as Derek Attridge observes, her first name is not revealed in the course of the novel, so the proper nomenclature for critical discussions of this character should be 'Mrs Curren'. See Derek Attridge, 'Trusting the Other: Ethics and Politics in J. M. Coetzee's *Age of Iron*', *South Atlantic Quarterly*, 93 (Winter 1994), 1, 59–82 (79).

2 There is also a sense of personal poignancy for the author in the novel's engagement with mortality. The dedication comprises three sets of initials, referring to both of Coetzee's parents, and to his son, all of whom died in the 1980s. (See Gallagher, *A Story of South Africa*, p. 194.) Just as the death of Coetzee's mother in 1985 puts a moving complexion on the composition of *Age of Iron*, so does the death of Coetzee's son in 1989 make the tortured father/son theme in *The Master of Petersburg* particularly poignant.

3 For an excellent account of the issue of otherness in the novel see Derek Attridge, 'Trusting the Other'.

4 Thabane reveals he is 43, having been born in 1943: the present of the novel is thus 1986 or 1987 (*AI*, 92).

5 Useful summaries of the period can be found in: William Beinart, *Twentieth-Century South Africa* (Oxford University Press, 1994); John Pampallis, *Foundations of the New South Africa* (London: Zed Books, 1991); Nigel Worden, *The Making of Modern South Africa* (Oxford: Blackwell, 1994). See also Paul B. Rich's essay, 'Literature and Political Revolt in South Africa: The Cape Town Crisis of 1984–86 in the Novels of J. M. Coetzee, Richard Rive and Menan du Plessis', *SPAN: Journal of the South Pacific Association for Commonwealth Literature and Language Studies*, 36 (October 1993), 471–87.

8. PRODUCING THE DEMON: *THE MASTER OF PETERSBURG*

1 Zinovy Zinik, 'The Spirit of Stavrogin', *TLS*, 4 March 1994, 19.
2 See Richard Pevear, 'Foreword' to *Demons*, translated by Richard Pevear and Larissa Volokhonsky (London: Vintage, 1994), p. vii.
3 For a note on the pros and cons of reinstating the suppressed chapter see Gary Saul Morson, *Narrative and Freedom: The Shadows of Time* (New Haven: Yale University Press, 1994), p. 295.

4 On this point see Pevear, 'Foreword', p. xv.

5 John Bayley, 'Doubles', *New York Review of Books*, 17 November 1994, 35–6 (35).

6 Zinik, 'The Spirit of Stavrogin', 19.

7 'Breyten Breytenbach and the Censor', in *De-Scribing Empire: Post-Colonialism and Textuality*, edited by Chris Tiffin and Alan Lawson (London: Routledge, 1994), pp. 86–97 (pp. 94–6). A different version of this essay is collected in *Giving Offense*.

8 There is a connection here with Frantz Fanon's enactment of the Hegelian struggle for recognition in the colonized's drama of consciousness. In this struggle, as Homi Bhabha writes, 'the peremptory self of the present disavows an image of itself as an originary past or an ideal future and confronts the paradox of its own making': foreword to *Black Skin, White Masks* (London: Pluto Press, 1996), pp. vii–xxvi.

9 *Demons*, translated by Richard Pevear and Larissa Volokhonsky, pp. 706, 712.

10 Mikhail Bakhtin, *Problems of Dostoevsky's Poetics*, translated by Caryl Emerson (Manchester University Press, 1984), pp. 242–6. In his review of Joseph Frank, *Dostoevsky: The Miraculous Years, 1865–1871*, Coetzee makes reference both to dialogics, and to the question of censorship and the suppressed chapter in *The Devils* (*New York Review of Books*, 42, 4, March 2 1995, 13–16.)

11 Gary Saul Morson and Caryl Emerson, *Mikhail Bakhtin: Creation of a Prosaics* (Stanford University Press, 1990), pp. 241–3. See also Bakhtin, *Problems of Dostoevsky's Poetics*, pp. 73, 299.

12 Morson, *Narrative and Freedom*, pp. 129–32.

13 Ibid., p. 295.

14 Virginia Woolf, *Collected Essays*, edited by Leonard Woolf, 4 vols. (London: Hogarth Press, 1966–7); vol. 1 (1966), p. 330.

15 Derek Attridge, 'Oppressive Silence' in *Critical Perspectives on J. M. Coetzee*, edited by Huggan and Watson, pp. 168–90 (pp. 171, 186).

16 Philip R. Wood, 'Aporias of the Postcolonial Subject' 1, 181–95 (194–5).

17 For an alternative, and bleaker, interpretation of the novel's ambivalences see Stephen Watson, 'The Writer and the Devil: J. M. Coetzee's *Master of Petersburg*', *New Contrast*, 22 (1994), 4, 47–61. Watson's reading leads him to larger questions of redemption and damnation, especially through a negative view of the novel's final chapter, and the 'psychic schism' he feels it suggests (52).

18 For a critique of this see Benita Parry, 'Speech and Silence in the Fictions of J. M. Coetzee', in *Critical Perspectives on J. M. Coetzee*, edited by Huggan and Watson, pp. 37–65.

19 This is an observation which finds a parallel in the purpose of Gordimer's *Burger's Daughter*, announced famously in that novel's epigraph from Lévi-Strauss: 'I am the place in which something has occurred.' The comparison is instructive in that Gordimer's novel of white revolutionary identity presents the construction of self in a way which, technically, parallels Coetzee's observations on dialogism.

20 Coetzee, 'Breyten Breytenbach and the Censor', pp. 90–1; Bakhtin, *Problems of Dostoevsky's Poetics*, p. 202.

21 'Breyten Breytenbach and the Censor', p. 91.

22 Nadine Gordimer, *Burger's Daughter* (London: Cape, 1979), pp. 209–10.

23 David Attwell, with some hesitancy, has suggested something similar, arguing that 'Coetzee's affiliations do seem postmodern in many respects, and if it were still admissible to talk in this fashion, we might speak of his willingness to rethink the modernist heritage in the context of South Africa's violent postcoloniality as a kind of heroism'. 'Afterword', *Critical Perspectives on J. M. Coetzee*, edited by Huggan and Watson, pp. 213–16 (p. 215). On the evidence of another essay, however, we might expect Coetzee, with his characteristic complex vision, to demur. Writing on Vargas Llosa, he shows himself sensitive to the dangers inherent in setting writing up as a rival to politics, since 'the risk run by the writer-as-hero is the risk of megalomania' (*GO*, 47).

Select bibliography

WORKS BY COETZEE

BOOKS

Dusklands (Johannesburg: Ravan Press, 1974; Harmondsworth: Penguin, 1983)

In the Heart of the Country (London: Secker and Warburg, 1977; Harmondsworth: Penguin, 1982)

Waiting for the Barbarians (London: Secker and Warburg, 1980; Harmondsworth: Penguin, 1982)

Life and Times of Michael K (London: Secker and Warburg, 1983; Harmondsworth: Penguin, 1985)

Foe (London: Secker and Warburg, 1986; Harmondsworth: Penguin, 1987)

White Writing: On the Culture of Letters in South Africa (New Haven: Yale University Press, 1988)

Age of Iron (London: Secker and Warburg, 1990; Harmondsworth: Penguin, 1991)

Doubling the Point: Essays and Interviews, edited by David Attwell (Cambridge, Mass.: Harvard University Press, 1992)

The Master of Petersburg (London: Secker and Warburg, 1994)

Giving Offense: Essays on Censorship (University of Chicago Press, 1996)

UNCOLLECTED ESSAYS AND INTERVIEWS

'Samuel Beckett's *Lessness*: An Exercise in Decomposition', *Computers and the Humanities*, 7 (1973), 4, 195–8

'Nabokov's *Pale Fire* and the Primacy of Art', *UCT Studies in English*, 5 (1974), 1–7

'Speaking: J. M. Coetzee' (interview with Stephen Watson), *Speak*, 1 (1978), 3, 21–4

'Surreal Metaphors and Random Processes', *Journal of Literary Semantics*, 8 (1979), 1, 22–30

'A Note on Writing', in *Momentum: On Recent South African Writing*, edited by M. J. Daymond, J. U. Jacobs and Margaret Lenta (Pietermaritzburg: University of Natal Press, 1984), pp. 11–13

'J. M. Coetzee: Interview' (Folke Rhedin), *Kunapipi*, 6 (1984), 1, 6–11

'An Interview with J. M. Coetzee' (Jean Sévry), *Commonwealth Essays and Studies*, 9 (1986), 1, 1–7

'Two Interviews with J. M. Coetzee, 1983 and 1987', (Tony Morphet), *Northwestern University Triquarterly*, 69 (1987), 454–64

'The Novel Today', *Upstream*, 6 (1988), 1, 2–5

'An Interview with J. M. Coetzee', *Contemporary Literature*, 33 (1992), 3, 419–31

'A Betrayed People', review of *Frontiers: The Epic of South Africa's Creation, and the Tragedy of the Xhosa People* by Noël Mostert, *New York Review of Books*, 40, 1–2, 14 January 1993, 8–10

'Resisters', review of *In No Uncertain Terms: A South African Memoir* by Helen Suzman, and *Return to Paradise* by Breyten Breytenbach, *New York Review of Books*, 40, 20, 2 December 1993, 3–6

'Breyten Breytenbach and the Censor', in *De-Scribing Empire: Post-Colonialism and Textuality*, edited by Chris Tiffin and Alan Lawson (London: Routledge, 1994), pp. 86–97

'The Heart of Me', review of *Under My Skin: Volume One of My Autobiography, to 1949* by Doris Lessing, *New York Review of Books*, 41, 21, 22 December 1994, 51–4

'Meat Country', *Granta*, 52 (Winter 1995), 41–52

'The Artist at High Tide', review of *Dostoevsky: The Miraculous Years, 1865–1871* by Joseph Frank, *New York Review of Books*, 42, 4, 2 March 1995, 13–16

'Palimpsest Regained', review of *The Moor's Last Sigh* by Salman Rushdie, *New York Review of Books*, 43, 5, 21 March 1996, 13–16

WORKS ABOUT COETZEE

Attridge, Derek, 'Oppressive Silence: J. M. Coetzee's *Foe* and the Politics of the Canon', in *Decolonizing Tradition: New Views of Twentieth-Century 'British' Literary Canons*, edited by Karen R. Lawrence (Urbana: University of Illinois Press, 1992), pp. 212–38. (Also, in modified form, as: 'Oppressive Silence: J. M. Coetzee's *Foe* and the Politics of Canonisation', in *Critical Perspectives on J. M. Coetzee*, edited by Graham Huggan and Stephen Watson, pp. 168–90)

'Trusting the Other: Ethics and Politics in J. M. Coetzee's *Age of Iron*', *South Atlantic Quarterly*, 93 (Winter 1994), 1, 59–82

Attwell, David, 'The Problem of History in the Fiction of J. M. Coetzee', *Poetics Today*, 11 (1990), 579–615; also in *Rendering Things Visible: Essays on South African Literary Culture*, edited by Martin Trump (Athens: Ohio University Press, 1991), pp. 94–133

J. M. Coetzee: South Africa and the Politics of Writing (Berkeley: University of California Press, 1993)

'Afterword' to *Critical Perspectives on J. M. Coetzee*, edited by Graham Huggan and Stephen Watson (London: Macmillan, 1996), pp. 213–16

Bayley, John, 'Doubles', *New York Review of Books*, 17 November 1994, 35–6

Beressem, Hanjo, '*Foe*: The Corruption of Words', *Matatu*, 2 (1988), 3–4, 222–35

Berthoud, Jacques, 'Writing Under Apartheid', *Current Writing: Text and Reception in South Africa*, 1 (1989), 1, 77–87

Bishop, G. Scott, 'J. M. Coetzee's *Foe*: A Culmination and a Solution to a Problem of White Identity', *World Literature Today*, 64 (1990), 1, 54–7

Castillo, Debra A., 'The Composition of the Self in Coetzee's *Waiting for the Barbarians*', *Critique*, 27 (1986), 2, 78–90

Colleran, Jeanne, 'Position Papers: Reading J. M. Coetzee's Fiction and Criticism', *Contemporary Literature*, 35 (Autumn 1994), 3, 578–92

De Kock, Leon, 'Literature, Politics and Universalism: A Debate Between Ezekiel Mphahlele and J. M. Coetzee', *Journal of Literary Studies*, 3 (1987), 4, 35–48

Dodd, Josephine, 'Naming and Framing: Naturalization and Colonization in J. M. Coetzee's *In the Heart of the Country*', *World Literature Written in English*, 27 (1987), 2, 153–61

'The South African Literary Establishment and the Textual Production "Woman": J. M. Coetzee and Lewis Nkosi', *Current Writing*, 2 (1990), 1, 117–29

Dovey, Teresa, 'Coetzee and His Critics: The Case of *Dusklands*', *English in Africa*, 14 (1987), 2, 15–30

The Novels of J. M. Coetzee: Lacanian Allegories (Craighall: Donker, 1988)

Du Plessis, Menan, 'Towards a True Materialism', *Contrast: South African Literary Journal*, 13 (1981), 4, 77–87

Du Plessis, Michael, 'Bodies and Signs: Inscriptions of Femininity in John Coetzee and Wilma Stockenstrom', *Journal of Literary Studies*, 4 (1988), 1, 118–28

Eckstein, Barbara, 'The Body, the Word, and the State: J. M. Coetzee's *Waiting for the Barbarians*', *Novel*, 22 (1989), 2, 175–98
The Language of Fiction in a World of Pain (Philadelphia: University of Pennsylvania Press, 1990) (incorporates preceding essay in a chapter dealing also with *Michael K*)

Edgecombe, Rodney, 'The Oracular Voice', in *International Literature in English: Essays on the Major Writers*, edited by Robert L. Ross (New York: Garland, 1991), pp. 637–46
'A Source for an Incident in J. M. Coetzee's *Life and Times of Michael K*', *Notes on Contemporary Literature*, 22 (1992), 1, 7

Fokkema, Aleid, 'Character as a Subject in Language: Some Reflections on J. M. Coetzee's *Foe*', *New Comparisons: A Journal of Comparative and General Literary Studies*, 9 (1990), 170–9

Gallagher, Susan VanZanten, 'Torture and the Novel: J. M. Coetzee's *Waiting for the Barbarians*', *Contemporary Literature*, 29 (1988), 2, 277–85
A Story of South Africa: J. M. Coetzee's Fiction in Context (Cambridge, Mass.: Harvard University Press, 1991)

Gardiner, Allan, 'J. M. Coetzee's *Dusklands*: Colonial Encounters of the Robinsonian Kind', *World Literature Written in English*, 27 (1987), 2, 174–84

Gilmer, Joan, 'The Motif of the Damaged Child in the Work of J. M. Coetzee', in *Momentum: On Recent South African Writing*, edited by M. J. Daymond, J. U. Jacobs and Margaret Lenta (Pietermaritzburg: University of Natal Press, 1984), pp. 107–20

Gitzen, Julian, 'The Voice of History in the Novels of J. M. Coetzee', *Critique: Studies in Contemporary Fiction*, 35 (1993), 1, 3–15

Glenn, Ian, 'Nadine Gordimer, J. M. Coetzee, and the Politics of Interpretation', *South Atlantic Quarterly*, 93 (Winter 1994), 1, 11–32
'Game Hunting in *In the Heart of the Country*', in *Critical Perspectives on J. M. Coetzee*, edited by Huggan and Watson, pp. 120–37

Goddard, Kevin, John Read and Teresa Dovey, *J. M. Coetzee: A Bibliography* (Grahamstown: National English Literary Museum, 1990)

Gräbe, Ina, 'Postmodernist Narrative Strategies in *Foe*', *Journal of Literary Studies*, 5 (1989), 2, 145–82

Gray, Rosemary, 'J. M. Coetzee's *Dusklands*: Of War and War's Alarms', *Commonwealth Essays and Studies*, 9 (1986), 1, 32–43

Gray, Rosemary, et al., 'Round Table on the Works of J. M. Coetzee', *Commonwealth Essays and Studies*, 9 (1986), 1, 50–8

Hall, Barbara, 'The Mutilated Tongue: Symbols of Communication in J. M. Coetzee's *Foe*', *Unisa English Studies*, 31 (1993), 1, 16–22

Harvey, C. J. D., '*Waiting for the Barbarians*', *Standpunte*, 34 (1981), 3–8

Hawthorne, Mark D., 'A Storyteller Without Words: J. M. Coetzee's *Life and Times of Michael K*', *Commonwealth Novel in English*, 6 (1993), 1–2, 121–32

Heider, Sarah Dove, 'The Timeless Ecstasy of Michael K', in *Black/White Writing: Essays on South African Literature*, edited by Pauline Fletcher (Cranbury, NJ; Associated University Presses, 1993), pp. 83–98

Hewson, Kelly, 'Making the "Revolutionary Gesture": Nadine Gordimer, J. M. Coetzee and Some Variations on the Writer's Responsibility', *Ariel*, 19 (1988), 4, 55–72

Huggan, Graham, 'Philomela's Retold Story: Silence, Music, and the Post-Colonial Text', *Journal of Commonwealth Literature*, 25 (1990), 1, 12–23

Huggan, Graham, and Stephen Watson (eds.), *Critical Perspectives on J. M. Coetzee* (London: Macmillan, 1996)

Irlam, Shaun, review of *White Writing*, *Modern Language Notes*, 103 (1988), 5, 1147–50

Joffe, P., 'The Naming of Michael K: J. M. Coetzee's *Life and Times of Michael K*', *Nomina Africana*, 4 (1990), 1, 89–98

Jolly, Rosemary Jane, 'Territorial Metaphor in Coetzee's *Waiting for the Barbarians*', *Ariel*, 20 (1989), 2, 69–79

Colonization, Violence, and Narration in White South African Writing: André Brink, Breyten Breytenbach, and J. M. Coetzee (Athens: Ohio University Press, 1996)

Kierop, Karin van, 'Mythical Interpretation of J. M. Coetzee's *Life and Times of Michael K*', *Commonwealth Essays and Studies*, 9 (1986), 1, 44–9

Kinzie, Mary, 'The Cure of Poetry: On the Discipline of Word and Spirit in Conditions of Dryness: An Essay with Admonishments from the Works of Louise Bogan, J. M. Coetzee, and Other Poets', *Southwest Review*, 76 (1991), 4, 456–78

Knox-Shaw, Peter, '*Dusklands*: A Metaphysics of Violence', *Commonwealth Novel in English*, 2 (1983), 1, 65–81

Lane, Richard, 'Embroiling Narratives: Appropriating the Signifier in J. M. Coetzee's *Foe*', *Commonwealth Essays and Studies*, 13 (1990), 1, 106–11

Macaskill, Brian, 'Charting J. M. Coetzee's Middle Voice', *Contemporary Literature*, 35 (1994), 3, 441–75

Macaskill, Brian, and Jeanne Colleran, 'Reading History, Writing Heresy: The Resistance of Representation and the Representation of Resistance in Coetzee's *Foe*', *Contemporary Literature*, 33 (1992), 3, 432–57

Maes-Jelinek, Hena, 'Ambivalent Clio: J. M. Coetzee's *In the Heart of the Country* and Wilson Harris's *Carnival'*, *Journal of Commonwealth Literature*, 22 (1987), 1, 87–98

'The Muse's Progress: "Infinite Rehearsal" in J. M. Coetzee's *Foe'*, in *A Shaping of Connections: Commonwealth Literature Studies – Then and Now* (Sydney: Dangaroo Press, 1989), pp. 232–42

Maher, Susan Naramore, 'Confronting Authority: J. M. Coetzee's *Foe* and the Remaking of *Robinson Crusoe'*, *International Fiction Review*, 18 (1991), 1, 34–40

Maltz, Minna Herman, 'Dual Voices and Diverse Traditions in Coetzee's *Waiting for the Barbarians'*, *Unisa English Studies*, 28 (1990), 1, 22–32

Marais, Michael, 'Interpretative Authoritarianism: Reading/Colonizing Coetzee's *Foe'*, *English in Africa*, 16 (1989), 1, 9–16

'Languages of Power: A Story of Reading Coetzee's *Michael K/ Michael K'*, *English in Africa*, 16 (1989), 2, 31–48

'"Omnipotent Fantasies" of a Solitary Self: J. M. Coetzee's "The Narrative of Jacobus Coetzee"', *Journal of Commonwealth Literature*, 29 (1993), 2, 48–65

Martin, Richard G., 'Narrative, History, Ideology: A study of *Waiting for the Barbarians* and *Burger's Daughter'*, *Ariel*, 17 (1986), 3, 3–21

Mayoux, Sophie, 'J. M. Coetzee and Language: A Translator's View', *Commonwealth Essays and Studies*, 9 (1986), 1, 8–10

McDaniel, Ellen, 'Quiet Heroism in *The Life and Times of Michael K'*, *Notes on Contemporary Literature*, 15 (1985), 1, 11–12

Merivale, Patricia, 'Ambiguous Frontiers: *Waiting for the Barbarians* as Topographical Parable', in *Proceedings of the XIIth Congress of the International Comparative Literature Association*, edited by Roger Bauer, et al. (Munich: Iudicium, 1990), vol. II, pp. 272–6

Moses, Michael Valdez, 'Caliban and His Precursors: The Politics of Literary History and the Third World', in *Theoretical Issues in Literary History*, edited by David Perkins (Cambridge, Mass.: Harvard University Press, 1991), pp. 206–26

'The Mark of Empire: Writing, History, and Torture in Coetzee's *Waiting for the Barbarians'*, *Kenyon Review*, 15 (1993), 1, 115–27

Moses, Michael Valdez (ed.), *The Writings of J. M. Coetzee* (Durham, N.C.: Duke University Press, 1994) (*South Atlantic Quarterly*, 93 (Winter, 1994), 1 (special issue))

'Solitary Walkers: Rousseau and Coetzee's *Life and Times of Michael K'*, *South Atlantic Quarterly*, 93 (Winter, 1994), 1, 131–54

Muller, Helene, 'Who is Michael K?', *Standpunte*, 38 (1985), 41–3

Neumann, Anne Waldron, 'Escaping the "Time of History"? Present Tense and the Occasion of Narration in J. M. Coetzee's *Waiting for the Barbarians'*, *Journal of Narrative Technique*, 20 (1990), 1, 65–86

Newman, Judie, *The Ballistic Bard: Postcolonial Fictions* (London: Arnold, 1995) (includes chapter on *Waiting for the Barbarians* and *Foe*)

Nicholson, Maureen, 'If I Make the Air Around Him Thick With Words: J. M. Coetzee's *Foe*', *West Coast Review*, 21 (1987), 4, 52–8

Olsen, Lance, 'The Presence of Absence: Coetzee's *Waiting for the Barbarians*', *Ariel*, 16 (1985), 2, 47–56

Parrinder, Patrick, 'What His Father Gets up to', *London Review of Books*, 12, 13 September 1990, 17–18

Parry, Benita, 'Speech and Silence in the Fictions of J. M. Coetzee', in *Critical Perspectives on J. M. Coetzee*, edited by Graham Huggan and Stephen Watson, pp. 37–65

Penner, Dick, 'Sight, Blindness and Double-Thought in J. M. Coetzee's *Waiting for the Barbarians*', *World Literature Written in English*, 26 (1986), 1, 34–45

'J. M. Coetzee's *Foe*: The Muse, the Absurd, and the Colonial Dilemma', *World Literature Written in English*, 27 (1987), 2, 207–15

Countries of the Mind: The Fiction of J. M. Coetzee (Westport: Greenwood Press, 1989)

Petersen, Kirsten Holst, 'An Elaborate Dead End? A Feminist Reading of Coetzee's *Foe*', in *A Shaping of Connections: Commonwealth Literature Studies – Then and Now*, edited by Hena Maes-Jelinek, Kirsten Holst Petersen and Anna Rutherford (Sydney: Dangaroo Press, 1989), pp. 243–52

Phelan, James, 'Present Tense Narration, Mimesis, the Narrative Norm, and the Positioning of the Reader in *Waiting for the Barbarians*', in *Understanding Narrative*, edited by James Phelan and Peter J. Rabinowitz (Columbus: Ohio State University Press, 1994), pp. 222–45

Post, Robert M., 'The Noise of Freedom: J. M. Coetzee's *Foe*', *Critique: Studies in Contemporary Fiction*, 30 (1989), 3, 143–54

Renders, Luc, 'J. M. Coetzee's Michael K: Starving in a Land of Plenty', in *Literary Gastronomy*, edited by David Bevan (Amsterdam: Rodopi, 1988), pp. 95–102

Rich, Paul, 'Apartheid and the Decline of the Civilization Idea: An Essay on Nadine Gordimer's *July's People* and J. M. Coetzee's *Waiting for the Barbarians*', *Research in African Literatures*, 15 (1984), 3, 365–93

'Literature and Political Revolt in South Africa: The Cape Town Crisis of 1984–86 in the Novels of J. M. Coetzee, Richard Rive and Menan du Plessis', *SPAN: Journal of the South Pacific Association for Commonwealth Literature and Language Studies*, 36 (October 1993), 471–87

Roberts, Sheila, 'A Questionable Future: The Vision of Revolution in White South African Writing', *Journal of Contemporary African Studies*, 4 (1984–5), 1–2, 215–23

'Post-colonialism, or the House of Friday: J. M. Coetzee's *Foe*', *World Literature Written in English*, 31 (1991), 1, 87–92

'Cinderella's Mothers: J. M. Coetzee's *In the Heart of the Country*', *English in Africa*, 19 (1992), 1, 21–33

Rody, Caroline, 'The Mad Colonial Daughter's Revolt: J. M. Coetzee's *In the Heart of the Country*', *South Atlantic Quarterly*, 93 (Winter 1994), 1, 157–80

Sévry, Jean, 'Variations on the Works of J. M. Coetzee', *Commonwealth Essays and Studies*, 9 (1986), 1, 18–31

Smith, Rowland, 'The Seventies and After: The Inner View in White, English-Language Fiction', in *Olive Schreiner and After: Essays on Southern African Literature in Honour of Guy Butler*, edited by Malvern van Wyk Smith and Don Maclennan (Cape Town: David Philip, 1983), pp. 196–204

Spivak, Gayatri Chakravorty, 'Theory in the Margin: Coetzee's *Foe* reading Defoe's *Crusoe/Roxana*', in *The Consequences of Theory*, edited by Jonathan Arac and Barbara Johnson (Baltimore: Johns Hopkins University Press, 1991), pp. 154–80

Splendore, Paola, 'J. M. Coetzee's *Foe*: Intertextual and Metafictional Resonances', *Commonwealth Essays and Studies*, 11 (1988), 1, 55–60

Stephenson, Glennis, 'Escaping the Camps: The Idea of Freedom in J. M. Coetzee's *Life and Times of Michael K*', *Commonwealth Novel in English*, 4 (1991), 1, 77–88

Strauss, Peter, 'Coetzee's Idylls: The Ending of *In the Heart of the Country*', in *Momentum: On Recent South African Writing*, edited by M. J. Daymond, J. U. Jacobs and Margaret Lenta (Pietermaritzburg: University of Natal Press, 1984), pp. 121–8

Viola, André, 'Survival in J. M. Coetzee's Novels', *Commonwealth Essays and Studies*, 9 (1986), 1, 11–17

Wade, Jean-Philippe, 'The Allegorical Text and History: J. M. Coetzee's *Waiting for the Barbarians*', *Journal of Literary Studies*, 6 (1990), 4, 275–88

Wagner, Kathrin M., ' "Dichter" and "Dichtung": Susan Barton and the "Truth" of Autobiography', *English Studies in Africa*, 32 (1989), 1, 1–11

Watson, Stephen, 'Colonialism and the Novels of J. M. Coetzee', *Research in African Literatures*, 17 (1986), 3, 370–92; reprinted in *Critical Perspectives on J. M. Coetzee*, edited by Huggan and Watson, pp. 13–36

'The Writer and the Devil: J. M. Coetzee's *Master of Petersburg*', *New Contrast*, 22 (1994), 4, 47–61

Williams, Paul, '*Foe*: The Story of Silence', *English Studies in Africa*, 31 (1988), 1, 33–9

Wood, Philip R., 'Aporias of the Postcolonial Subject: Correspondence with J. M. Coetzee', *South Atlantic Quarterly*, 93 (Winter 1994), 1, 181–95

Wood, W. J. B., '*Dusklands* and "The Impregnable Stronghold of the Intellect"', *Theoria*, 54 (1980), 13–23

'*Waiting for the Barbarians*: Two Sides of Imperial Rule and Some Related Considerations', in *Momentum: On Recent South African Writing*, edited by M. J. Daymond, J. U. Jacobs and Margaret Lenta (Pietermaritzburg: University of Natal Press, 1984), pp. 129–40

Wright, Derek, 'Fiction as Foe: The Novels of J. M. Coetzee', *International Fiction Review*, 16 (1989), 2, 113–18

'Chthonic Man: Landscape, History and Myth in Coetzee's *Life and Times of Michael K*', *New Literatures Review*, 21 (1991), 1–15

'Black Earth, White Myth: Coetzee's *Michael K*', *Modern Fiction Studies*, 38 (1992), 2, 435–44

Zamora, Lois Parkinson, 'Allegories of Power in the Fiction of J. M. Coetzee', *Journal of Literary Studies*, 2 (1986), 1, 1–14

Zinik, Zinovy, 'The Spirit of Stavrogin', *TLS*, 4 March 1994, 19.

OTHER WORKS CITED

Appiah, Kwame Anthony, *In My Father's House: Africa in the Philosophy of Culture* (London: Methuen, 1992)

Armbruster, Frank E., Raymond D. Gastil, Herman Kahn, William Pfaff and Edmund Stillman, *Can We Win in Vietnam? The American Dilemma* (London: Pall Mall Press, 1968)

Ashcroft, Bill, Gareth Griffiths and Helen Tiffin (eds.), *The Post-colonial Studies Reader*, (London: Routledge, 1995)

Bakhtin, Mikhail, *Problems of Dostoevsky's Poetics*, translated by Caryl Emerson (Manchester University Press, 1984)

Barthelme, Donald, *Sixty Stories* (London: Secker and Warburg, 1989)

Beinart, William, *Twentieth-Century South Africa* (Oxford University Press, 1994)

Bhabha, Homi K., foreword to Frantz Fanon, *Black Skin, White Masks* (London: Pluto Press, 1996), pp. vii-xxvi.

The Location of Culture (London: Routledge, 1994)

Boehmer, Elleke, *Colonial and Postcolonial Literature* (Oxford University Press, 1995)

Brink, Carel Frederik and Johannes Tobias Rhenius, *The Journals of Brink and Rhenius, being the Journal of Carel Frederik Brink of the Journey Into Great Namaqualand (1761–2) made by Captain Hendrik Hop, and the Journal of Ensign Johannes Tobias Rhenius (1724)*, translated by E. E. Mossop (Cape Town: The Van Riebeeck Society, 1947)

Brydon, Diana, 'The White Inuit Speaks: Contamination as Literary Strategy', in *Past the Last Post: Theorizing Post-Colonialism and Post-Modernism*, edited by Ian Adam and Helen Tiffin (Hemel Hempstead: Harvester, 1991), pp. 191–203

Cavafy, C. P., *Collected Poems*, translated by Edmund Keeley and Philip Sherrard (London: Chatto & Windus, 1990)

Chapman, Michael, *Southern African Literatures* (London: Longman, 1996)

Defoe, Daniel, *Robinson Crusoe* (1719; Harmondsworth: Penguin, 1982)
Roxana (1724; Harmondsworth: Penguin, 1987)
Selected Writings of Daniel Defoe, edited by James T. Boulton (Cambridge University Press, 1975)

De Man, Paul, *Allegories of Reading: Figural Language in Rousseau, Nietzsche, Rilke, and Proust* (New Haven: Yale University Press, 1979)

Derrida, Jacques, *Of Grammatology* (Baltimore: Johns Hopkins University Press, 1976)

Dostoevsky, Fyodor, *Demons*, translated by Richard Pevear and Larissa Volokhonsky (London: Vintage, 1994)

During, Simon, 'Postmodernism or Post-colonialism Today', *Textual Practice*, 1 (1987), 1, 32–47; extract printed in *The Post-colonial Studies Reader*, edited by Ashcroft, Griffiths and Tiffin, pp. 125–9

Fanon, Frantz, *The Wretched of the Earth* (1961; Harmondsworth: Penguin, 1990)
Black Skin, White Masks (London: Pluto Press, 1996)

Foucault, Michel, *The Foucault Reader*, edited by Paul Rabinow (London: Penguin, 1991)

Frede, Dorothea, 'The Question of Being: Heidegger's Project', in *The Cambridge Companion to Heidegger*, edited by Charles Guignon (Cambridge University Press, 1993), pp. 42–69

Gordimer, Nadine, *A Guest of Honour* (London: Cape, 1971)
The Black Interpreters (Johannesburg: Ravan Press, 1973)
Burger's Daughter (London: Cape, 1979)
'The Idea of Gardening', *New York Review of Books*, 2 January 1984, 3–6

Gray, Stephen, *Southern African Literature: An Introduction* (Cape Town: David Philip, 1979)

Harvey, David, *The Condition of Postmodernity* (Oxford: Blackwell, 1990)

Hegel, G. W. F., *Phenomenology of Spirit*, translated by A. V. Miller (Oxford University Press, 1977), pp. 116–17

Heidegger, Martin, *Being and Time*, translated by John Macquarrie and Edward Robinson (Oxford: Blackwell, 1962 (reprinted 1995))

Hutcheon, Linda, 'Circling the Downspout of Empire', in *Past the Last Post: Theorizing Post-Colonialism and Post-Modernism*, edited by Ian Adam and Helen Tiffin (Hemel Hempstead: Harvester, 1991), pp. 167–89

Jameson, Fredric, *Postmodernism, or, the Cultural Logic of Late Capitalism* (London: Verso, 1991)

Kafka, Franz, *The Complete Short Stories*, edited by Nahum N. Glatzer (London: Mandarin, 1992)

Lukács, Georg, *Writer and Critic*, translated by Arthur Kahn (London: Merlin Press, 1978)

The Meaning of Contemporary Realism, translated by John and Necke Mander (London: Merlin, 1979)

McHale, Brian, *Postmodernist Fiction* (1987; reprinted, London: Routledge, 1991)

Morson, Gary Saul, *Narrative and Freedom: The Shadows of Time* (New Haven: Yale University Press, 1994)

Morson, Gary Saul and Caryl Emerson, *Mikhail Bakhtin: Creation of a Prosaics* (Stanford University Press, 1990)

Pampallis, John, *Foundations of the New South Africa* (London: Zed Books, 1991)

Sangari, Kumkum, 'The Politics of the Possible', *Cultural Critique*, 7 (1987), 157–86; extract printed in *The Post-colonial Studies Reader*, edited by Ashcroft, Griffiths and Tiffin, pp. 143–7

Schreiner, Olive, *The Story of an African Farm* (1883; Oxford University Press, 1992)

Slemon, Stephen, 'Monuments of Empire: Allegory/Counter-Discourse/Post-Colonial Writing', *Kunapipi*, 9 (1987), 1–16

'Post-Colonial Allegory and the Transformation of History', *Journal of Commonwealth Literature*, 23 (1988), 1, 157–68

Thiher, Allen, *Words in Reflection: Modern Language Theory and Postmodern Fiction* (University of Chicago Press, 1984)

Tiffin, Helen, 'Post-Colonial Literatures and Counter-Discourse', *Kunapipi*, 9 (1987), 3, 17–34

Visel, Robin, 'A Half-Colonization: The Problem of the White Colonial Woman Writer', *Kunapipi*, 10 (1988), 3, 39–45

Watt, Ian, *The Rise of the Novel: Studies in Defoe, Richardson and Fielding* (1957; reprinted, Harmondsworth: Penguin, 1981)

Wikar, Hendrik Jacob, *The Journal of Hendrik Jacob Wikar (1779), and the*

Journals of Jacobus Coetsé Jansz (1760), and Willem van Reenen (1791), translated by A. W. van der Horst and E. E. Mossop (Cape Town: The Van Riebeeck Society, 1935)

Woolf, Virginia, *Collected Essays,* edited by Leonard Woolf, 4 vols. (London: Hogarth Press, 1966–7); vol. 1 (1966)

Worden, Nigel, *The Making of Modern South Africa* (Oxford: Blackwell, 1994)

Index